Y0-BUP-148

Building and Managing a Web Services Team

Building and Managing a Web Services Team

Nancy Cox

HD
30.37
.C69
1997
West

•A15048 581146

I(T)P® A Division of International Thomson Publishing Inc.

New York • Albany • Bonn • Boston • Detroit • London • Madrid • Melbourne
Mexico City • Paris • San Francisco • Singapore • Tokyo • Toronto

Copyright © 1997 by Van Nostrand Reinhold

I(T)P® A division of International Thomson Publishing Inc.
The ITP logo is a registered trademark used herein under license

Printed in the United States of America

For more information, contact:

Van Nostrand Reinhold
115 Fifth Avenue
New York, NY 10003

International Thomson Publishing GmbH
Königswinterer Strasse 418
53227 Bonn
Germany

International Thomson Publishing Europe
Berkshire House 168-173
High Holborn
London WCIV 7AA
England

International Thomson Publishing Asia
221 Henderson Road #05-10
Henderson Building
Singapore 0315

Thomas Nelson Australia
102 Dodds Street
South Melbourne, 3205
Victoria, Australia

International Thomson Publishing Japan
Hirakawacho Kyowa Building, 3F
2-2-1 Hirakawacho
Chiyoda-ku, 102 Tokyo
Japan

Nelson Canada
1120 Birchmount Road
Scarborough, Ontario
Canada M1K 5G4

International Thomson Editores
Seneca 53
Col. Polanco
11560 Mexico D.F. Mexico

All rights reserved. No part of this work covered by the copyright hereon may be reproduced or used in any form or by any means—graphic, electronic, or mechanical, including photocopying, recording, taping, or information storage and retrieval systems—without the written permission of the publisher.

The ideas presented in this book are generic and strategic. Their specific application to a particular company must be the responsibility of the management of that company, based on management's understanding of their company's procedures, culture, resources, and competitive situation.

1 2 3 4 5 6 7 8 9 10 QEB FF 01 00 99 98 97 96

Library of Congress Cataloging-in-Publication Data

Cox, Nancy.
    Building and managing a Web services team / Nancy Cox.
        p.   cm.
    Includes index.
    ISBN 0-442-02274-3
    1. World Wide Web servers—Management.   2. Business enterprises—Computer networks—
Planning. 3. Business enterprises—Computer networks—Management 4. Intranets (Computer
networks)—Design and construction.   5. Computer network architectures.   I. Title.
HD30.37.C69   1996
658'.05467—dc20   96-41389
                                                                                      CIP

*To the full moon on the wooden deck
in the shower garden.*

C O N T E N T S

CHAPTER 3

Purchasing Web Hardware and Software 75

CHAPTER 4

Selecting Internet and Web Service Providers 125

CHAPTER 5

Staffing and Outsourcing 159

CHAPTER 10

Providing External Web Business Services 325

A C K N O W L E D G M E N T S

I would like to publicly acknowledge the contributions of the following friends and colleagues for their support and technical knowledge so generously given: Steve Huber, Marie Wrobel, Tom Manley, Frankie Chea, Selvyn Scott, Skip Slone, Reggie Jones, and Joanne Helfrich. I would like to thank John Boyd of Van Nostrand Reinhold for his expertise in developing the work. I also appreciate Carol McClendon, Neil Levine, and Mike Sherry for believing from the beginning in the need for this book.

Nancy A. Cox
Orlando, Florida
August 30, 1996

Overall Charter and Strategy for Web Business Services

"Since we have such a short timeframe to accomplish so many tasks, let's get started on these six top priority items, shall we?" Three pairs of eyes simultaneously blinked in agreement as Chris scrolled through the project plan. The Fremont office would be relocating, moving into a larger space in less than thirty days, and much remained to be done.

"Jason, would you please get quotes from three reputable moving companies and arrange for all the utilities at the new site?"

"Sure, Chris, and I'll contact our phone company and have our service and equipment relocated as well."

"Great! Leslie, would you take bids from three interior decorating firms and arrange for new stationery to be printed?"

"Will do, Chris."

"And, Sydney, here is the revised lease agreement. Would you have our lawyer look it over? And please notify all our customers, suppliers, and other interested parties of the move."

"Sure will, Chris. And would you like for me to check on the delivery dates for the new computer equipment as well?"

"Oh, absolutely! Please post your progress on these items by noon tomorrow on the company bulletin board. And, thanks everyone!"

The next day, status entries began to pour in detailing the team's progress. Jason had searched the Internet for moving companies within the firm's zip code handling large office moves, had accessed the home pages of the top five, filled in their request for quote forms, received electronic bids from three who could accommodate the tight time frame, and had selected the lowest bidder. Then Jason had accessed the home pages of Fremont Power and Light, the public utilities, and telephone companies; requested a relocation of service and equipment; electronically paid the deposits and fees required; and received confirmation messages from all of them.

Leslie had sent a customized infobot out on the Web to seek out the three top interior decorating firms in the city. Leslie then held videoconferences with them, viewing prototype 3-D floor plan designs, annotating them, and selecting the patterns and fabrics for the furniture, draperies, and wall coverings. Electronic design boards were attached to the e-mail message Leslie sent to Chris for final approval. Leslie had also attached the electronic quote received from the printer, along with several samples of business stationery that had been electronically purchased.

Sydney had held a videoconference with the attorney who was vacationing in Martinique and they made some minor adjustments to the lease agreement. This was then e-mailed using the language translator to the landlord in Barcelona for review. Sydney composed an announcement including the hyperlink to the firm's home page to all the customers, suppliers, and other organizations in the firm's database, then mass e-mailed and posted it on the firm's Help Desk and Customer Support Web pages. The firm's home page had been updated with a "NEW" hyperlink to a virtual reality view of the new office, a location map, the new telephone number and address. The delivery of the new computer equipment was also on schedule according to the shipping notice received electronically from Allied Computers in Boston.

Chris leaned back from the computer with a satisfied look. "Now, it's time to launch the media campaign detailing all our new products and services. Let's see how the new interactive brochure is coming along," she said, clicking the Marketing Department's organization chart image on the internal home page as the late afternoon traffic outside her window began to build.

In this fictional scenario, the World Wide Web was used repeatedly as a business tool, enhancing the many ways the Fremont office conducted business, both internally and externally. All of the components of the Web featured are either generally available today or in development. Web tools now provide a simple, intuitive user interface, electronic mail, multimedia displays of information, simultaneous document sharing, sophisticated search capabilities, bulletin board systems, and electronic forms access. New features just emerging as part of the Web's offerings include videoconferencing, virtual reality with 3-D images and animation, and secure electronic funds transfers. At the cutting edge in this scenario are the infobot software agent and multiple language translation capabilities.

It's not enough, though, just to know that these Web features exist or, perhaps, rush to install them. The organization must first step back for a moment from this compelling portal to the information universe and determine how this technology meshes with the overall vision and mission of the organization and how this new technology can be best applied to the organization's most basic business applications and processes. Only then will the enterprise be able to successfully implement this new and emerging technology for access to internal employees as well as external customers, suppliers, etc., in ways most profitable and beneficial to all. This chapter focuses on sweeping trends fueling the Information Age, typical Web business services, the benefits and limitations of using Web technology, how to create a charter for implementing Web services, and how to market that service within the enterprise.

Trends

To create a vision of the future, it is first imperative that the organization examine not only trends, events, and forecasts that apply to the realm of computers, but also those that most profoundly affect our lives in general. Only by recognizing both micro (computer industry) and macro (U.S. society and global) trends can organizations find ways to profit from them.

COMPUTER INDUSTRY TRENDS

In a scant 20 years, we have come from computing power residing only in the large data centers of government or mammoth corporations to having over 25% of all U.S. households equipped with personal computers offering processing power and connectivity once available only in science fiction. We now wear more computing power on our wrists than was used to plot rocket trajectories in the early days of the space program. And yet, we are not even fully immersed in the Information Age; we are still testing the waters, just beginning to share the information gleaned from various computer means.

The computing trends of processing power doubling every 18 months, miniaturization, reduced cost of owning the newest technology, and relative ease of use are fueling the Information Age by enabling individuals to use personal computers in unprecedented numbers. Couple this trend with that of sharing the information developed on the personal computers and you have the "wired generation," where communicating with other people, applications, and machines is a not only a requirement but a simple fact of life. In no arena will this urge to connect be more illustrative than that of the exponential growth of computing networks in general and the Internet in particular.

The Internet and World Wide Web Growth

The Internet, a network of networks connecting computers throughout the world, was developed in the 1970s by the U.S. Department of Defense to connect government agencies with defense contractors, research companies, and academic institutions. The Net languished for several years with its traditional user base. Then the World Wide Web was designed at the CERN particle physics laboratory in Switzerland in 1989 to assist scientists in sharing research information. In 1993 came the widespread release and adoption of an Internet user interface application created by the National Center for Supercomputer Applications. Dubbed Mosaic, this client software enabled non-technical users to easily navigate the Internet, transfer files, exchange electronic messages, and search for information. Mosaic used a simplified form of an internationally-standard document structuring language, thus promoting widespread industry acceptance. Today, the Internet user base has shifted dramatically from the traditional domains of government, military, and education to the burgeoning commercial sector (see Table 1.1). In three years this sector has experienced a growth rate of over 600%. The "urge to connect" trend is also noteworthy as the number of network domains has increased over 1,700% in the same timeframe.

In the eight years for which statistics are available, traffic on the Internet has grown from a mere dribble of 85 million packets per year to

Table 1.1	The Internet Becomes "Commercialized"—Number of Hosts in Top Level Domains					
Year	Commercial	Government	Military	Education	Network	Organizations
1995 (July)	1,743,390	273,855	224,778	1,411,013	300,481	201,905
1996 (July)	3,323,647	361,065	431,939	2,114,851	1,232,902	327,148
Source: http://www.nw.com/zone/WWW/dist-byname.html						

60 billion packets annually, as shown in Table 1.2. This exponential growth reflects the major Internet trends of increased numbers of users, increased numbers of networks connected, increased commercialization, and increased file sizes to accommodate multimedia such as audio, video, and large document transfers.

Along with the overall growth in the Internet, the World Wide Web specifically has boomed. Table 1.3 shows the WWW growing from virtual non-existence in 1991 to accounting for 21% of all Internet traffic in April of 1995. Where is the growth coming from? File transfer, the mainstay of the Internet, is shrinking as this capability is used more frequently from the browser screen. This sharp growth curve is expected to continue as more and more companies, networks, and countries come online and use browsers to navigate and interact with the Web.

Table 1.2	Growth in Internet Traffic
Year	**Traffic in Millions of Packets**
1989	468
1990	2,466
1991	5,868
1992	12,153
1993	24,016
1994	45,283
1995	60,399
1996 (projected)	96,000
Source: NSFNet Statistics (http://nic.merit.edu/nsfnet/statistics/)	

Table 1.3   Percent of Growth in World Wide Web Traffic

YEAR	WWW	File Transfer	Telnet	E-Mail	News
1991	0	20	17	8	10
1992	0	25	13	8	10
1993	0.002	24	15	7	9
1994	3	41	6	6	10
1995	21	14	8	6	8
1996 (est.)	25	12	6	10	9

Source: NSFNet Statistics (http://nic.merit.edu/nsfnet/statistics/)

Who's Open for Online Business?

As of this writing, 152 countries have connections to the Internet, with over 50% of them coming online since 1992. The number of networks installed ranges from the United States with over 28,000 to 20 countries with only one connection—for example, Angola, Cook Islands, and Mali. The rather high-tech countries generally are the ones with the most networks installed (see Table 1.4).

Table 1.4   Top Ten Countries, Country Codes, and Networks Installed

Rank	Country	Country Code	Networks Installed (7/96)
1	United Kingdom	UK	579,492
2	Germany	DE	548,168
3	Japan	JP	496,417
4	United States	US	432,727
5	Canada	CA	424,356
6	Australia	AU	397,460
7	Finland	FI	277,207
8	Netherlands	NL	214,704
9	France	FR	189,786
10	Sweden	SE	186,312

Source: http://www.nw.com/zone/WWW/dist-byname.html

Figure 1.1   On-Line Scotland Home Page

Figure 1.1 shows one of the top Web sites in the world, called On-Line Scotland (http:// www.ibmpcug.co.uk/~ecs/region.htm). This home page illustrates the type of information typically presented, the colorful and fun display, and the hyperlinks used by those accessing the page.

Internet networks in the various U.S. states tend to follow population counts, with California and New York having the most nets installed and South Dakota ranking number 50 with 15 networks connected.

Table 1.5	Top Ten States, State Codes, and Networks Installed		
Rank	State	State Code	Networks Installed (1995)
1	California	CA	4,832
2	New York	NY	2,152
3	Massachusetts	MA	2,005
4	Virginia	VA	1,964
5	Texas	TX	1,341
6	Ohio	OH	1,233
7	New Jersey	NJ	1,208
8	Maryland	MD	1,178
9	Washington	WA	972
10	Pennsylvania	PA	919

Source: NSFNet Statistics (http://nic.merit.edu/nsfnet/statistics/)

These top-ranked states represent the major online markets for businesses and other organizations (see Table 1.5). Again, all states are experiencing increasing numbers of network connections to the Internet.

For a home page a little closer to home, take a look at the page for cable television's Science Fiction Channel (http://www.scifi.com) shown in Figure 1.2. Again, this page demonstrates the consistent look and feel of information presented using Web technology. SciFi also includes several icons that lead to the Freezone (an area where consumers can download free video clips), the ScheduleBot (where you can see today's program schedule linked to more information about the shows), the Bboard (public forums on all manner of science fiction related subjects), and the Trader (an online store promoting science fiction merchandise).

U.S. Society and Global Trends

Several key trends shaping our national society and affecting the world at large are being facilitated by the computing trends discussed above. The most glaring trend is the globalization of society. National government boundaries are fraying at the edges as technology, ideas, and cultural norms bleed across the borders. Hierarchical structures are

Figure 1.2   The Sci-Fi Channel's Home Page

tumbling as national governments, corporations, and other entities flatten. The European Community, with its common currency, and the Pacific Rim are good examples of people from widely divergent backgrounds and cultures banding together to manufacture and deliver products and services worldwide on an unprecedented scale. The Internet and the World Wide Web support this globalization trend as one of the primary technological vehicles to spread global culture. In locating products, services, and information, we have come from asking "What is your street address?" to "What is your telephone number?" to "What is your fax number?" to "What is your e-mail address?" to finally, "What is your URL?"

The next sweeping trend to impact our lives at large is customization. Even though major markets are banding together to achieve a global presence, the individuals within those markets still demand that products and services be customized to meet their specific needs. This trend will lead to the demassification of markets, where special orders will become the norm. Organizations need to provide uniquely beneficial ways for individuals to use their products and services. For example, even though you can go into a McDonald's anywhere in the world and see the basic menu, each restaurant offers specialties for the particular area, such as soy sauce in Honolulu or Coke in liter-sized cups in Nuremburg. The WWW offers organizations the ability to customize their electronic offerings to customers, such as asking users which online magazines they want to receive and automatically sending them.

A third trend in the environment at large is the shortening of product development cycles. Consumers now expect new products, services, and enhancements to be available faster and at less cost; i.e., better, cheaper, faster. In using the WWW, organizations can notify consumers much more quickly of new products and services in a more efficient and less expensive manner.

Typical Web Business Services

The Web is most accepted today as a strategic information delivery tool. Web services typically fall into two categories of providing information: a source for static information and a source for dynamic information. Static information, which does not change or need updating very often, includes company policies and procedures, manuals, newsletters, etc. Dynamic information changes minute by minute within an organization and would include the telephone directory, conference room bookings, electronic catalogs, training class registrations and records, financial reports, and travel reservations. Other Web services include electronic mail, customer service/help desk, and links to customers, suppliers, and other entities. Web business services are more fully discussed in Chapters 9 and 10 of this book.

Although so many Web sites are now operational, the vast capabilities of the technology are still not deployed in most online locations. The presentation of text remains the single most common usage of Web technology. Thousands of Web home pages provide textual information, along with hyperlinks to more textual information. The next most common service is that of electronic messaging; users may send their comments or requests from a Web page. Only within the previous six months (a decade in Web years) have more interactive, animated, and application-based services started to appear. Table 1.6 lists the more common uses of Web technology within the more forward-thinking enterprises today, arranged from the simple static variety to more complex and dynamic applications.

Table 1.6   Common Uses of Web Technology

Web Services	Description
Policies, procedures, and manuals	Company policies, operating procedures, and technical manuals are placed online for wider dissemination, faster access and update, and keyword search capability
Communications	Company newsletters, event notification, press releases
Forms templates	Frequently-used electronic forms provided for download, completion, and exchange via e-mail
Organizational charts	Text or image and text charts for all defined organizations within the enterprise
"WIN" reports	Major new business contracts or technology wins for organization-wide dissemination
Newsgroups	Bulletin board-like forum for the exchange of ideas and information on specified topics
Employee resumes and interest profile	It's not who you know or what you know, but who knows what you know. Online resumes with skill summaries, experience, relocation preferences, and other interests. E-mail access to the employee from the resume.
Lessons learned	Listing of historical lessons learned, categorized by topic, such as software version, hardware platform, etc.
Standard products	Listing of company-standard products for desktops, network equipment, hardware, software, and communications

Continued

Table 1.6 Common Uses of Web Technology *(continued)*	
Web Services	Description
Fun stuff	Share-a-ride commuting partners, hobby clubs, local restaurants, direction maps, community events, etc.
Project management system	Interactive access to project plans, reports, team rosters, and documents arranged by project/program. Dynamic view of project funds expenditures.
Telephone directory	Listing of all employees, along with related information, such as physical location, mail point, closest fax machine, department code, etc.
Electronic software distribution	Users download software from the Web page using the Web's file transfer capabilities
Electronic messaging	Simple electronic mail access from the Web pages, reply or notification to user's mail system in-box
Education and training	Listings of classes, employee training records, interactive download of computer-based training courses, class registrations
Conference room scheduling	Reservation system for scheduling conference rooms, audio/visual equipment, and catering services
Employee benefits	Interactive benefits quote, selection and verification, benefits records and disbursements
Job postings	External and internal access to currently-available jobs with e-mail response capability
Web crawler	Search engine for all home pages, content, etc., associated with the Web and/or all information, objects, etc., stored in enterprise databases or warehouses
Products and services catalog/brochure	Image-laden listing of all products and services with easy ordering capability in a secure credit card/funds transfer environment
Collaborative computing	Sharing of complex drawings, document, and diagrams interactively with annotation features
Just-in-time ordering system	Parts inventory database access with automatic ordering at specified inventory levels
Travel system	Official Air-line Guide with hotel and rental car information, reservation, and travel expense reimbursement capability
Customer service/ Help Desk	Interactive customer access for problem reporting, tracking and resolution. Customer's product/service suite viewable by Customer Service representative.
Network monitoring and administration	Interactive dynamic network configuration, system monitoring, and administration

Benefits and Management Concerns

"Why should we create a Web site?" "What happens if we do?" These are the two questions most frequently asked when an organization considers the creation of a home page. While the Web is simple, fast, feature-rich, interactive, and can be nimbly used in many ways as described previously, implementing Web technology within the organization raises several concerns. Management must balance the benefits with the issues that Web service deployment raises within the enterprise. The overall benefits and limitations of deploying an Internet presence within an enterprise are discussed in this section and summarized in Table 1.7.

BENEFITS OF USING WEB TECHNOLOGY

The Web brings to the information table a wealth of benefits aimed at organizations as well as individuals. Web technology is highly suited to

Table 1.7 Summary of Web Benefits and Limitations	
Web Benefits	Web Limitations
Global in scope	Unproven new technology
Easy, intuitive GUI access via browsers	Lack of security features
Low-cost access	Lack of performance management
Low- or no-cost software	No customer support
Low-cost hardware	Requires an Internet connection
Runs on all platforms	Software programming language incompatibilities between versions
Standardized file transfer	May not scale for large enterprises with intense interactive applications
Standardized document creation	Difficult to maintain content over time
Standardized network protocol, TCP/IP	Animation, video, audio slow
Reduces paper/printing costs	Unfiltered information may overwhelm users
Reduces marketing/sales costs	Not all employees may have personal computers
Increases productivity via faster search capabilities	

facilitating the societal and global trends discussed previously. In general, Web services are:

- Global
- Customizable
- Faster
- Cheaper
- Better

Global

A marketer's dream, the World Wide Web is global in scope, providing easy, one-click access to information stored on connected computers anywhere in the world. The Web provides an open market with equal access for all participants. The Web user interacts with the services in a demand or pull manner in which the flow of information can be controlled by the requester of that information, regardless of where the user is located.

Customizable

Web technology easily lends itself to the customization of products and services based on the capability of fast updates to information and the feedback received from consumers visiting the Web site. Product offerings can be tailored to the individual consumer by permitting the selection of criteria and submittal of the choices to database and manufacturing processes. For example, a consumer can request a disability insurance quote, select from the various permutations of the plans offered, and submit the quote request via electronic mail. The company can create a customized policy for the consumer and e-mail all the forms to the customer for further processing. In the near future, we will be sending software agents out to conduct specific tasks, such as ordering customized Levi's jeans based on measurements or 3-D body images submitted to the manufacturer.

Faster

The Web is faster in more ways than one. Web services can be implemented and deployed rapidly as compared to the development time of traditional distributed applications. Access to information is quick and will become even quicker as individuals upgrade their modems to at least 28.8 Kbps, corporations establish T1 access to their Internet Service Providers, and the Internet itself completes the installation of T3 backbone services. File transfer, even of large and complex files, is faster than using traditional network methods.

Cheaper

The Web is less expensive than traditional information dissemination media in several ways. First, connecting to the Web, either by using the company's in-place network or by leasing access to a service provider, is cheaper than the historic point-to-point or one-to-many type network access arrangements. Connections are flat-rate and not usage or distance sensitive as is the case with today's Value Added Network (VAN) service providers. A connection can be made for as little as $150 per month in most major markets.

The second cost advantage is that all or most of the software required to establish a Web client/server offering is either free from Internet sources or quite reasonable in cost from commercial companies. The hardware is also usually reasonable, especially if an existing file server can be used.

Offering text-based information and forms routing through the Web service will result in a reduction in the cost of printing, distributing, and storing paper documents.

Lastly, the Web offers marketing and sales capabilities to a global audience of sophisticated consumers at far less cost than traditional direct mail, print media, television, or radio.

Better

"Better" is quite a subjective description, but there are several advantages for using the Web to provide services. As a productivity-enhancing tool, the Web offers point-and-click access, global search capabilities, sub-second response times in most areas, and a common look and feel to the information presented. The Web browsers are available for every hardware computing platform and operating system, and the information can be accessed from every platform as well. The Web also offers a standards-based file transfer technique, document creation language, and network protocol in the form of TCP/IP.

Having a Web presence also places the organization on the forefront of the movement to go online, offering open access to all connected users anywhere, at any time. This places the enterprise on the cutting edge of the globalization trend.

MANAGEMENT CONCERNS WITH WEB TECHNOLOGY

Management concerns in creating an external presence on the Web or in providing an intranet service within the organization generally fall into the following categories:

- Access
- Cost
- Data protection
- Keeping current

Access

The management concern with the nature of access to the Web services can be seen from three perspectives. First, the organization is now accessible and "open"—open for business, open to customer inquiries and requests, open to the flow of information, and open in terms of security breaches. Products are now under development to enable the flow of information, but to do so in more secure and circumspect ways.

Access also has to do with who in the organization will have Web capability. If only the professional staff has personal computers, the goals of wide dissemination of company information and interactive access to Web applications will be short-changed.

Finally, when the Web service is available to all employees in the organization, what will they be permitted and able to access? Will this be controlled by management under an appropriate use policy? The organization must address internal as well as external access to Web services.

Cost

While the cost to create a Web presence is relatively low, the cost to manage the Web business service can be more extensive. The Web services will "take off" and users will demand that their applications, documents, plans, news topics, etc., be placed on the Web server in a timely fashion. Managing this user demand, as well as providing a secure, fault-tolerant environment with good response rates, is costly in terms of personnel, hardware, software, and communications.

Data Protection

Providing secure access to the Internet for internal users and secure access to the enterprise from external Web site users is a major concern of network managers today. The Internet provides very few tools to establish a secure Web presence. Work is, however, underway in filling in the security gaps, such as user authentication, access control, encryption, digital signatures, etc.

Another concern in this area is protecting the content of the Web pages from corruption, either intentional or accidental. If anyone can gain access to the Web server or another user's computer accessed by a hyperlink and place unseemly information there, then the organization must have suitable controls in place to prevent this type of access.

Keeping Current

Another major issue in creating a fully-functional Web service is that of how to keep the information content and home page design current. In a short amount of time, an organization may have thousands of Web pages in their system, each with content that could very well become outdated. Unless policies and procedures are in place, content owners may not remember to update their pages, leaving users to access outdated information. Some companies design a "last updated" field on the page and when a certain threshold is reached, send a message to the content owner that the content needs to be reviewed and revised, if required.

Chartering the Web Business Service

How do you launch a Web business service within your enterprise? The process of creating a Web presence—installing the hardware and software and generating the Web pages—is relatively easy and, in many organizations, technical people have already gone ahead and placed Web home pages out there. The difference here is that in order to provide reliable, consistent, available, and intuitive access to the Web, the organization must have at least a minimal structure in place. Whether this is referred to as the Web development team on a small scale or the Web services organization in a larger enterprise, an entity of some sort should be formally chartered to provide these services.

The process for chartering a Web business service may be too involved for a very small organization, but the steps discussed below and shown in Figure 1.3 are necessary in defining the nature of the service within a full-scale operation.

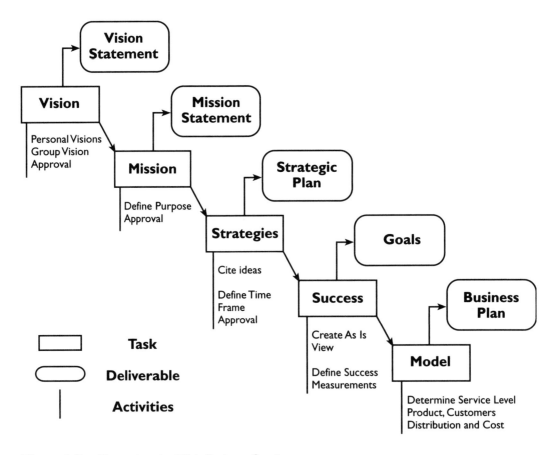

Figure 1.3   Chartering the Web Business Service

CREATING THE VISION

The very first step in chartering a Web business service is to create a vision statement. A vision is a view of the preferred future that those who share that view want to create. The vision statement will stand in stark relief to the way things are at present and will create a level of discomfort. The poetic, compelling vision will inspire people to want to move forward toward it, making the necessary changes and sacrifices required along the way.

A vision statement is the focus for the new service as the participants in that vision want it to become. The vision should have an associated longer range timeframe such as five or ten years. The statement does not necessarily have to mention any technology, any physical means used to achieve the vision. It can be simple, almost slogan-like, as in the "Healthy People in a Healthy World" vision of SmithKline Beecham or describing the Web as the "embodiment of all human knowledge" in the CERN vision. It can be far more descriptive, as demonstrated by the vision of the Electronic Messaging Association shown on page 20.

Sample vision statements for a start-up Web services organization could be:

"Linking people, business, and government with the universe of information."

"Building relationships to acquire global wisdom."

"Connecting people, processes, and technology for universal change."

The process to arrive at a vision statement that is compelling and shared is to assemble the current staff interested in providing a Web business service and poll them for their own personal visions of the future. Common themes can then be identified and worked into a vision statement that the group will share and to which they can wholeheartedly commit. The approved vision statement should be published on all documents relating to the chartering of the service and can be used as a slogan or logo on the subsequently-developed Web pages.

A vision statement is not fixed for all time. Change is the only constant we have today and this rapid transformation will continue. The trends discussed earlier will persist, evolving along the way; and world events

---

Electronic Messaging Association's Vision Statement

The information revolution is driving changes so profound that we compare its impact to the emergence of printing, writing, and speech. Electronic communications are global and becoming pervasive. Traditional organizations are meeting challenges more effectively, working and competing with new organizations to meet the changing needs of society. The critical applications of users and information products and services are moving up the value chain as messaging and similar applications are driven into the infrastructure.

Key ways that individuals live and work are changing. Individuals are empowered by the information revolution to have greater ability to participate and to have a true sense of accomplishment, contribution, and satisfaction.

Pervasive electronic communication dramatically alters the economies of scale for a wide range of activities and significantly reduces the barriers to corporate partnerships and other forms of collaboration. Organizations will sharpen their focus on primary competencies, creating new opportunities to provide corollary products and services independent of organizational structure or geographic location. Governments find that society's goals are easier to achieve through public participation in enhanced governance.

The EMA serves as a catalyst in the rapid evolution of electronic communications. EMA and its members will shape, drive, and consciously create changes and identify relevant strategies and processes. Rather than sinking further into a divided society of information "haves" and "have-nots" with less for all, the EMA and its members will increase the likelihood that the information revolution will work for everyone, leveraging universal electronic communications to enable people, businesses, and governments to achieve their fullest potential.

---

may slow down or propel them forward. Annually, you will want to have another vision planning session to assess your progress, recommit to the vision, or modify it in the event of any dramatic shifts.

ESTABLISHING THE MISSION

The mission of the Web services organization is actually the purpose for its being. What will the service do? Who is the service for? Typical mission statements for a start-up Web business service could be

"To foster the exchange of information in a full Web business services environment to all employees and customers."

"To provide an open forum of information exchange among all employees and between the company and its customers and suppliers through the use of World Wide Web technology."

"To widely distribute corporate electronic information to all employees and customers in a timely and reliable manner by means of the World Wide Web."

Again, establishing the mission involves tossing ideas around among the interested staff until a statement fits, and then publishing it frequently thereafter. The mission statement will also need to be reviewed annually to determine if the focus of the service organization has changed in any way that would impact the stated purpose.

DESIGNING SUCCESS MEASUREMENTS

One of the areas often overlooked in this stage of business charter development is to define ways to measure the success of the organization's mission. In other words, how will you know if you are successful?

To measure success, you first have to know where you are right now, to analyze the current situation. This analysis becomes the baseline or benchmark from which to measure your progress. For example, how many users within the organization have access to the Internet? How many have Web browser software? How are documents distributed today? How much does this cost? How much paper is consumed by the enterprise and at what cost? How many telephone calls does the Help Desk get daily? How much does it cost to distribute software to your users today by traditional means? How much was the last direct mail campaign and how many sales did it generate?

Gathering these statistics will enable you to formulate success measurements for the new Web business service. Typical success measurements might be:

"80% of all internal users have Web connectivity by year end."

"Document printing, distribution, and storage costs have been reduced by 50% within the first year of the service."

"Service calls to the Help Desk have been reduced by 30% in the first month the external Web page was placed into production."

"The Web's electronic catalog generated 25% more sales than the last direct mail campaign."

After the "as is" analysis has been conducted and the success measurements identified, the service organization should monitor their progress on a continual basis. When one of the measurements has been fulfilled, this must be communicated to your management and your customers. Placing an attention-getting award icon on your home page with a link to more information in a press release format is a good place to inform people of your successes.

FORMULATING STRATEGIES

Strategies are high-level activities and timeframes that move the service toward the preferred future as outlined in the vision statement. This becomes your action plan to start and sustain the Web business service. What needs to be done; when will it start; when will it end; who will do it? These strategies should be formulated from creative and bold ideas that will direct the Web services organization forward to fulfill the vision. A brainstorming session would be helpful here to bubble up all the ideas and suggestions.

What emerges from your planning session is a high-level strategic plan for the Web business service with the following elements:

- Strategy
- Time frame
- Responsible entity

As the services organization moves forward in time, these strategies will need to be adjusted. Action plans will be completed, success measurements will be achieved, and the vision may have shifted somewhat in response to the micro and macro trends discussed previously.

MODELING THE BUSINESS SERVICE

To successfully model the Web as a business service—whether for internal or external users—the product and target consumers must be specifically defined, as well as the means of distributing the product, where the consumer can obtain it, and how much it will cost. These elements, along with the items already discussed, will form the business plan for the new Web business service.

Selecting the Web Business Service Level

The first decision to make is what level of service to offer—whether to offer internal or external Web services. Several different approaches are available, ranging from using the Web as an internal application only or flinging the electronic doors to your business wide open. As shown in Figure 1.4, essentially four levels of service can be offered using Web technology.

- Pure intranet
- Pure Internet
- Hybrid
- Open system

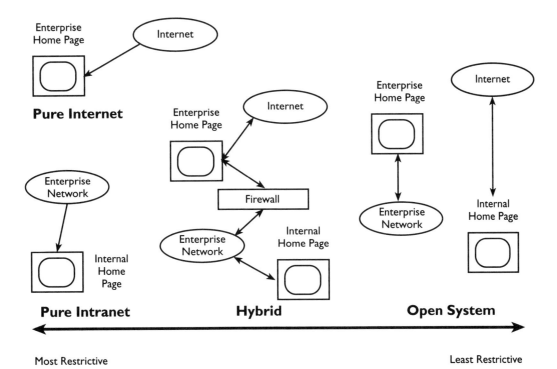

Figure 1.4   Selecting the Level of Service to Provide

Pure Intranet

A strictly internal Web business service, frequently referred to as an "intranet," provides a Web site or a number of networked sites that are within the enterprise and visible and available only to each other. This is a closed architecture and the focus is on using Web technology for internal use only. The users do not have access to the outside world through their Internet browser. In this case, the enterprise has made the decision that the Web will be used as an internal information access and distribution tool with no links to the Internet. This is the most restrictive service level to offer but has an advantage in the area of management control over how users spend their time interacting with the system.

Pure Internet

The enterprise may decide to launch a Web business service that presents a home page only to the outside world who gain access through the Internet. The business presents essentially a storefront window, but no "in" doorway. There are no links to the inside of the business, no electronic mail hyperlink, no comment form or registration; the site is strictly to provide information as a roadside billboard would do for a passing motorist. This is also a very restrictive environment to offer as it provides no access for the calling customer to assistance or more information, but it's a lot less labor intensive.

Hybrid

The hybrid approach is the most common implementation of Web technology today. Organizations establish a corporate Web site, giving access to customers, suppliers, and other parties from the Internet. Hyperlinks, embedded in the external home page and subsequent pages, direct the calling public to more information or applications. Users internal to the enterprise also have a Web site or network of sites, and access their internal home page by means of their desktop browser. Internal users are given access to the Internet and can partake of the services offered there, such as search capabilities and hyperlinked access to computers the world over. Some organizations do restrict access to certain sites that they find objectionable for the workplace or the capability to transmit sensitive or proprietary data over the Internet. External users are prohibited from entering the network of the enterprise by means of security features such as proxy servers and firewalls, which will be discussed in Chapter 8.

Open System

The least confining service level to offer is that of a totally open system. The Web server acts as an open doorway to the calling public and to the internal users. There are no prohibitions on what Internet services can be accessed or where in the internal network an external user can go. You are open 24 hours for business and there are no locks on the doors. Most enterprises shudder to even consider this as an option due to security and privacy reasons, but the technology does support this level of service.

For our purposes within this book, we will select the hybrid service level as the working model for the Web business services organization. It is the most frequently applied approach in Web deployment today and will enable us to explore more services, options, techniques, etc. Now that we know how we are going to offer the service, we need to specify and define the product.

The Product

What is it that will be offered to the consumer? What are we selling? The product the Web organization will offer is information, which will be displayed, distributed, and linked on the system. It is imperative that the Web services initiators have a clear idea or vision of what the product is and how it will be electronically communicated to the target consumers. It would be beneficial to review the list shown previously of typical Web services for product ideas.

The product may be the electronic distribution of software, such as application programs, music, video, books, reports, magazines, newsletters, online translation services, etc. The product may be an electronic brochure describing the business, an online catalog filled with images of the goods offered (automobiles, flowers, coffee, T-shirts), an insurance policy quote form, or a myriad of different things the business markets. The business may also just want to raise the level of awareness about the organization, as in the case of an association or an annual charity benefit.

The product is also an image—a presence, if you will—of the organization made available through Web technology, such as that of a theme park, national park, or museum. The image portrayed by the home page is vitally important, as this is the storefront, the first snippet of knowledge the consumer has about the organization.

The organization's home page must be designed in such a way that users are encouraged to return to the page again and again, can interact with up-to-date information, use the hyperlinks, easily purchase or download the products, request further information, and have a little fun in the process. Pointers for home page design will be more fully illustrated in Chapter 4.

The Target Market

Using the hybrid service level approach, the target market at a high level will be both internal and external customers. To get more specific, these customers must be identified, counted (if possible), and segmented into groups or categories. This analysis of the target customer enables the content and the hyperlinks of the home page to be more effectively written to appeal to a specific market segment.

Internal Customers

The first internal customer for the new Web business service will most often be the Corporate Office. The CO will want an external Web presence to market the company's products and services and to provide more information about the company, such as annual reports, press releases, etc., to the interested public. The CO also has many shelves full of policies, plans, and procedures. Huge, unwieldy static documents such as these can be managed more effectively, updated and searched more quickly, and made available to a wider audience of internal users than by traditional paper or e-mail means. The CO will also want to place an overview of the company, the location, pertinent address information, and organization charts on the Web server, as well as video keynote speeches and graphical presentations.

Human Resources is the next most likely internal customer. HR has static information such as the Employee Handbook or relocation information that benefits from being placed on the Web. HR also has a need to provide job postings to both internal and external candidates. HR may want to provide a personal home page for every employee that can be interfaced with the job posting application. HR may manage the corporate telephone directory. If so, this would be an excellent item to place on the Web.

Education and Training could place the class schedule on the Web, permit online search capability and registration for classes. Personnel training records, certifications, and classes and seminars attended could also be made available to internal users through the Web. Eventually, the internal user could request computer-based training courses right from their desktop, playing them from their Web browsers and interacting with the course work.

Sales and Marketing are internal customers who want to know statistical information, such as exactly how many external customers are accessing the organization's home page, what their Internet address is, what hyperlinks are used, how the customers navigate through the information presented, etc. Emerging software will provide this type of feedback to the Sales and Marketing department.

Finance would benefit from being an internal customer, as they have financial reports, labor statistics, budget expenditures, and related information that can be placed on the Web.

Customer Service/Help Desk areas can offer their calling customers an electronic means to have their questions answered, product information dispensed, and trouble tickets tracked.

Planning, Engineering, and Manufacturing benefit from using Web services for project management, action item postings, progress reports, and placing project documents online for group viewing and collaboration.

Finally, all employees with access to the Web service will be target customers. Employees need up-to-date information about policy changes, benefits information, contract wins, pricing revisions, software and hardware standards, jobs, and so much more.

External Consumers

Who are your external customers? Theoretically, they are the 30 million or so users worldwide connected today to the Internet—truly a mass electronic market. But, on closer inspection, they do share some common characteristics as shown by the data in the third Internet survey conducted as part of the Hermes project at the University of Michigan (http://www.umich.edu/~sgupta/hermes/survey3). The survey of

Internet users found that the majority of respondents were male, well-educated, in professional occupations, and had an above average income.

Even though these demographics of Web users may not fit in with your target customer, you may be compelled to establish a Web presence based on competitive pressure. Do a search of the Web for keywords in your competitors' company names or product suites, and see.

How do you reach these external customers? First, advertise your Web page address in your current marketing literature. For example, in your next magazine advertisement, drop in your Web address along with an offer for a free screen saver or video clip. Publish your Web address in every piece of correspondence that goes to your customer base—product information, invoices, shipping notices—putting it right up there with your street address, telephone, and fax numbers. List your Web address in Internet search engines such as InfoSeek Net Search, Deja News Research Service, Lycos, Yahoo, etc., as well as in any compendium of who's on the Web (the "Internet Yellow Pages," for example).

Product Distribution

How and where will your target customers obtain your product? If your Web service essentially provides only information to your calling customers, your product will be distributed when the customer accesses your home page. If your product is software or music, video, magazines, or literature, a customer must interact with your organization's home page to obtain the product. If the product is free, the home page will then have an area where the customer can select the product and download it immediately. If not, the customer will complete the payment and distribution form and electronically mail it back to your organization for processing. The use of credit cards, third party financing, and "e-cash" or digital funds is just starting on the Internet today. The ramifications of this emerging technology will be discussed in Chapter 10.

Product Cost

How much will the internal users and external customers pay for the products and services the Web business service will provide? Determining the product's cost to the customer involves measuring the cost to design, implement, and maintain the Web business service. These costs are then rolled into the cost of the product which is offered electronically. The organization's profit margin is then applied to the total cost of the product and a price to the customer is established. The process of determining costs and establishing pricing, billing, accounting, and internal chargeback scenarios will be explored more completely in Chapter 6.

Summary

Establishing a Web business service organization can either be a snap—just install the free client and server code, write some pages, and open for business—or it can require extensive planning. Traditional business management principles can be applied to the development of a Web service to provide the organization with a more practical, long-range viability. In this first chapter we explored the phenomenal growth of the World Wide Web, cited typical business services that can be offered using Web technology, and discussed the benefits and limitations of using the Web as a strategic information delivery tool. We then illustrated the process required to develop a charter and justification for the launch of the service and provided solid business case-type material on vision and mission creation, setting service levels and modeling the business. Our focus will now turn to the more technical aspects of launching the Web service—that of the underlying architecture and system components of the internal and external Web sites.

Designing the Web Services Architecture

The underlying architecture that enabled the Fremont office's extensive use of Web technology to quickly accomplish tasks didn't happen by accident. Each component of the system was judiciously planned and designed to meet the business requirements as set forth by the office's managers, administrators, and end users. From these initial requirements, a Web services architecture or road map was designed to facilitate and enhance the core business activities over both the short and long term.

In this chapter we will explore the development of a Web business services architecture. The building blocks of this plan will be based on the Internet and Web architectural framework in place today, with an eye toward future developments in Web technology. We will analyze architectural components such as the system requirements, the network, the Web server, the client system, application content, as well as management and financial systems. As these pieces are snapped into place, a basic architectural design for Web services will emerge, well-suited for organizations of all sizes.

Internet and Web Architecture Today

The Internet and the World Wide Web both follow a traditional client/server architecture. This framework is a necessary foundation for the highly-decentralized and platform-independent nature of the Internet and the Web. Understanding this framework is essential in designing a compatible and fully-functional Web services architecture for the enterprise.

CLIENT/SERVER ARCHITECTURE

In its most basic form, the client/server architecture has three components: a client computer, a server computer, and a network connecting the two of them. This arrangement, as shown in Figure 2.1, is a collaborative model used to accomplish distributed tasks. The client, usually residing at the end user's computer, directs a request to the server, transmitting it across the network. The server handles the request by directing a response over the network back to the client. For example, a client requests access to a word processor application residing on the server. The server provides the client with access to the application program and the end user begins interacting with the word processor to create a document.

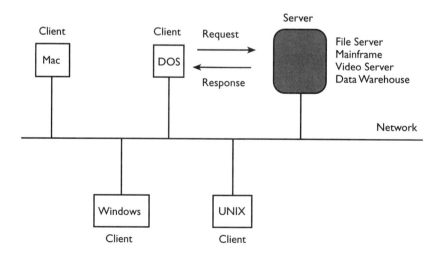

Figure 2.1   Client/Server Architecture Model

The client might also be a personal digital assistant, laptop computer, palmtop computer, a television with a smart set-top box, a wrist watch, as well as the more typical desktop personal computer or work-station. In some cases, the client may be a mainframe computer. The client may also operate as a server.

The server typically is a higher-end personal computer acting as the repository of data for the clients on the network. The server contains such shared resources as application programs, network access, and data and files too large to be stored on the client's system. The server generally requires multi-gigabyte hard disk storage as well as higher levels of RAM (16MB and up). The most common type of server is the file server, a storehouse of data, programs, and shared resources for the clients that reside on a Local Area Network (LAN). Data ware-houses are also classified as servers since they respond to requests for data on demand. The server may also act as a client. The roles of client and server may reside on a single computer and may occur simultaneously. Today's multitasking computer operating systems enable this working arrangement.

Figure 2.2 illustrates the client/server architecture of the Internet and the WWW today. High-capacity backbone frame relay switches using a high-speed T3 network infrastructure transmit requests and responses between the clients and the servers. The domestic Internet has four Network Access Points (NAPs) for entry to the backbone and runs a collection of protocols under the umbrella of TCP/IP that provide such services as electronic messaging, World Wide Web, file transfer, and management. The U.S. Internet connects with other Internets in vari-ous countries, forming the global electronic communications commu-nity. The Internet has recently undergone significant improvements in the area of transmission speeds, moving from a T1-based backbone to that of T3. The enormous growth in the number of users, the amount of traffic generated, and the increased file sizes prompted this major network upgrade. The Internet is also moving from a transport-based network to an application-based network, with the focus shifting from connectivity to application interoperability.

For more information and network diagrams on the new Internet architecture, go to http://www.merit.edu/.internet.html and http://www.iab.org/iab/overview.html.

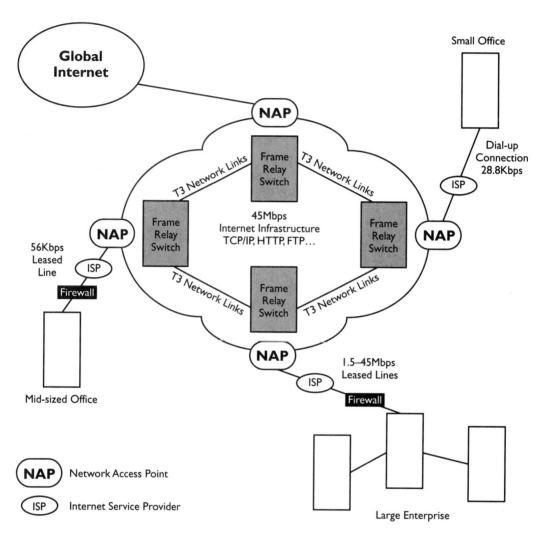

Figure 2.2   Internet and WWW Architecture Today

DISTRIBUTED NATURE OF THE WEB

The Web personifies the client/server paradigm by connecting thousands of server computers with thousands of client computers over the vast network of the Internet. In peer-to-peer fashion, Web clients request hyperlinked information located on Web servers and the responses travel over the Internet back to the clients. The Web is a global presentation system enabling the searching, locating, accessing, and display of the myriad forms of digital information. The distributed nature of the Web, functioning within the client/server model, facilitates the use of shared data, collaborative computing, and concurrent engineering. The fundamental characteristics of the Web—its lack of central ownership, its "openness," and its ever-changing nature—all contribute to the phenomenal growth of the Web and the amount of information available to end users.

Web Services Requirements

How does the overall architecture of the Internet and the World Wide Web mesh with the organization's requirements for a Web business service? What is the current configuration of the organization's computing environment? Requirements, or what the administrators and users expect the system to do, must be gathered and ranked prior to initiating the design of an architecture for the Web business service. The new system must fulfill management's and the end user's expectations or the deployment will not be successful over the long term. Establishing the Web services requirements enable the selection, configuration, and deployment of the new system. They also become part of the system acceptance criteria used in migrating the new Web services from a test to a production environment.

REQUIREMENTS GATHERING

The process of gathering the requirements for the new Web business service follows a continuum, from a very simple approach for a small organization to a lengthy and complex process for a very large, highly-distributed enterprise.

At its simplest, requirements can be collected from a few interested parties, creating a brief checklist of features and functions that the system should offer, then ranking them according to which items have highest or lowest priority. This list is then used to evaluate the products and services required to create the Web services system.

The more complex process involves first establishing a Web services requirements team composed of information managers, technical administrators, UNIX professionals, customer support representatives, and end users. The deliverable of this process is the formal system requirements definition. The following steps briefly illustrate the process:

1. Form the requirements team.
2. Gather input from industry and trade organizations.
3. Gather input from current news publications and trade journals.
4. Poll end users and administrators for required and desired functions and features. Polling can be accomplished by taking a survey; circulating a questionnaire; conducting personal interviews, demonstrations, and presentations; analyzing relevant data such as the cost of printing within the organization; and so on.
5. Generate the draft requirements definition.
6. Submit to all team members and interested parties for further input.
7. Generate the formal system requirements definition.
8. Obtain management approval.

During the entire requirements gathering process, the team must focus on what the users and managers of the system want. Figure 2.3 depicts a few of the highly-desirable features and functions that end users most often request in a new Web services system. This list is, of course, different from that requested by the management and administrators, as depicted in Figure 2.4.

REQUIREMENTS MATRIX

After the formal system requirements definition has been approved by management, the team then decides, for each item, whether it is a hard requirement (essential, a must have) or whether it is just desirable (a want, nice to have). The requirements, along with their designation as either a must or a want are placed into a table or spreadsheet, forming a requirements matrix, a concept developed by Kepner-Tregoe. This matrix will then be used to evaluate the potential products and services under consideration for the new system. The matrix will also be used to test the system against the stated requirements prior to accepting and placing it into production. We will add more detail to the requirements matrix in the next chapter when we discuss the acquisition of system services, hardware, and software.

Figure 2.3   What the Web Users Want

CREATING TESTABLE REQUIREMENTS

In formulating the requirements definition, each requirement listed must be phrased in such a way as to be measurable or testable. The wording must specify exactly what the product or service should do in order to successfully meet this requirement. For example, to state that "the system must be available to the end users" is not testable or measurable because the definition of "available" has not been defined or specified. A better way to state this requirement would be "the system shall be available to the users 99.99% of the time." Creating testable requirements up front in the process, even though it is a bit more time consuming, will pay major dividends during the product selection and system acceptance testing phases.

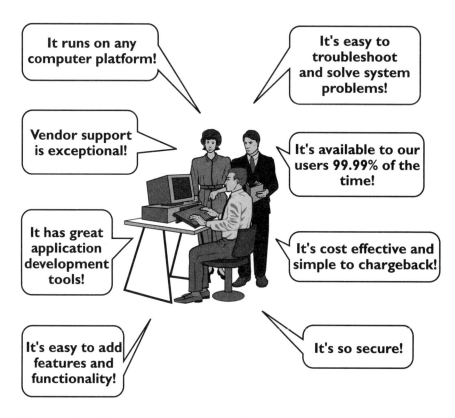

Figure 2.4 What the Management and Administrators Want

FORMULATING THE "AS IS" CONFIGURATION

Before the new or upgraded architectural model can be designed, an organization needs to perform an analysis of their current computing environment. This "As Is" model takes a snapshot of the organization's network infrastructure; all hardware computing platforms; the software on those machines, including operating systems, applications, utilities, and versions; the number of users; and any existing connections to the Internet, Value Added Network providers, or online services. The analysis will also show how the users are using the existing computing environment, what types of data are being exchanged, and the size of the files, thus giving clues about the network speed required to support the multimedia capabilities of the new Web service. This survey will enable the Web services deployment team to determine what additional hardware and software purchases and/or upgrades are required to launch the new service and how to reconfigure the network to handle the new demands of the service.

Architectural Components

The design of the Web services architecture flows from the functional and administrative/management requirements definition. Users, managers, and administrators have specified exactly what the system is to do and how it is to behave. From this documentation of the musts and wants for the system, an architectural model that satisfies these requirements will be built. As illustrated in Figure 2.5, the Web services architecture has several components. These pieces fit together to provide not only a framework for the initial service offering, but a foundation for new services and enhancements as demanded by growth and technological advances. This section will explore the Web services architectural components, including the advantages of a layered

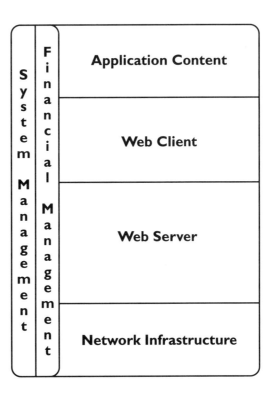

Figure 2.5   The Web Services Architectural Components

architectural approach, the network infrastructure, the Web server, the Web client, and the application content. System and financial management are also briefly addressed here as part of the overall architecture.

LAYERED ARCHITECTURE APPROACH

In the early days of computing, the application process was not shielded from the underpinnings of the network. The application process required knowledge of the data routing between two systems on the network. The routing codes used in the network needed to be known by all the concentrators and routers along the way. Routing codes were not standardized between networks, creating a great deal of overhead in the application code and severely restricting the overall design of the network.

In the late 1970's, an international standards-making body called the International Standards Organization (ISO) began work on a new approach to data communications. This approach focused on a layered architecture. A "layer" is a subgrouping of interrelated functions that are performed at the request of adjacent layers, as shown in Figure 2.6. The layer (n) makes requests of the adjacent layer (n–1 or n+1).

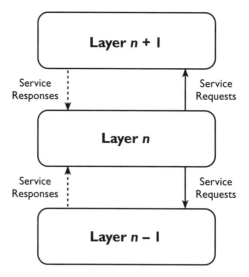

Figure 2.6   Concepts of a Layered Architecture

The adjacent layer then responds to the request and the exchange of data ensues. Each layer performs a unique set of tasks. When two cooperating systems are communicating, the interaction occurs in a peer-to-peer manner. For example, layer 1 in System A communicates with layer 1 in System B to establish the physical connection.

ISO's seven-layer architectural model, called the Open Systems Interconnection (OSI-X.200) standard, offered several distinct advantages. First, the application process became just a user of the network, and was effectively shielded from anything that went on in the network. Second, the application program developers now did not have to build knowledge of the communications system into the program. The overhead of the program code was reduced and applications became more portable. Lastly, each layer only had to have knowledge of the layer either directly above or below it. This meant that changes made in one layer would not affect all the layers, lending more stability to the communications system. The model also permitted the cooperating systems to become more "open," using widely-known international standards, instead of proprietary data communications architecture specific to one vendor.

The Internet rests on a layered architecture very similar to that of the ISO model. The Internet uses the Transmission Control Protocol/Internet Protocol (TCP/IP), discussed later in this chapter, while the ISO open systems model uses the OSI protocol. As can be seen from the comparison diagram in Figure 2.7, the OSI model can be roughly mapped to the layers in the Internet protocol stack. The Internet model combines the application, session, and presentation layers of the OSI model into its application layer; it uses TCP for its transport protocol and IP as the network protocol. A brief description of the unique responsibilities of each of the layers in both models is included in the diagram.

NETWORK INFRASTRUCTURE

Infrastructure refers to the fundamental functions and characteristics of the network and can also be considered the network's backbone. The network infrastructure for a Web service has four basic components as depicted in Figure 2.8: network topology, network physical media, network technology, and network speed. These four elements are the nec-

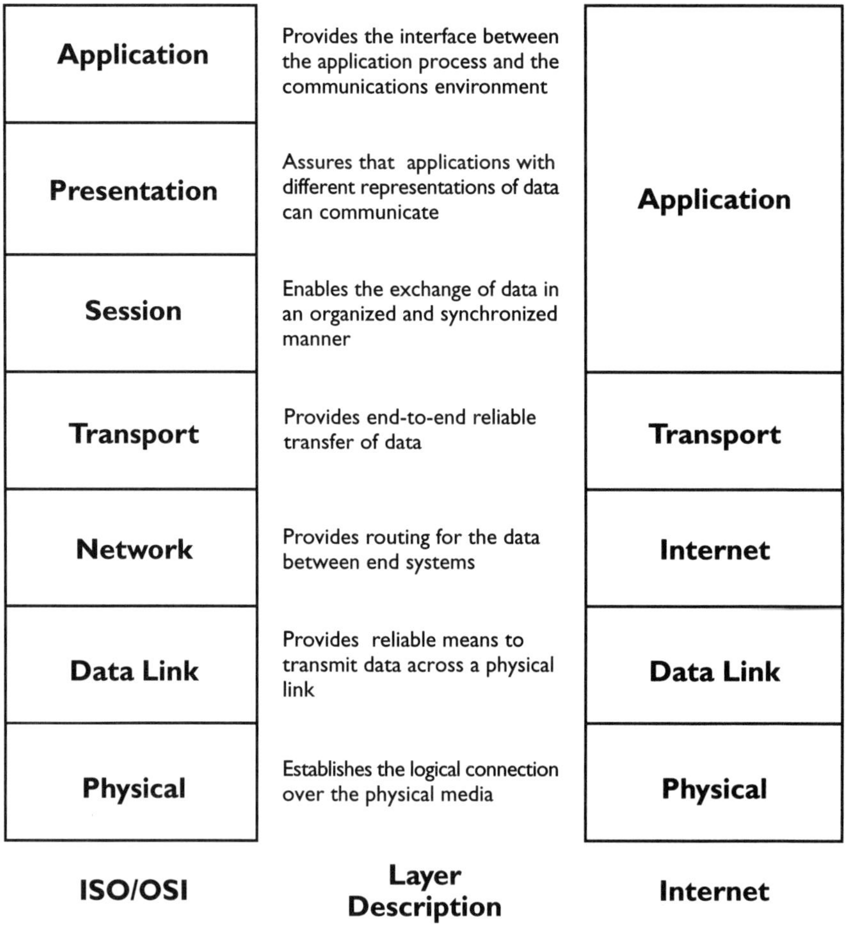

ISO/OSI	Layer Description	Internet
Application	Provides the interface between the application process and the communications environment	**Application**
Presentation	Assures that applications with different representations of data can communicate	
Session	Enables the exchange of data in an organized and synchronized manner	
Transport	Provides end-to-end reliable transfer of data	**Transport**
Network	Provides routing for the data between end systems	**Internet**
Data Link	Provides reliable means to transmit data across a physical link	**Data Link**
Physical	Establishes the logical connection over the physical media	**Physical**

Figure 2.7   Comparison of Internet and OSI Architectures

essary building blocks for creating a network infrastructure that will provide robust and reliable communications for the Web business services initially, and with careful planning, over the long term.

Network Topology

The network topology is the manner in which the network is arranged or designed. The topology defines the way devices are arranged along the physical network media. Typically, five network topologies are in common use today within large and small organizations. The devices on the network may be arranged in a star, ring, bus, tree, or hybrid fashion, as shown in Figure 2.8.

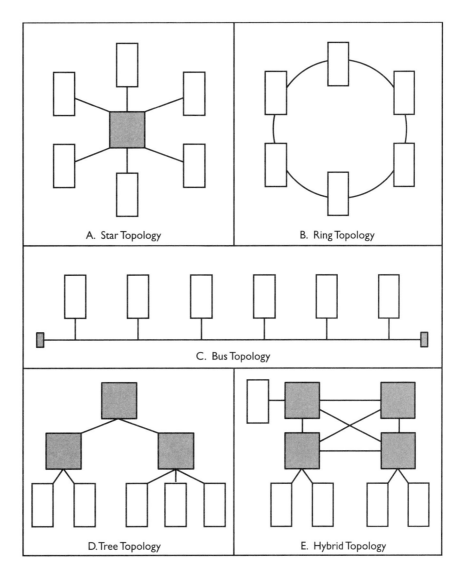

Figure 2.8 Network Topologies

Star

In the star network design, the devices on the network are connected to a central hub or host computer. This arrangement has two advantages. First, all the devices operate independently of one another; traffic will continue to flow even though one or more devices may become disabled. Second, all traffic is routed through the central controller, so routing information needs to be kept in only one location.

This decreases the amount of routing information that would normally reside at the end devices in the star.

The star network topology has a major disadvantage—should the central hub fail, all of the devices on the network become disabled. This single point of failure is mitigated in most enterprises by implementing redundant hardware and software at the central hub.

A Private Branch Exchange (PBX) telephone system is the most commonly known example of a star network topology.

Ring

The ring network topology arranges all the devices in a circle along the same physical media. While the devices are physically arranged in a star pattern, logically they form a ring. The computers, printer, file servers, and other devices are connected in a peer-to-peer fashion around the ring. This arrangement enables traffic to travel along the network even if one of the devices is inoperable.

The disadvantage of the ring network design is that each device must contain additional routing information to be able to pass data to the neighboring device(s). This increases the complexity of the network design.

IBM's Token Passing Ring network is an example of this type of network topology.

Bus

The bus (also known as a linear bus) topology places all the devices in the network in a line along the physical media. Each device monitors the network for data having its address and rejects data destined for any other device. A major disadvantage of this network topology is that all devices must depend on the same physical media. If the media stops functioning, all devices in the network are disabled.

In the bus network design, devices may be added or deleted easily, a device failure does not affect the flow of data, and the network as a whole is highly available and reliable.

The very popular Ethernet Local Area Network is based on the linear bus network topology.

Tree

In a tree networking topology the devices are arranged in a hierarchical pattern extending from the root of the tree to the branches. The tree is a more complex version of the star topology. Each device communicates only with one other device on the network, thus reducing the amount of overhead required to route the traffic. This topology is suited to high-traffic networks, since large amounts of data have no need to traverse the wide area network when communicating with a device on the same branch of the tree, as shown in Figure 2.8.

Hybrid

The hybrid networking topology combines elements from the star, ring, and tree arrangements. Also known as the mesh topology, this is the most complex network design and is typically used in large wide area networks, such as the Internet and geographically-distributed, autonomous divisions of a large corporation that wish to manage and control their own network connectivity. The devices are arranged in a star or ring manner, emanating from a network hub connected in a logical ring or star manner with other, similarly-configured hubs. While complex, this approach offers a high level of redundancy at the hub level.

Network Physical Media

After the network topology has been selected, the next option to explore is the physical media by which the devices on the network are connected. Several choices are available, ranging from the traditional twisted-pair and coax wiring to that of the emerging wireless network connections. An enterprise may already have a LAN in place, so wiring options may not be an issue. The Web service would simply ride the existing local area network, with a connection to the wide area network in larger organizations.

The choice of the physical media is an important one since many users will be simultaneously downloading home pages and images that require high-speed networks and consume much network bandwidth. When selecting the physical media for the deployment of the Web business service, pay particular attention to the top supported speed and the amount of bandwidth currently available for each medium. Select the media offering the highest possible speed and bandwidth at a price and degree of installation difficulty you can afford.

TP

TP, or twisted-pair, is traditional copper telephone cable. The distinct advantage of using TP as the transmission medium for the network is that this wiring is generally already installed within the organization. TP is also quite inexpensive to purchase and install. Today, users can achieve transfer rates of up to 10Mbps, but this medium is noisy. Using shielded twisted-pair lowers the noise level.

Coax

Coaxial cable is the most commonly-installed network physical media for data communications within enterprises of all sizes. A coaxial cable is thick and black and can be found in Ethernet and IBM network implementations. Speeds of 100Mbps are possible over Ethernet coax facilities using the 100Base-T standard. Organizations seeking increased network speeds at reduced installation costs are opting for the deployment of a thinner coax cable called 10Base-T.

Fiber

Fiber optic cable uses hair-thin glass media to carry lightwave signals. Fiber optic cable is not susceptible to electromagnetic interference as is unshielded twisted-pair. Fiber is a high-bandwidth, high-speed transmission medium capable of carrying light waves over great distances. While expensive to install today, fiber is becoming a more and more common implementation as greater speeds for multimedia delivery to the desktop are required. Used in conjunction with emerging technologies such as Asynchronous Transfer Mode (ATM) (discussed later in this chapter), 100Mbps transmission speeds to the desktop are possible.

Hybrid Fiber/Coax (HFC)

A hybrid fiber and coax approach called HFC uses fiber optic media for the backbone network and coax cabling to the desktop. This approach is beneficial in that the backbone's speed and bandwidth are increased, the network can be extended over greater distances, and the installation is still cost-effective to install and maintain.

Wireless

Wireless technologies are beginning to emerge as transmission media for data communications. The advent of infrared, cellular, microwave, satellite, and other technologies have facilitated the mobility of the end user; reduced the amount of cabling required within buildings; and made possible quick and easy adds, moves, and deletions of network devices. While wireless technologies do not yet offer the higher network speeds required for Web multimedia-type transmissions, better compression schemes are under development to facilitate the use of this media.

Network Technologies

The number of network technologies abound today, ranging from simple dial-up connectivity to sophisticated, high-speed, high-bandwidth service offerings. The network technology is a consideration in the organization's access to the Internet and in the network deployed within the enterprise. A discussion of the various network technologies available, their essential characteristics, and their advantages and limitations are explored in this section.

The various service offerings of Internet network access providers will be more completely discussed in Chapter 4.

Dial-up

The simplest type of network is a dial-up connection to another computer or network provider using a modem (or Modulator DEModulator device). Commercial modems today offer transmission speeds up to 28.8Kbps—the minimum acceptable speed for Web services. This type of network connectivity is suitable for home office users, very small businesses or branch locations, or very simple Web services. Either SLIP or PPP is needed for an organization to connect to the Internet using a dial-up arrangement. These protocols are discussed later in this chapter.

Dial-up networks are available in more areas and are inexpensive to install and maintain over time. The disadvantage of this type of network is the speed limitation. As the Web service or organization grows, the network speed may not provide an acceptable response time for the end users.

ISDN and SMDS are both higher-speed dial-up networking technologies discussed later in the section.

Ethernet

Ethernet is a mature networking technology that is the most common means of providing data communications within local area networks.

The technology most often uses basic thick coaxial cable. Ethernet has also been deployed using copper twisted-pair wiring, thin coaxial cable, and fiber optic media. While typically arranged in a linear bus network topology, Ethernet switches are now being installed to provide star-type connectivity for network devices in order to offer increased speeds and higher bandwidth to the desktop. Speeds of up to 10Mbps are traditionally supported, but enhancements such as Fast Ethernet and Isochronous Ethernet offer much faster speeds of up to 100Mbps.

ISDN

Integrated Services Digital Network is a high-speed, high-bandwidth network service offered by the local telephone companies. This networking technology is the digital replacement for the analog telephone network. While the technology has been around for years, it has been slow to gain market acceptance due to a lack of applications and availability in all areas. ISDN provides both voice and data transmission. The service offers basic digital connectivity at speeds up to 144Kbps and primary rates of 1.544Mbps.

ISDN is a dial-up facility that requires high-speed modem connectivity. The cost of this dial-up connection may be prohibitive for smaller enterprise or home office users and is not available in all areas.

An emerging technology dubbed B-ISDN, or Broadband Integrated Services Digital Network, is a networking standard under development. B-ISDN will provide higher speeds and bandwidth connectivity for larger enterprises.

SMDS

Switched Multimegabit Data Service is a local telephone company network service, offering speeds up to 45Mbps. The service has the ability to connect fiber optic, Ethernet, and token ring LANs in a metropolitan area using a dial-up connection. The advantage here is that the enterprise requires only one connection to the SMDS per each site, instead of installing a multiplicity of leased lines between sites. SMDS, due to its fundamental compatibility with ATM's fixed-cell technology, is seen by some as an acceptable migration path to ATM. This service will be replaced by ATM/SONET.

ATM/SONET

Asynchronous Transfer Mode is an emerging networking technology that holds the greatest promise for high-speed, high-bandwidth delivery of multimedia information required by sophisticated Web business services. Data types fueling the migration to ATM technology include medical imaging, collaborative engineering, videoconferencing, and the transfer of huge files. While the technology is fairly new, many companies have conducted pilots and are now migrating to production status.

The underlying technology is that of a fixed-cell packet comprised of 48 bytes of user data and 5 bytes of overhead routing data. This consistent cell length enables the network to transmit the packet at much greater speeds than that of traditional packet networks using variable-length packets. ATM offers a base speed of 25Mbps and, at the present, can provide up to 622Mbps. Trials are underway that offer network speeds of 2.5Gbps.

An advantage of ATM technology is its independence regarding physical media. ATM can run over twisted pair, coax, fiber optic and wireless media. Another advantage is that the fixed-cell technology reduces the delays present in packet networks, thus making it well-suited to carrying multimedia data, such as that of a Web service.

Synchronous Optical Network is a networking standard used for the transfer of data over fiber optic media. SONET uses Broadband ISDN to achieve speeds of 13Gbps. Using ATM technology in conjunction with SONET-based fiber optic networking enables the reliable transfer of real-time videoconferencing, video on demand, and medical imaging.

Frame Relay

Frame relay provides for the transfer of variable-length packets between computer systems across a packet network. The technology establishes a permanent virtual circuit between the computer systems and offers a guaranteed speed and availability. This network arrangement sets up a virtual local area or wide area network that reduces the need for multiple leased lines between sites.

Frame relay assumes the end devices to be intelligent, and so does not provide for the delays incurred by offering error checking. Therefore, frame relay networks typically transmit data faster than X.25 networks. Because frame relay has been around for a while, it is available and well-supported in most areas through public network providers such as CompuServe, AT&T, Sprint, Regional Bell Operating Companies, and MCI.

Frame relay, in conjunction with ATM technology, today forms the upgraded backbone infrastructure of the Internet.

X.25

X.25 is an international standard networking technology widely adopted and deployed in many countries. While the network speed is slow—just under 2Mbps—the technology does provide superior error-checking capability and is useful for connecting remote computers and terminals to hosts. This technology is simple and inexpensive to deploy and operate, but is not suited for high-speed networking demands such as a very active and sophisticated Web business service.

Cable TV

The major cable television carriers have been merging for some time with information delivery-type companies in an effort to offer interactive services to the home. These services now include video on demand, home shopping, bill payment, and video games—all delivered by means of the broadband cable network. The potential of this networking service is limitless. Eventually, users will be able to respond to public opinion polls, enjoy interactive music, make and receive telephone calls, and participate in real-time videoconferencing—all from the privacy of their own homes.

Many cable TV providers are also entering the business arena. For example, the Cable News Network (CNN) now offers the capability to receive continuous news feeds within a window on a user's personal computer. Since most corporations have quite an extensive coaxial cable physical plant already installed, the use of this type of networking technology is appealing.

Wireless

Wireless networking technology has emerged as a beneficial means to connect remote users to the host system and reduce the time and expense to add, move, and delete devices from the network. This technology today does not offer the high speeds and bandwidth required for the more complex Web services; and it is also relatively expensive to install initially. However, more sophisticated compression schemes are under development to enable wireless networking technology to better meet the needs of future Web service offerings.

Network Speed

Consideration of the speed at which a network transmits data is of paramount importance in designing the Web services architecture. Internet service providers offer a variety of network speeds, depending on the needs of the organization. Network speed is also a primary consideration when designing the organization's intranet. To determine the acceptable network speed, another look must be taken at the "As Is" configuration and the new Web services requirements. The organization must consider the vision it established for the service to allow for growth in the network speed.

Several options exist today in the area of network speed, ranging from simple modem connectivity to that of a very sophisticated network design using high-speed routers and switching hubs. The slowest acceptable speed capable of handling a Web service that provides minimal document transfer, simple graphics, and electronic messaging would be a dial-up modem connection running at 28.8Kbps. The Internet backbone has recently been upgraded to T3 service, providing an infrastructure speed of 45Mbps. Now being tested in the film industry are experimental network infrastructures that enable concurrent engineering on huge multimedia files traversing a network at speeds exceeding 1Gbps.

Typically, a medium to large organization will connect to an Internet service provider with a switched 56Kbps or T1 leased line. Significant growth in the transmission of huge multimedia files, interactive applications requiring subsecond response times, and the exponential increase in the number of users of Web services are driving organizations toward higher-speed Internet and intranet connectivity. Should an organization initially deploy a Web service using one of the slower-speed options, care should be taken to ensure that the network components can be easily and cost-effectively upgraded to higher speeds as the demand increases. A comparison of network technologies and speeds is shown in Table 2.1.

Table 2.1 Comparison of Network Technologies and Speeds	
Network Technology	Maximum Speed
Modem	28.8Kbps
Switched 56	56Kbps
T1	1.5Mbps
ISDN	1.5Mbps
X.25	1.5Mbps
Frame Relay	2Mbps
T3	45Mbps
Fast Ethernet	100Mbps
FDDI	100Mbps
SMDS	150Mbps
T4	274Mbps
B-ISDN	600Mbps
ATM	622Mbps
SONET	13.271Gbps

As revealed in the table, the various networking technologies offer a somewhat bewildering array of network speeds. The Web services network must be designed to support the fast and reliable transfer of information, ranging from simple text messages to that of complex images. A careful analysis of how the network is physically and logically constructed will reveal areas where the speed changes. Since the network is only as fast as the slowest link, planning a higher-speed backbone infrastructure in conjunction with compatible speeds to the desktop will ensure that end users have acceptable response times.

INTERNET NETWORK PROTOCOLS

Before data transmission can occur across the physical media and after the logical connection for the session has been established, the two collaborating computers perform a "handshake" involving the exchange of a specifically-formatted sequence of bits. Protocols form the "rules of engagement" for the transfer of data between systems, offering the exchange of specific information located within pre-defined areas of the bit stream. Each participating computer expects this sequence and, upon receiving it, can then open the session to further data interchange. Without the exchange of this protocol information, the orderly transfer of data between cooperating systems would not take place.

In actuality, the Internet is composed of an entire suite of protocols described in documents called Request for Comments (RFC) with an associated document number. For example, RFC 822 describes the SMTP protocol.

Several protocols are present within the layered architecture of the Internet. Lower-level Internet network protocols that handle the bit stream between the computers are TCP/IP, SLIP, and PPP. Additional protocols have been developed to handle more complex data types, such as electronic messaging (SMTP), news (NNTP), management information (SNMP), file transfers (FTP), and World Wide Web hypertext (HTTP). These application-oriented protocols are layered on top of the lower-level protocols.

In reality, large networks tend to be heterogeneous, in that they run multiple protocols. For example, a wide area network connecting a number of geographically dispersed locations might run the Internet Protocol as well as proprietary protocols such as DECnet and AppleTalk. The Internet itself is moving toward a multi-protocol implementation as it begins to incorporate the OSI networking suite and TCP/IP.

The protocols discussed in this section are typically those most often encountered in provisioning a Web business service.

TCP/IP

Transmission Control Protocol/Internet Protocol is the fundamental networking protocol suite of the Internet. Widely adopted and implemented, TCP/IP is the most frequently-used protocol within organizations today. This ubiquity stems from the insistence by the Department of Defense on the use of TCP/IP over the ARPANET, the forerunner of the Internet. All educational institutions, federal agencies, defense contractors, and research organizations communicating over the Internet had to use TCP/IP. Another reason is that TCP/IP is used in Ethernet Local Area Networks, a common LAN implementation in organizations of all sizes. TCP/IP provides for the reliable transfer of data between two cooperating systems. It is an open network protocol, meaning that it was developed in the public domain and offers a set of specific recommendations and guidelines for network deployment. TCP/IP is not proprietary; it is neither developed or supported by a particular vendor.

In the future, we will see even greater interoperability between TCP/IP and other networking protocols such as OSI, Novell's IPX, and SNA (IBM's System Network Architecture). All three of these protocols now offer some means to carry TCP/IP traffic over their own network in the form of tunneling or other special means.

The newest release of the Internet Protocol, IP Version 6 (also known as IPng or IP next generation), will offer several enhancements to this venerable network protocol. A "flow id" in a new header field will be used to facilitate the movement of massive multimedia information such as video and audio across the Internet.

SLIP

The Serial Line Internet Protocol is a simple protocol that enables Internet Protocol traffic to be transmitted between two devices over a single point-to-point dial up link. The devices may be routers, servers, or client workstations. Since basic SLIP does not support compression, the CSLIP (Compressed Serial Line Internet Protocol) is now becoming available in newer modems.

PPP

Point-to-Point Protocol is similar to SLIP in that it facilitates the transmission of Internet Protocol traffic over a point-to-point link. PPP also supports OSI, DECnet, Novell's IPX, and AppleTalk and can be used over a leased line as well as a dial-up line. Due to PPP's capability of assigning IP addresses, remote users can also establish network connections. PPP is fast surpassing SLIP as the protocol of choice for connecting to the Internet.

HTTP

Based on TCP/IP, Hypertext Transport Protocol is the protocol used on the World Wide Web. This set of rules enables a user to request hypertext objects (Web pages) from a Web server and have the information transferred back over the Internet.

FTP

Also based on TCP/IP, the File Transfer Protocol enables users to fetch and store files over the Internet. Files from simple text to complex multimedia and compound documents can be quickly and easily exchanged between cooperating systems using FTP. The protocol can be configured to require a user ID and password prior to the display of the files located on the FTP server, or it can provide open access in which only the word "anonymous" is required as the password. The facility supports two transfer modes, ASCII and binary. FTP is recommended when file sizes exceed 10MB as it is far quicker and more reliable than current electronic messaging file transfer capabilities.

SMTP

Simple Mail Transfer Protocol is the underlying protocol for the store-and-forward electronic messaging application used on the Internet. SMTP enables a user to send and receive simple text messages, store those messages, send and receive attachments, including those with multimedia content. It also provides a uniform and consistent addressing scheme.

Coupled with MIME (Multipurpose Internet Mail Extensions), SMTP permits the exchange of much larger and more complex data types, such as images, video, and audio.

SNMP

Simple Network Management Protocol is used to gather management information on all devices connected to the network. The protocol uses a query and response messaging scheme. This throughput, traffic, feature, and error data can then be used to compile historical trending information. The information is collected in a database called the Management Information Base (MIB), which is then queried.

NNTP

The Network News Transfer Protocol is responsible for providing access to Internet news groups (Usenet News, and NetNews), bulletin board systems, and conferencing. NNTP permits news articles on the Internet to be posted, distributed, and retrieved.

RSVP

Reservation Protocol, under development by the Internet Engineering Task Force (IETF), will enable the time-dependent streams of data contained in multimedia files to flow smoothly across the Internet without the delays or latency experienced today.

WEB SERVER SYSTEM

In designing the Web server system, three architectural components must be addressed: server hardware, server software, and network access. Care should be taken to examine the requirements gathered above, as well as usage and growth projections, to ensure that all three of these components will enable the Web business service to prosper at launch and into the future.

Hardware Configuration

Three basic hardware platforms exist today, and all have Web server capabilities. The most common hardware platform is UNIX due to the fact that the Internet is UNIX-based. More software applications have been developed for the UNIX platform, although the surge in Internet interest has shifted development resources to the other hardware platforms.

Choosing the fastest and largest machine that suits the enterprise's needs and budget will ensure that the system will meet the increasing demands for service in an intense Web business environment. In selecting a hardware platform, consideration should be given to the machine's processor speed, disk capacity, and amount of random access memory (RAM) available. These factors control the machine's performance and will be discussed in the following section for each hardware platform.

As an example, a smaller organization with a simple Web service may opt for a 75MHz processor with a 750MB hard drive and 16MB of

RAM. A large organization with a highly-sophisticated and well-frequented Web service will benefit from a 100+ MHz machine with a 1GB hard drive and 64MB of RAM. The reason for the large hard drive recommendation is that the Web service will be storing a large number of Web documents, will contain the log files for the service, and will store the indexes of the Web search facilities, among other system files and utilities. Large organizations may also opt to segment their service offerings and place them on separate servers. For example, a separate electronic messaging server or a separate video server may be implemented.

These are the minimum suggested configurations, and individual organizations may vary in their requirements and funding.

An enterprise may have already standardized on hardware platforms for both client and server computer systems. If so, the choice for Web server hardware has already been made. Just the size of the system, what software to run, and the type of network access need to be decided.

UNIX
The UNIX workstation is the most widely-implemented hardware platform for Web servers today. The workstation offers high performance, a robust application suite, built-in TCP/IP, and is fully scalable for growth and enhancements. UNIX workstations are available from several manufacturers including Sun Microsystems, Silicon Graphics, Hewlett-Packard, and Digital Equipment Corporation.

PC
The personal computer as a Web server is not as commonly deployed. The reason is that the Windows operating system is not multitasking and requires an enormous amount of overhead to run, which negatively impacts the system's performance. Personal computers running DOS and UNIX are more frequently used as proxy servers or as firewalls in the Internet network infrastructure. The Windows NT operating system is a move toward higher performance for Microsoft in the server arena, and more Web servers running Windows NT may emerge.

Mac
Apple Computer Inc. manufactures the Macintosh line of desktop computers. With the recent release of the Power Mac line, Apple has

positioned itself as a player in the Web server arena. Macs have always been popular as client workstations due to their superior graphical user interface and ease of use. Today, the high-end Power Macs are a good choice as the hardware platform for the Web business service.

In smaller organizations, or those which opt for simple Web services such as electronic messaging and small text-only document delivery, the Mac platform called the Performa will be sufficient.

For large organizations whose Web services are sophisticated, with thousands of accesses a day, the Power Mac line is the better choice in the Macintosh product suite. These systems have built-in audio-visual capabilities, a CD-ROM drive, and an intuitive and easy-to-use graphical user interface.

Web Server Software

Selecting the server software for a high-quality Web business service can be a rather daunting task. Many options exist in the areas of operating systems, applications, communications, and administration. The goal is to provide a fully-functional Web server capable of offering a suite of enhanced features and capabilities to the Web clients. Not every organization will desire or be able to provide all the different types of software discussed in this section (see Table 2.2). The selection of the software suite must be tailored to the needs, vision, and

Table 2.2 Web Server Software

Web Server Software	Description
Accounting software	Billing and chargeback of system services
Application development software	Developer tools, such as Sun's Java, to create new application programs
Application program interfaces	APIs—program specifications used to link Web applications to other applications
Calendaring and scheduling	Productivity tools that enable users to schedule their time and resources, such as conference rooms
C compiler	Programming tools used in the development of application code

Continued

Table 2.2   Web Server Software *(continued)*

Web Server Software	Description
CGI tools	Common Gateway Interface tools provide interactive forms and statistics
Communications software	Provides network access
Conferencing (data) software	Enables documents to be viewed and sometimes annotated simultaneously by multiple users
Configuration and management tools	Utilities to design, configure, and manage the Web service
Conversion tools	Translate files between disparate applications
Credit card software	Application program designed to handle online purchases made with credit cards
Electronic commerce software	Electronic Data Interchange (EDI), along with other tools such as e-mail, electronic funds transfer (EFT), etc.
E-mail software	Electronic messaging application program, such as SMTP/MIME, cc:Web, etc.
HTML authoring software	Used to design and create Web pages
Gateways	Provides access to other systems and applications, such as enterprise data warehouses
Logging and analysis tools	Measures the amount of traffic on the Web system and provides statistical analyses and trending information
Multimedia tools	Enables the delivery of multimedia over the Web—audio, video, animation
Monitoring	Web server and extended network monitoring for problem determination, isolation, and resolution
Security software	Proxy server, access control, user authentication and authorization
TCP/IP software	Essential network software for Internet access
Virus protection	Software to enable the scanning of files retrieved from Internet and Web information sources
Videoconferencing	Provides videoconferencing capabilities to multiple users
Viewers	Enables files created by disparate applications to be displayed without running the application
Web crawlers	Provides keyword search and indexing capabilities for internal and external Internet resources
Web server software	Application program providing the server software for the Web service

budget of the enterprise. Most of the software tools described here also have a client side, which is discussed in the section entitled "Web Client Software Tool Set" a little later in this chapter

Operating System Software

In general, Web server software can run on any widely-adopted operating system including UNIX, Windows or Windows NT, DOS, and Mac OS. Again, the choice of UNIX as the operating system for the Web server is beneficial in that software is created for the UNIX environment first, then developed for other operating systems. UNIX is also the most commonly-implemented operating system for Web servers today. UNIX includes TCP/IP software and is a high-performance multitasking operating system, something a very active and multi-functional Web server requires. UNIX is available from several companies, most notably Solaris from SunSoft, UnixWare from Novell, and Open Server from the Santa Cruz Operation (SCO).

Application Software

Application software can be the server side of applications, application program interfaces, or application development tools. These tools provide the ability to create new software programs, link application programs, and provide database access. Applications, such as electronic messaging, group calendaring and scheduling, fax integration, and videoconferencing, can be served to the Web client side of the client/server equation.

Communications Software

The Web server must have communications software in order to access the network. The server must be running TCP/IP. This protocol is available built into the UNIX operating system. Several commercial versions of TCP/IP are also available, including Chameleon from NetManage, PC/TCP from ftp Software, and MacTCP from Apple.

System Administration Tools

Web server system administration software provides tools and utilities to configure, maintain, administer, monitor, recover, and secure the system. These tools are required to design, operate, and protect the system on a daily basis.

The features and functionality of various Web server software product offerings will be more thoroughly discussed and compared in Chapter 3.

Network Access

The server requires access to the network. Access can be made directly to an Internet Service Provider (ISP) by a dial-up connection via modem or by using a Local Area Network (LAN) connection. The LAN connection requires a network interface card (NIC) of the type designed for the particular LAN, such as Ethernet, token ring, or fiber.

WEB CLIENT SYSTEM

The computing environment selected for the client side of the Web business service also needs to be as robust as the enterprise's budget and needs require. The Web client system, similar in design to the Web server system, is composed of the hardware platform, client software, and network access. Again, the recommendations made here are just that—recommendations. Each enterprise will tailor the Web client system to meet its own requirements.

Hardware Configuration

The hardware platform should be, at a minimum, an MPC Level II machine or equivalent. An MPC Level II is a standard multimedia 486SX 25MHz personal computer with at least 4MB of RAM and a 160MB hard drive. The machine should also have a high resolution color monitor, CD-ROM drive, and 16-bit sound card, as well as a network access card or a 28.8Kbps modem. With this system, a user can access all the features and functions offered by the Web business service and have an acceptable response time when interacting with the World Wide Web for searching and downloading documents and images. This is a very inexpensive system, although a far greater amount of computing power may be acquired today at a slightly higher, but reasonable cost.

Again, UNIX workstations offer the highest performance and are fully compatible with the TCP/IP network protocol of the Internet. Not all companies can afford to provide UNIX workstations for their employees due to the expense. Also, UNIX workstations are more common in engineering, scientific, and academic environments; so support for them is somewhat lacking in business environments. Here, the personal computer or Macintosh computer are more widely implemented. Web client software is multi-platform, and the choice of the hardware for the client side would be predicated on what the enterprise is using today, what future computing environment is anticipated, and what the cost will be to acquire new or upgraded hardware for the Web business service implementation.

Hardware options for the Web client will be more thoroughly explored in the next chapter.

Web Client Software Tool Set

The following section describes the tools most effective in providing a highly interactive and intuitive client interface to the Web. Not all the services and tools listed here will be provided by every Web services organization. The cost to provide and support the various tools may be too high for smaller enterprises. The organization should view this list, summarized in Table 2.3, as a suggested tool set and tailor their service offerings accordingly. The organization may deploy a minimal tool set initially and continue to add enhancements as funds and support become available.

Table 2.3   Web Client Tool Set Summary

Web Client Tool Set	Description
Archie	Utility for searching filenames for keywords
Bitnet	Discussion group mail server
Browser	Client interface to WWW, Internet, and intranet services
Compression utilities	Software to compress files prior to sending them over the Internet or intranet
Database access	Access to corporate and/or external databases
Decompression utilities	Software to decompress files that arrive in compressed format (zipped, stuffed, self-extracting archives, uuencoded)
E-mail	Electronic messaging capability
Finger	Utility to locate a specific user or host
FTP	File Transfer Protocol—Utility for the exchange and storage of files
Fax integration	Enables a user to send and receive faxes from the browser

Continued

Table 2.3 Web Client Tool Set Summary *(continued)*	
Web Client Tool Set	**Description**
Forms	Defines fields for user-specified requests and electronic response
Gopher	User interface for Archie as well as other utilities
Image maps	Pictures with embedded hyperlinks to another document, graphic, or image
Internet relay chat	Channels devoted to specific topics for real time queries and responses
Internet talk	Capability to communicate in real time with one other user
Listserve	Mail distribution utility for groups of users
News	Access to intranet and Internet news groups (Usenet)
Print capability	Permits a user to send a file to a local or remote printer
Search engines	Enables user to perform keyword searches of internal and external information sources
Telnet	Enables login to remote hosts
Translators	Software to convert files from one application program to another
Videoconferencing	Capability to view another user or users in real time with audio for face-to-face sessions
Virus protection	Software to enable the scanning of files retrieved from Internet and Web information sources
WAIS	Wide Area Information System—Utility for searching documents based on keywords
Web crawler	Utility that seeks all Web pages in a defined domain and indexes them as well as key words on the Web pages
WHOIS	Search for user, network, and domain

The Web Browser

The fundamental resource in the Web client software tool set is the Web browser. So, of paramount importance is the particular WWW browser selected. The browser, or the client interface to the Web, is the portal through which end users will discover and navigate the vast realm of knowledge that is the Web. The browser must be flexible enough to offer easy and intuitive access to the more common Internet tools as well as access to custom services developed by the Web business services organization.

Web browsers may be acquired as public domain software at no cost, as shareware with a minimal cost, or as a commercial off-the-shelf (COTS) product for which there are per user and/or site licensing fees depending on the size of the enterprise. In some organizations, only COTS products are selected for enterprise-wide deployment due to on-going support requirements.

The most popular Web browsers today are NCSA's Mosaic, Netscape Navigator, and Microsoft Internet Explorer. These browsers offer such basic features as a colorful graphical user interface, point-and-click selection of hypertext links, image loading, menu-driven and icon feature selection, and access to print facilities, search tools, and directories.

The specific features and functionality of various Web browser product offerings will be more thoroughly discussed and compared in Chapter 3.

Traditional Internet Resources and Tools

The resources and tools in this section have been available for some time on the Internet. The Web business service product offering should provide access to as many of these tools as possible to enable the end users to take advantage of the robust resource-sharing capabilities of the Internet. Additional tools are described in Table 2.3.

E-Mail

One of the most basic and beneficial Web client software tools to offer end users is the ability to exchange electronic messages with the entire user base of the Internet, now numbering 30 million. With SMTP (the Internet mail protocol discussed previously) the user benefits from a simple addressing scheme and the ability to send simple text messages as well as complex multimedia files using MIME (Multipurpose Internet Mail Extensions).

Search Engines

User access to the myriad of available tools used to conduct online searches is another crucial feature to offer in the Web services client software tool set. As productivity enhancing tools, search engines can be very simple, with just a one keyword search parameter, or they can be highly complex, including multiple words, phrases, fuzzy searches, wildcard searches, and less-than, equal-to, or greater-than search parameters. The user benefits from these search engines by having ready access to online information stored in the vast reaches of the Internet universe, by interacting quickly and easily with the system, and by enjoying fast response of the system to queries. Several search engines are now commonly available to Internet users, including gopher, WAIS, WHOIS, Yahoo, InfoSeek, and Lycos. The home page of the Yahoo search engine (http://www.yahoo.com) is illustrated in Figure 2.9. Also, a fairly new search resource is that of the WWW Virtual

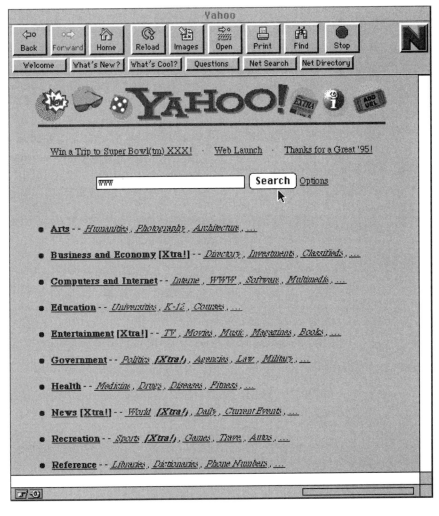

Figure 2.9   Yahoo Search Engine Home Page

Library, a distributed subject catalogue which can be seen at the following address:

http://www.w3.org/pub/DataSources/bySubject/Overview.html

News

Access to the Internet's news groups (Usenet) gives users an opportunity to stay current on topics of interest and relevancy to the organization. User's can interact with this resource by simply reading the content of the various news articles or they may become more involved by posting, retrieving, and distributing articles.

FTP

The Internet's File Transfer Protocol is an elemental service for users to access remote computer hosts and download or upload files ranging from simple text to large documents, audio, or video. Providing users with this utility will reduce the amount of traffic generated on the organization's electronic messaging systems by users attempting to transfer very large file attachments.

Telnet

Telnet is also an elemental Internet service enabling users to log onto remote host computers and access files and services there. A user can establish a connection with the remote computer and accomplish tasks just as if the remote host resided on the user's own local machine. This capability facilitates fast and easy file transfers and the use of other services.

Additional Resources and Tools

The Web business service should also offer users the following additional resources and tools. In most cases, the application and utility software can be found in the public domain or are available from commercial sources. Table 2.3 summarizes the tools discussed below as well as a few additional resources.

Translators

Users of the new Web service will be exchanging a fair number of application files using the Internet functions of FTP, Telnet, and electronic messaging. When a user receives a file that was created by an application program not resident on the recipient's client system, the exchange of information screeches to a halt. The user cannot "open" the file. End users must have several translators to convert an application file into a format compatible with another application quickly and easily. For example, suppose a user receives a WordPerfect file and only has Word for Windows resident. The user must be able to employ a translator to convert the file into Word for Windows format or lose the ability to display and manipulate the content of the word processor file.

Compression/Decompression Utilities

As the Web services user base increases, two things will happen. First, the users will be interacting more with the service offerings, placing a heavier demand on the network. Second, the users will be retrieving and sending ever larger and more complex files, particularly those with multimedia content, such as images, video, audio, graphics, animation, etc. This sharp increase in the amount of traffic on the network can be mitigated by providing users with compression and decompression utilities. The compression utility enables a user to dramatically shrink the size of a large file prior to sending it out over the network. This reduces the traffic on the network considerably and also reduces the amount of disk space required to store the file at the user's workstation. To display the file, the user decompresses it, restoring the file to its original size and content.

Forms

Electronic forms offer end users interactivity with the Web site. Users can fill in a text field on the Web page, click on a button, and transfer their query back to the server. The Web server then processes the request; linking with databases, documents, etc.; and sends the formatted response back to the client. Search engines now use forms extensively, with online purchasing expected to jump the current usage to new heights.

Fill-in forms enable a user to accomplish tasks such as signing a guestbook, registering for further access to the Web site's wonders, requesting information, providing comments and feedback, and searching for information located on the Web server. Since forms can be linked to databases and indexed by means of scripts, users can access and obtain more information interactively from the Web page than would be possible without forms. An example of a form located on a Web page is

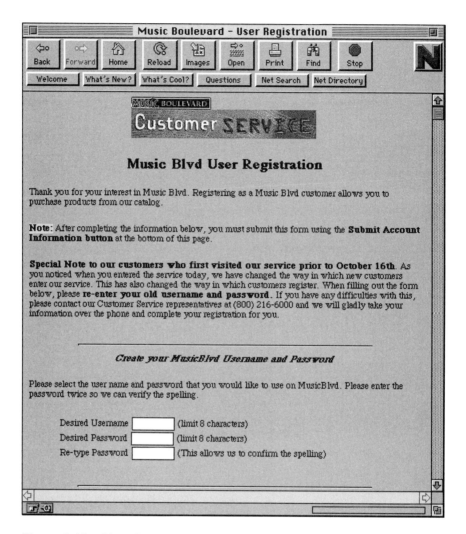

Figure 2.10   Music Blvd User Registration Form

shown in Figure 2.10. This is the Music Blvd registration page that enables users to establish an account for ordering music selections (http://www.musicblvd.com). The form requests a user password and goes on to collect credit card information, billing and shipping addresses, e-mail address, and phone numbers.

Web Crawlers
A Web crawler is an application program that searches home pages of a user-specified domain and indexes them along with keywords on

those pages. A user can then query the Web crawler for information by using a keyword search. Crawlers can be used to search the organization's home pages and subsequent pages in order to provide users with a virtual database of all documents stored on Web sites within the enterprise.

Database Access

Through the use of forms and scripts, an organization can provide users with access to all internal databases. The simple fill-in form with an intuitive graphical user interface can return search results from the very simple to highly complex in nature. Information that resides in corporate databases can now be accessed by anyone with a Web browser, regardless of the computing hardware platform or operating system software.

Videoconferencing

Real-time desktop videoconferencing, while cost prohibitive in terms of labor and equipment just a few years ago, has become one of the hottest applications emerging in enterprises today. New, cost-effective software and hardware, coupled with high-speed networks and sleek compression schemes, have brought this technology to the individual user's desktop. Offering videoconferencing as part of an enhanced Web service is definitely worth considering, especially if employees travel a great deal and require quick decision timeframes across multiple locations and time zones.

Virus Protection

Users will be downloading quite a bit of information from the World Wide Web and should have virus protection tools available. These tools are generally available in the public domain or through commercial sources. They are inexpensive and well-worth the investment in time to provide them for the entire internal user base. Huge files may be zipped, stuffed, and otherwise compressed and may contain insidious viruses that execute at the moment the file is decompressed. Users may also FTP files that contain viruses from any one of a number of innocuous-sounding sources. Policies that outline the steps to follow in dealing with information gleaned from unknown and untrusted sources should be created and communicated to users, including proper downloading and what to do in the event of a virus attack.

Client Network Access

The Web client system also requires access to the network in order to interact with the Web server. Access can be made by a dial-up connection via modem or can be made using a Local Area Network (LAN) connection. The LAN connection, as with the server, requires a network interface card (NIC) of the type designed for the particular LAN, such as Ethernet, token ring, or fiber optic.

APPLICATION CONTENT

The most important component of the architectural model from the user perspective is the content of the Web business service application. Content is what the user accesses and interacts with on a session-by-session basis. The content is structured within the service's home page and subsequent pages. These pages then provide links to the organization's databases, documents, and objects, such as images, animation, audio, and video, as well as links to the external World Wide Web and the Internet. The developers and owners of this application content need to have a clearly-defined set of agreed-upon objectives in designing the content for the Web business service. The objectives of providing application content by a Web business service may be stated as follows:

- Application content will offer a level of consistency in the display and representation of information within the Web service.
- Application content will be updated often and be maintained by the various content owners.
- Application content will make use of enhanced Web service tools to encourage frequent use.
- Application content will offer relevant links to other Web sites and services.

Consistency

In providing the content for the Web business service, the application developers and content owners should offer their information to the users in a consistent manner. This doesn't mean that rigidly-defined rules for the placement of a print button or the "mail to:" field need to be set in stone within the organization. The users will, however, benefit from a consistent approach in the reduction of both time to access features and labor costs to train users (through developing online help tutorials or other suitable documentation). Some level of uniformity is desirable in the design of application content over time.

Frequent Updates

The content of the Web business service application needs to be updated frequently. Users will not return to a completely static site—"been there, done that." The owners of the application content must make it a priority to conduct periodic reviews of their information on the Web pages and update them accordingly. Each time a page is updated, the new items are collected and displayed in a special area usually termed "What's New." Users frequently accessing the page will check this area first before continuing on to the subsequent or linked pages. While it requires an investment in time and labor to provide frequent updates, the users will perceive the page as fresh each time and will continue to access it often.

Enhanced Tools

The application content must be presented in a light-hearted, entertaining, and intuitively easy manner to ensure that users frequent the Web service. Web tools such as HTML to provide hypertext links, image maps as point-and-click links, and fill-in forms for interactive feedback and user requests are some of the tools previously discussed in the sections on Web client and server systems. When used with flair and an eye for informing the user in an entertaining way, the Web service will be used more often and by more people.

Advanced tools such as Virtual Reality Modeling Language (VRML) and Java enable Web developers to present the application content in an animated and jazzy way. VRML is used to create three dimensional virtual worlds through which a user can navigate. Virtual malls and trade shows use this technology to present their content, products, and services. Java is an application development tool that enables the creation of applets—small programs—that bring animation to the Web page. With tools such as these, the application content of the Web business service becomes entertaining and dynamic, ensuring repeat visits by users.

Links

Hyperlinks to other Web sites and other internal Web pages are also an integral part in providing a high-quality, highly-interactive Web business service. Up-to-date lists of interesting and relevant sites and pages can be placed in an area on the Web page called "Hot List" or "Links to Other Sites." The user then clicks on the particular topic of interest and the system automatically sends the site's URL internally or out to the World Wide Web. The advantage of having links is that access time to locate information is greatly reduced and the user benefit in productivity gain is immeasurable. The disadvantage is that these links, like the application content itself, must be tested and updated often to prevent users from encountering dead links.

MANAGEMENT SYSTEM

The Web services management system extends throughout the architectural model, touching all components, as discussed previously. This system provides the organization with administrative, configuration, and management tools and utilities that facilitate the smooth on-going operation of the entire Web business service. Such tools include system monitoring, problem identification, isolation and resolution, configuration management, help desk, security, and disaster recovery. These items will be discussed in more depth in later chapters.

FINANCIAL SYSTEM

The financial system also touches all of the Web business service architectural components. The system enables the enterprise to collect usage statistics and monitor such on-going costs as labor and support, storage, hardware and software purchases, maintenance and licensing fees, copyright royalty payments, and network communications charges. These costs are then charged back to the organization on a per-user basis, at the departmental or division level, or as part of the corporate overhead flow down. Each organization will have its own unique means of cost allocation. Including the financial system in the architectural design will ensure that the need for the collection of usage statistics and costs will not be overlooked. More details on budgeting and cost allocation will be discussed in a later chapter.

Putting It All Together

Many options for each of the architectural components have been discussed in this chapter. The Internet offers quite an array of protocols;

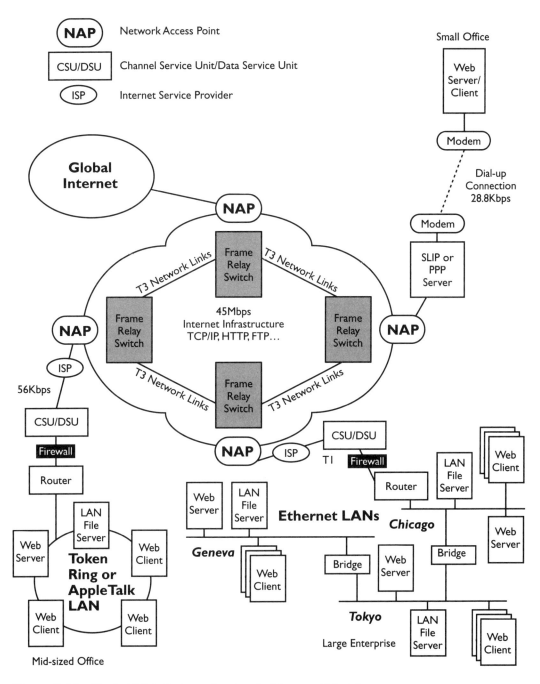

Figure 2.11   Typical Web Business Service Architectural Model

networks can be configured for several speed, wiring, and technological options; and the hardware and software associated with the client/server paradigm within the overall architecture also offer many choices. Now it's time to snap some of these pieces together and show a typical model. Again, this model is a series of recommendations, not a rigidly-prescribed road map for a particular organization.

The diagram in Figure 2.11 illustrates the components of a typical Web business service architectural model for small, medium, and large organizations, as well as the interface to the Internet. Basically, the diagram shows the enterprise connected to an Internet Service Provider, who then accesses the Internet backbone infrastructure through one of the four main Network Access Points. The exponential growth of the Web, along with the increase in the file sizes of multimedia data types such as audio, video, animation, and virtual reality, will drive the network speeds and bandwidth to much higher levels than are depicted here today.

Summary

In this chapter, an architectural model was designed to provide consistent, reliable, and robust Web services to internal and external users. A discussion of the manner in which the Internet at large is architected facilitated the design of an architecture compatible with the layered design of today's Internet and WWW services. The organization's requirements for the Web business service were defined and ranked as musts or wants. An "As Is" architectural design was created to use as a baseline in making system upgrades and acquisitions. Architectural components such as the network infrastructure, the Web server, the client system, the management and financial systems, as well as the application content were explored and recommendations for services, configurations, features, and functionality were offered. Lastly, a suggested architecture for organizations—ranging from small, remote sites to multi-geographic locations—was illustrated based on the options considered in the chapter's previous sections.

In the following chapter, the decisions made in designing the Web business service architecture will now be standardized and the specific hardware, software, and communications services required to launch and maintain the service will be analyzed and compared.

3

Purchasing Web Hardware and Software

"The trouble with standards is the second 's,'" lamented Jason as he scanned the electronic request forms submitted by users asking for new or enhanced Web application software and services.

"Isn't that the truth!" agreed Chris, "We have every hardware platform and operating system out there and selecting just the right product for our user base is like trying to find the potato peeler in the kitchen gadget drawer."

The Fremont office had standardized on a Web server and client suite of hardware, software, and services which made subsequent decisions to add functionality a little easier. Standardizing was a natural byproduct of the extensive hardware, software, and service acquisition process that the Fremont office conducted prior to launching the new Web business service.

This chapter will explore the process used to purchase and acquire the hardware, software, and services defined in the Web architectural model. The process outlined is comprehensive and, in its entirety, suitable for large enterprises. Smaller organizations will want to tailor this process to meet their own requirements. The benefits of standardizing on a product and service mix are discussed, and detailed product comparisons are then offered as a means to narrow the search for that ultimate potato peeler.

The Acquisition Process

In most instances, the product to be acquired is not unique within the industry. Competition is fierce in the Internet arena today, offering customers a wealth of choices in hardware, software, and services. While competition is the foundation of our economy and beneficial in terms of features, functionality, availability, and cost, the task of sorting through the maze of competing products can be quite daunting. This section presents a more structured methodology for selecting and acquiring products and services that reduces the cost and the amount of time required to reach a decision. The acquisition process is illustrated in Figure 3.1. For each phase, a list of tasks is shown, along with the specific deliverable for that phase.

INDUSTRY ANALYSIS

An excellent first step in this process is to conduct a paper analysis of all the competing products and services within the particular architectural component proposed for acquisition. Several publications within the computer industry offer timely test drives, evaluations, product comparisons, and reports that can be used to shorten the acquisition process. Also, going out on the Internet to look for information on a particular product or service will be beneficial, as this information is often times more candid and up-to-date than that published in traditional media. An industry analysis reduces the time required to refine the requirements matrix and narrow the number of products to be considered more thoroughly.

To conduct the industry analysis, gather all the relevant research material and quickly scan the information, focusing on the high-level musts that were identified on the Requirements Matrix. Eliminate any products and services that do not have even one of the musts. At the

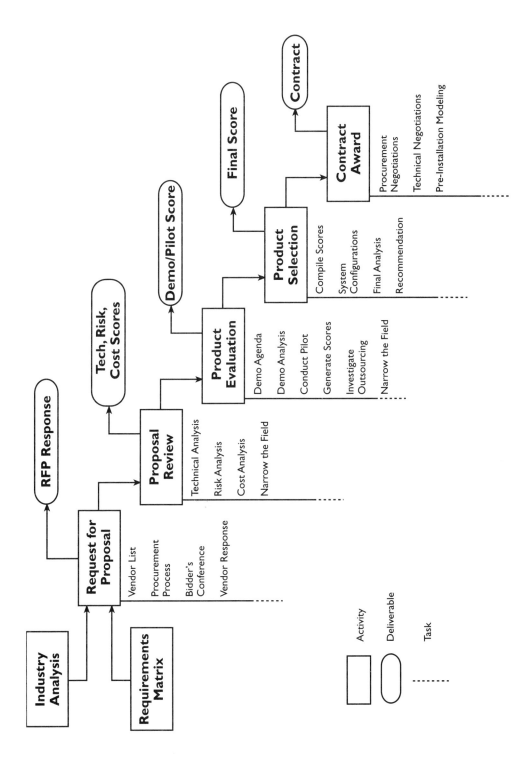

Figure 3.1 The Acquisition Process

end of this activity, a shorter list of products and services to be evaluated will emerge.

REFINING THE REQUIREMENTS MATRIX

Generated in the previous phase, the Requirements Matrix addresses the features and functionality of the new Web business system. The matrix lists all the required and desired features in terms of *musts* and *wants*. In this phase, the wants will be given a weight between 1 and 10. A weight of 1–4 indicates an item with relatively low importance to the evaluation team; a weight of 5–7, medium importance; and a weight of 8–10, high importance. Only the wants are given a weight, as the musts require a yes or no response. If the particular product does not meet at least one must, that product will be eliminated from the competition. Therefore, it is extremely important to reach agreement within the team as to which items will be musts. As an option, the team might elect to have no musts and list only the weighted wants, so as to more thoroughly evaluate all the relevant products and services.

As the hardware, software, or service features are analyzed, each item is then given its own individual score between 0 and 10, following the same importance scale as for the weights. A 0 means that either the product or service did not have the particular feature or that the outcome of the analysis was so low as to not merit a score. The weight and the score are then multiplied to give the weighted score. After all the weighted scores for the various competing products are totaled, the products are ranked, usually with the top three to five products or services remaining in the running for the acquisition. The deliverable for this phase is the completed Requirements Matrix, an example of which is illustrated in Figure 3.2, showing all the technical scores for the hardware, software, and services evaluated.

REQUEST FOR INFORMATION OR PROPOSAL

In larger corporations with more stringent procurement policies, the evaluation team may have to generate a Request for Information (RFI). This document is an invitation to as many vendors as possible to provide general information on their products and services, as well as budgetary pricing. Typically, an RFI would contain the Require-

	A	B	C	D	E	F	G
				WSO3Req			
1							
2		Web Business Services Requirements Matrix					
3							
4	Paragraph	Requirement	Must	Want/Weight	Vendor Score	Weighted Score	
5							
6	1.0	Web Server Software					
7	1.1	Hardware Platforms Supported					
8	1.1.1	UNIX	M				
9	1.1.2	Mac		5	0	0	
10	1.1.3	Win 3.1	M				
11	1.1.4	Win NT		10	10	100	
12	1.1.5	Win 95		7	7	49	
13	1.1.6	OS/2		3	0	0	
14	1.2	Networking Support					
15	1.2.1	TCP/IP	M				
16	1.2.2	Novell Netware		8	8	64	
17	1.3	Administration					
18	1.3.1	GUI Based Configuration		8	6	48	
19	1.3.2	GUI Based Maintenance	M				
20	1.3.3	Remote Diagnostics	M				
21	1.4	Logging					
22	1.4.1	CERN/NCSA Common Log Format	M				
23	1.4.2	Automatic Archival of Log Files		9	7	63	
24	1.4.3	Customizable Log Entries		9	5	45	
25	1.5	Performance Measurement					
26	1.5.1	Real-time performance statistics		8	6	48	
27	1.6	Security					
28	1.6.1	Requires Password	M				
29	1.6.2	Supports S-HTTP		8	8	64	
30	1.6.3	Proxy Server Included		8	0	0	
31	1.7	Documentation					
32	1.7.1	On-line Tutorials		7	9	63	
33	1.7.2	Clear, Concise Documentation		8	5	40	
34							
35							

Sheet1 / Sheet2 / Sheet3 / Sheet4 / Sheet5 / Sheet6 / Sheet7 /

Figure 3.2   Sample Web Services Requirements Matrix

ments Matrix in a Technical Specifications section, management and administration requirements, and general procurement-oriented requirements. The Requirements Matrix that actually goes to the vendors should not show the weights of the wants. It is more beneficial to the organization if the vendors think that all items have equal importance. The Requirements Matrix, along with the descriptions of the items, form the Technical Specifications. This list of numbered items is then used as the structured format that the vendors use when submitting their response. This way, all the responses are alike in format and easier for the evaluation team to score.

The RFI does not require the company to make a purchase decision. Rather, the purpose of this document is to gather industry and trade input to further refine the requirements, access the current state and the direction of the industry regarding particular products and services, and assist in eliminating some of the products and services that offer fewer features and functionality.

The Request for Proposal (RFP) or Request for Quote (RFQ), however, are far more formal documents that, in most organizations, require the company to purchase the sought-after product or service. The RFP would contain the same basic sections as the RFI, with the addition of company bidding instructions, a schedule of events and due dates, contractual and purchasing information, procedures, and requirements. Again, the RFP is distributed to as large a vendor list as is required by policy, and the vendors respond with information and pricing. During this phase, the organization may choose to answer questions submitted by the vendors either electronically or in writing. The organization may also hold a bidder's conference, which all or most of the vendors would attend, to more thoroughly and openly discuss the technical and general requirements of the RFP.

PROPOSAL REVIEW

During the Proposal Review phase of the acquisition process, the vendors' responses to the organization's RFP have been received and are ready to be analyzed. Based on the information contained in the RFP, the evaluation team and procurement will conduct three separate analyses—technical, risk, and cost—which will lead to three separate scores for each of the responding vendors. These scores will be combined with the product evaluation score (discussed in the next section) to create an overall evaluation score for the vendor. This overall score is used to rank the vendors and to recommend to management which particular products and services should be acquired to launch the new Web business service.

Technical Analysis

The evaluation team performs the technical analysis by measuring the product or service against the stated requirements in the matrix. The team members individually review each vendor's response to the Requirements Matrix. Each line item is researched and given either a yes or no response for the musts or a score for the wants. The team then convenes to discuss each line item and decide on a team score. Arriving at a team score can be quite a lively experience, as people sometimes have widely-divergent ideas on how well a particular product or service satisfies the intent of the line item. Some teams throw out the highest and lowest individual scores, then average the remaining scores to get a team score. Other teams arrive at a consensus score through the magic of group dynamics.

The deliverable for this activity is the final technical score for each of the responding vendors.

Cost Analysis

Based on the cost worksheets included in the Request for Proposal, each vendor should have submitted detailed pricing information as part of their response. The evaluation team and the procurement representative both review these costs simultaneously. The evaluation team is looking for costs aligned with their requirements matrix. These are costs that fit the architectural model discussed in Chapter 2. Procurement, on the other hand, is looking for costs that can be divided into capital that will be depreciated over time and expense that will be charged out within the same year.

A larger organization at this point may want to formulate a Business Case for the acquisition of the product or service. For this document, all relevant costs and savings or revenue generated are gathered and analyzed. The costs for the new product or service are contrasted with the costs of doing business today. The tangible benefit of a return on investment (ROI) is then calculated for the deployment; any intangible benefits such as productivity enhancement, retaining an existing contract, or improving the information architecture of the entire organization are considered. In the final analysis, the company—after reviewing all the relevant costs and benefits of the product or service acquisition—will either go ahead with the acquisition, table it for further research, or allocate the funds to another acquisition altogether.

The deliverable for this activity is the final cost analysis score for each of the responding vendors.

Risk Analysis

In assessing the risks associated with the acquisition of a product or service, several factors must be considered. The most important one is that of vendor viability. How long has the company been in business? Are they financially sound? How well do they support their product or service? Another important risk is that of time. How long will it take to implement the acquired product or service? If it takes an inordinately long period of time, the requirements originally agreed upon may shift, the project may lose its executive champion, or the product itself may be removed from the market. Another risk to consider is a technical risk. In what stage of the product life cycle is the proposed product? Is the product standards-based? Is the product open or proprietary?

Each risk identified is then given a weight. The risk associated with the particular vendor is then scored, just as in the Requirements Matrix, but with one exception—the risk score is a negative number and it is subtracted from the total of all the other scores. This way, a very high-risk vendor will not make it into the final selection round.

The deliverable for this activity is the final risk analysis score for each of the responding vendors.

PRODUCT EVALUATION

The product evaluation phase can take the form of one or more of the following methodologies:

- Demonstrations
- Customer site visits
- Prototyping
- Pilots

The above list runs from the least to the most time-consuming of the methodologies. For each of them—an agenda in the case of the demonstrations, and site visits or a full blown project plan for the prototype and pilot—should be in place so that the vendors may be consistently scored as to their results. The agenda or project plan should be constructed so as to provide adequate feedback on the most important requirements and those that could not be convincingly scored based on the RFP response. This is the "Show Me" part of the acquisition process, permitting the vendor to gain more information about what the organization really wants and likes, and permitting the evaluation team to get a "feel" for how the vendor will support them and work with them in the future.

Demonstrations may be held either at the organization's location, at a customer site, at a trade show, or at the vendor's offices. Creating an agenda for the demo is time well spent; it will focus the evaluation team and the vendor on the most important features and functions of the product or service, thereby cutting down on the marketing hype. The vendor should have a copy of the demo agenda far enough in advance to tailor the demo specifically to your organization. The vendor should be required to show only hardware and software that is commercially available today, not anything in the beta stage.

Site visits enable the organization to see a working system in another customer's location. Care should be taken to select a customer that has a similar computing environment as the organization, with a similar product/service mix, traffic situation, and number of users. When visiting, be sure to meet with the employees actually involved in the day-to-day operation and maintenance of the system, rather than just the IT manager. Question them about the ease of installation and maintenance, the vendor support, the frequency of product/service updates, etc., as well as the technical requirements.

Prototyping the new product or service is a rapid means to demonstrate the capabilities of the new Web business service without conducting an extensive pilot. The hardware and software required for the prototype can generally be acquired from the prospective vendor(s) at no charge. To build a successful prototype, a team composed of technical people, managers, administrators, customer support people, and especially end users must be formed. Prototyping is an iterative process. The developers will mock up some applicable screens for the team to view, and the feedback from this review will be rolled into the next iteration of the prototype. Gradually, a model of the new system will emerge that suits the needs and requirements of all parties involved. Prototyping provides a working skeleton of the new system and, when used for in-house demonstrations, can gather more support for the system within the organization.

Pilots of the new Web business service are the most complex, labor-intensive, and time-consuming methodology to use for the product evaluation activity. However, by really "lifting the hood" on the products and services, the organization can gain valuable information, learn lessons, and shake out any show-stoppers well before the system goes into production. The pilot could be a small feature set of the new Web service running on a few designated workstations, such as those of the evaluation team and some end users. The pilot could also be confined to a workgroup in a particular division with a hard requirement for a particular tool set that will be offered by the new Web business service. For example, the pilot might be in Human Resources, connecting all the HR representatives with benefits information and providing a Web home page for external job recruitment. Whatever the extent of the pilot, the evaluation team will score the vendor(s) on their overall performance during this activity.

The deliverable for this activity is the final product evaluation score for each of the responding vendors.

Investigating Outsourcing

At this point in the acquisition process, the team has enough information to investigate the possibility of outsourcing the Web business service to a provider of such services. The team knows exactly what the requirements for the service are, how much they will cost to deploy and operate, and how many people will be required to manage the system. The vendors may be queried for an outsourcing price now or this may have been part of the original RFP. The team will then analyze the cost of the outsourcing against the cost of deploying and running the system in-house. Benefits to the organization, such as keeping their Web expertise within the firm and controlling the service, must be contrasted with the advantages of turning the whole scenario over to the vendor.

PRODUCT SELECTION

The product selection activity involves such tasks as compiling all the scores generated to date, configuring the system for the last time, conducting the final analyses, documenting the results, and making a formal recommendation to management for approval to purchase the required Web business service hardware and software.

In compiling the scores, each of the four scores contributing to the final recommendation for a product need to be given a weight expressed as a percentage, so that one particular score does not unduly influence the decision. For example, the cost of the product may rank 25%, the technical 25%, the risk 35%, and the product evaluation 15%. All the scores are then recomputed according to their assigned weights, and a ranking of all the vendors emerges.

The system may need to be configured one last time based on the vendor's responses to the RFP. Items such as traffic predictions and hardware capacity may need to be rethought. The final system configuration is then part of the recommendation that goes to procurement for the last phase in the acquisition process.

All the scores, configurations, vendor responses, etc., are documented as part of the recommendation to management. This document will recommend all the products and services that were evaluated by their rankings. The document will also specify which vendor and which products and services are technically- and administratively-preferred by the evaluation team. This package is then analyzed by management and a decision is made to proceed to the contract award.

CONTRACT AWARD

In this final stage of the acquisition process, procurement takes the cost information and the final system configuration to the remaining vendors and typically asks for a Best and Final Offer (BAFO). The results of this offer generally cause a small number of vendors to surface that have the most technically viable products and services at a minimal cost with the least risk. If any final technical negotiations need to be performed, the evaluation team works with procurement to accomplish them. Contract award will include the delivery dates for the new hardware and software as well as a rollout plan or deployment schedule to launch the new service within the enterprise. After the contract(s) have been awarded, the evaluation team, working with the selected vendor(s), may also conduct pre-installation modeling of the Web business service. The project then moves on to the production planning stage.

Setting Standards

Within an organization there typically will be myriad computer hardware platforms, software packages, online services, and communications facilities. This hodgepodge evolves over time as various divisions and business units implement their own computing environments in an autonomous fashion, without having to interface their systems to others within the organization. This is all well and good until the enterprise wants to deploy a corporate-wide distributed application such as electronic messaging or time reporting. The notion of setting up a standard products list for the entire organization then gains attention. In the Web business service arena, whatever hardware, software, and services are selected for the initial deployment have the potential of becoming the standard for the organization. At the very least, consideration of standardizing on a Web server hardware platform, Web server software, a Web browser, and some of the tools discussed in the Chapter 2 has merit over the long term.

Establishing a standard suite of products and services for the enterprise has several advantages and limitations to be considered in this early stage of building the Web service.

BENEFITS

Standards benefit the end users and the organization as a whole in several ways. Adopting a standard suite of software and services reduces the end user's learning curve, the cost of maintaining and supporting numerous packages, and the time required to troubleshoot and resolve problems. Also, as new distributed applications are placed into production, testing them with the standard products is easier and less time-consuming. Interoperability among the diverse application programs and services is also enhanced. This is particularly important as the end users begin to electronically communicate within the global community.

CONSTRAINTS

Along with the benefits of adopting a standard set of products and services come several limitations or constraints. Users may find the set of products too confining for their immediate requirements. The standard products list may not be updated as quickly as the users need, since the evaluation and testing of new products and new versions of existing products are time-consuming and require labor to undertake. Once a standard is established within a company, the organization loses some leverage in dealing with the vendor(s) of those standard products. The organization may end up paying more for products than if the particular component competed once again in the open market.

Software and Hardware Selection

In Chapter 2 we designed the architecture for the new Web business service, discussing the many system components and how they fit together. This section provides more detailed information about the features and functions of various architectural components such as Web servers, client software, Internet service providers, Web service providers, and network services. For each component, a table compares the current product offerings, citing hardware platform and operating system compatibilities as well as giving source information.

SELECTING WEB SERVER SOFTWARE

Web server software is a key piece in the Web business service architectural design. Web server software today ranges from that of a very streamlined and simple feature set available free on the Internet to that of a robust, feature-rich application from major software vendors costing several thousand dollars. Today, the most popular Web server software is NCSA, which is free from the National Center for Supercomputer Applications (refer to Table 3.1). In selecting the appropriate Web software for the organization, a review of the requirements and the requirements matrix is in order. Not all of the features and functions discussed in this section will be beneficial to every organization from the initial deployment of the Web server. Each organization will have to tailor the Web server feature set to meet such business constraints as the budget, time, and existing hardware platforms or network protocols.

Web Server Software Features

The Web server software features detailed in this section are presented as an aid to selecting the best possible feature set for the particular organization. Addressed here are such topics as administration, performance, monitoring, directories, logging, and security.

Table 3.1 Survey of Web Server Software

Product Name	Vendor	Platforms Supported	Operating Systems Supported	Source	Cost
Alibaba	Computer Software Manufaktur	PC	Win NT, Win 95	www.csm.co.at	Commercial
Apache Server	The Apache Project	UNIX	UNIX	www.apache.org	Free
Apple Internet Servers	Apple	Power Mac	Mac OS	www.apple.com	Commercial
BASIS WEBserver	Information Dimensions	UNIX	UNIX	www.idi.oclc.org 800.328.2648	Commercial $5,000–25,000
BBN Internet Server	BBN Planet	Mac	Mac OS	800.632.7638	Commercial $9,895
CERN Server (httpd)	CERN	UNIX	UNIX, VMS	www.w3.org	Free
Communications Builder	The Internet Factory	PC	Win NT, Win 95	www.aristosoft.com	Commercial $495
CompassSearch Web Server	CompassWare Development	PC, UNIX	Win, UNIX	212.685.4220	Commercial $14,995
CyberServer	Ipswitch	PC, DEC Alpha	Win NT, AIX	617.246.1150	Commercial $695
CyberWeb	Tandem	UNIX	UNIX	www.tandem.com	Commercial
DataRamp	Working Set	PC	Win NT	617.576.1700	Commercial
Digital Internet Alpha Servers	Digital Equipment Corp.	Alpha	UNIX, Win NT	www.digital.com	Commercial $1,000–12,000

Continued

Table 3.1 Survey of Web Server Software (continued)

Product Name	Vendor	Platforms Supported	Operating Systems Supported	Source	Cost
EMWAC	European Microsoft Windows NT Academic Centre	PC	Win NT	emwac.ed.ac.uk/	Free
FirstClass Server	SoftArc	PC, Mac, UNIX	Win NT, Win 95, Win 3.X, Mac OS	800.364.1923	Commercial $495–1,900
FolkWeb Server	ILAR	PC	Win NT, Win 95	www.ilar.com	Shareware
FrontPage	Vermeer Technologies (Microsoft)	PC	Win NT, Win 95, Win 3.1	www.vermeer.com 617.576.1700	Commercial $695+
FTP Web Server	FTP Software	UNIX	UNIX	800.282.4FTP	Commercial $1,495
GoServe for OS/2	IBM	PC	OS/2	www2.hursley.ibm.com	Free
Global Access	Santa Cruz Operation	UNIX	UNIX	www.sco.com	Commercial
https	EMWAC	PC, Alphas	Win NT	emwac.ed.ac.uk	Free
Hype-It Web Servers	Cyklic Software	PC	DOS	800.4HYPEIT	Commercial $549–1,995
I/Net Web Server/400	IBM	AS/400	OS/400	www.ibm.com 616.344.3017	Commercial $1,250
InfoBase Web Server	Folio	PC	Win NT	www.folio.com	Commercial $6,995
Internet Office Server	CompuServe	PC, UNIX	Win NT, UNIX	800.sprynet	Commercial $599
Internet Server	Berkely Software Design	PC	UNIX, BSD/OS	info@bsdi.com	Commercial

Continued

Table 3.1 Survey of Web Server Software (continued)

Product Name	Vendor	Platforms Supported	Operating Systems Supported	Source	Cost
InterWare	Consensys Computers	PC	Win NT	800.338.1896	Commercial
InTEXT Web Server	InTEXT Systems	PC, UNIX	Win 3.X, UNIX	916.985.6008	Commercial $7,500
ISYS Web	Isys Odyssey Development	PC	Win 95, Win NT, Win 3.X	800.992.4797	Commercial
MacCommon LISP Server	MIT	Mac	Mac OS	www.ai.mit.edu	Free
MacHTTP	BIAP Systems	Mac	Mac OS	www.biap.com	Shareware
MindWare NT	Durand Communications Network	PC	Win NT	800.999.7771	Commercial $1,495+
MMB TEAMate	MMB Development Corp.	UNIX	UNIX	mmb.com	Commercial
MultiHost	New Frontiers Information Corp	UNIX	UNIX	www2.multihost.com	Commercial $495+
NaviServer	Navisoft	PC, UNIX	Win NT, UNIX	www.navisoft.com	Commercial NT: $1,500 UNIX: $5,000
NCSA Server (httpd)	NCSA	UNIX	AIX, HP-UX, IRIX, Linux, SunOS, Solaris, OSF/1	hoohoo.ncsa.uiuc.edu	Free
Net+Effects InfoNow Server	Net+Effects	UNIX	UNIX	www.net.effects.com	Commercial

Continued

Table 3.1 Survey of Web Server Software (continued)

Product Name	Vendor	Platforms Supported	Operating Systems Supported	Source	Cost
NetPublisher	Ameritech Library Services	PC	Win NT	netpub.notis.com	Commercial
Netra Internet Server	Sun Microsystems	UNIX	UNIX	www.sun.com	Commercial
Netscape Web Servers	Netscape Communications	PC, UNIX	Win NT, UNIX	home.netscape.com/	Commercial to $5,000
Netware Web Server	Novell	PC	DOS	corp.novell.com/ announce/webserv/	Commercial $995
OpenMarket Web Server	OpenMarket Corp.	UNIX	UNIX	www.openmarket.com 617.621.9500	Commercial $1,500–5,000
Oracle Websystem	Oracle	PC	DOS, Win 3.X	www.oracle.com 800.633.0596	Commercial
Personal Web Server	Vermeer	PC	Win 3.1, Win NT, Win 95	www.vermeer.com 617.576.1700	Commercial
phttpd	Signum Support AB	UNIX	Solaris	www.signum.se	Free
Plexus HTTP	Tony Sanders	UNIX	UNIX	www.earth.com	Free
Power MachTen	Tenen Intersystems	Power Mac	Mac OS	800.662.2410	Commercial $695
PowerWeb	PowerWeb	PC	Win NT		Commercial
Purveyor Web Server	Process Software Corporation	PC	Win NT, Win 95, VMS	www.process.com 800.722.7770	Commercial $1,995
Quarterdeck Web Server for Windows	Quarterdeck	PC	Win NT, Win 95, Win 3.1	www.quarterdeck.com	Commercial

Continued

Table 3.1 Survey of Web Server Software (*continued*)

Product Name	Vendor	Platforms Supported	Operating Systems Supported	Source	Cost
SafetyWEB	Spry	PC, UNIX	Win NT, UNIX	server.spry.com	Commercial
SAIC-HTTP Server	SAIC	PC	Win NT, Win 95	wwwserver.itl.saic.com	Free
SiteBuilder	American Internet Corp.	PC	Novell NetWare, DOS	www.american.com	Commercial $1,495
Slackware Professional Linux	Morse Telecommunication	PC, UNIX	UNIX	www.morse.net	Commercial $25
Spinner	Informationsvavarna	UNIX	UNIX	spinner.infovav.se	Free
Spry Web Server	Spry	PC, UNIX	Win NT, UNIX	server.spry.com	Commercial
Spyglass Server	Spyglass, Inc.	PC , UNIX	Win NT, UNIX	800.647.2201	Commercial
SuperWeb	Frontier Technologies	PC	Win NT	www.frontiertech.com	Commercial
Topic Information Server for WWW	Verity	PC, UNIX	HP-UX, Win NT, Win	www.verity.com	Commercial
VRServer	Tenet Networks, Inc.	PC	Win NT	619.736.8473	Commercial
WebFORCE	Silicon Graphics	UNIX	UNIX	www.sgi.com	Commercial
WebObjects	NeXT Computer, Inc.	PC	Win 3.X	800.879.6398	Commercial
WebQuest	Questar	PC	Win NT, Win 95	www.questar.com 800.925.2140	Commercial $379
Web Server 10	Intergraph, Corp.	PC	Win NT	800.345.4856	Commercial $3,995
WebServer 32	Quarterdeck	PC	Win NT, Win 95	www.quarterdeck.com	Commercial

Continued

Table 3.1 Survey of Web Server Software (*continued*)

Product Name	Vendor	Platforms Supported	Operating Systems Supported	Source	Cost
WebServer 40 Developer Edition	MDG Computer Services	Mac, Power Mac	Mac OS	708.622.0220	Commercial $995
WebSite	O'Reilly and Associates	PC	Win NT, Win 95	website.ora.com 800.998.9938	Commercial $495
WebSTAR	StarNine (Quarterdeck)	Mac	Mac OS	www.starnine.com/	Commercial $495–$795
Webware	EDIME	PC	Novell NetWare	www.edime.com.au	Commercial
WebWare 1.0	Open Software Foundation	UNIX	UNIX	www.osf.org	Free
Windows NT Web Alpha Server	Digital Equipment Corp.	Alpha	Win NT	www.digital.com	Commercial
WinHTTP	Robert Denny	PC	Win 3.1, WWG 3.11	rdenny@netcom.com	Free
WN server	John Franks	UNIX	UNIX	hopf.math.nwu.edu	Free
Worldgroup Internet Server	GALACTICOMM, Inc.	PC	DOS	www.gcomm.com/	Commercial $1,995

Administration

The Web server must be, of necessity, simple to configure, administer, and manage on a daily basis. An organization might select a Web server software package with a high level of pizzazz, like slick user interface screens or virtual reality tools. But if the administrator cannot make simple changes on the fly without having to bring the entire system to its knees, then your selection efforts will have been in vain. The administrative functions of the Web server software are of paramount importance in ensuring the smooth operation and maintenance of the Web business service.

The following administrative features are recommended for fully-functional Web server software.

- **Setup and Configuration**—From the initial setup of the Web business service to the ongoing configuration of the system, a **graphical user interface** is essential as a productivity-enhancement tool. The initial setup of the system may require **bulk loading** of user data, which is much more easily accomplished using GUI tools than text commands. The system administrator of an active site will be making continual changes to the system configuration as more Web pages and users come on line. The software may offer **form-based configuration** as well, which enables an administrator to make sweeping changes much more rapidly. The server software should also offer **configurable user groups**, not just a list of all the users. The ability to classify and categorize users into groups enables the administrator to perform tasks on large groups of users instead of on a large number of individuals. The server software should also support the ability to change the system, user, and group configurations online in real-time without restarting the server.

- **Maintenance**—The ongoing maintenance of the Web business service requires a **graphical user interface** in order to facilitate the smooth operation of the Web site. Typical maintenance features to look for are the capability to **generate reports** based on system traffic, user access, etc.; **remote maintenance** of the server while the server is operational; and the capability to **customize error messages**.

Performance

The most important consideration in the area of Web server performance, from the software standpoint, is the **number of supported** concurrent connections. A very active Web site may encounter hundreds of thousands of hits per day, so the number of users that can access the system at the same time becomes a discriminator in the selection of high-performance Web server software. Server software that supports a **32-bit** operating system architecture is also advisable for an active site.

The server software should provide **real-time performance measurement tools** and utilities to enable the system administrator to monitor the system, gather statistics, and provide trending information to management.

Load control capability enables the server software to better utilize the system resources to provide a higher quality of service for those accessing the site.

In addition, the Web server software should be **scalable**, able to handle an increase in traffic without necessitating a complete change in the software to another, more expensive version.

User Features
Features available from the server to users include **application launch,** the ability to start an application program such as a spreadsheet or word processing program while working natively. The server software should also provide a **graphical user interface**, the capability to **generate forms**, and **imagemap support**.

Web Page Development
The Web server software should include, at a minimum, tools used to create and maintain Web pages. Some active or differentiated Web sites will have a requirement for the capability of serving **multiple home pages** from the same server. **Conversion tools** enable documents existing within the enterprise to be easily converted into HTML format for inclusion as Web pages. **HTML editing and authoring tools** would enable the development of Web pages and perhaps include the capability for managing links to other documents or images. **CGI (Common Gateway Interface) support** is the standard for launching server-run scripts and enables the creation of forms to gather user input. **Script support** permits the real-time generation of HTML documents, images, etc., and enables links to be made between other

applications such as databases and electronic messaging systems. Support for program applets, such as **Java,** and programming languages, such as **C, Visual Basic, DOS, Perl, and VRML,** are also useful to have in the Web page development tool set. Support for **image file formats** such as GIF, TIFF, and JPEG enable graphics to be easily inserted into Web pages. The Web server software should also support **aliases,** which are used to reroute requests from one URL to another, and **server push,** the capability to send documents or images to users.

Database Access

The Web server software should, at a minimum, provide the **connectivity** and **file support** necessary to access databases. The software should be **compatible with major database software programs** such as Access, Excel, and FoxPro. The software should provide for access to information in **user-created databases** as well as **database management databases.** The database access feature should provide a **Web-based forms interface** to SQL or ODBC databases. The software should be **scalable,** as the needs for database access within the organization grow, and provide a built-in **search engine** for a wide variety of document types.

Directory

The Web server software should provide directory capabilities, including the generation of a **directory tree** and **user directories.** The server software should provide for different directory roots for different IP addresses and have the capability to **expand IP addresses.** The software should also provide **indexing** to facilitate the hierarchical organization of Web documents within the Web site. Such indexing should be automatic, dynamic, and provide for multiple indexes per directory.

Logging

The logging feature enables the system administrator to determine Web site usage, monitor performance, conduct server performance tuning, troubleshoot problems, and conduct other related tasks. Typical logging features include logs written in a **Common Log Format** (CERN/NCSA) to facilitate the sharing of information across disparate server software running on multiple servers within a large enterprise. The logging feature should provide for the **automatic archiving and cycling** of log files for storage and retrieval purposes. Log file entries should be customizable to suit the specific reporting needs of the organization. The Web server software should offer **multiple logs**, such as the number of site accesses, errors, services performed, audit trail and tracing, and real-time performance measurement.

Monitoring

Monitoring capabilities in Web server software should enable the system administrator to **detect broken hypertext links** before the users do. The administrator should also be able to look at the hierarchy of links, file names, document titles, labels, and URLs to detect any problems.

Security

Web server security features are of critical importance in not only preventing network access by unauthorized users, but also protecting the content on the Web site. Typical security features include **access control**, where the system administrator can prohibit access by domain name and by IP address, can change access control lists without restarting the server, and can establish file-level access control. User **authentication**, via passwords, smart cards, or digital signatures, ensures that the user attempting to access the system is actually the intended or permitted user. **Encryption**, especially public key, is also a highly sought-after Web server feature. The Web server should support **SSL** (Secure Socket Layer) and **S-HTTP** (Secure Hypertext Transport Protocol).

Some Web server software also provides **proxy server** capability. Proxy servers allow a user to have direct Internet access from behind an organization's firewall. To speed repetitive attempts to access external Web sites, **proxy server caching** may also be provided.

Additional Features

Some Web server software applications offer additional features such as **bulletin board systems, chat rooms, electronic mail, gopher** access and **listserv** capability.

The Web server should offer support for **additional protocols** such as FTP, SNMP, SMTP, and NNTP.

Web sites that expect a heavy amount of international users may want to specify **National Language Support** as one of their feature requirements.

This feature enables Web documents to be translated into different languages for display to the requesting user.

SELECTING FIREWALL SERVER SOFTWARE

The instant you connect your Web server to the Internet you are living in an electronic neighborhood with your front door unlocked! Firewall servers are so named because they provide an extremely valuable service in the electronic protection of your organization from outside intrusion. A firewall is a logical device that establishes a demarcation point between the outside network and the enterprise's private network, filtering the transmissions and providing access for only those specified as permissible by the organization. Some firewall solutions feature bundled hardware and software. Firewall features, like those of Web servers discussed previously, range from trim, free versions from Internet sources to those laden with such features as encryption and virus detection available in all price ranges from third party software vendors. Again, not all the features and functions discussed in this section will be required by every organization. Some mixing, matching, and tailoring to specific needs should be done to select the appropriate firewall server software for the particular organization. A survey of current firewall software is shown in Table 3.2.

Firewall Server Types

The first decision to make when selecting firewall server software is determining the type of firewall that will be deployed. Firewalls come in four versions:

- packet filters
- proxies
- circuit-level
- application-level

A packet filter firewall examines the standard TCP/IP header information of the packet for the IP source and destination address, then permits or denies access based on an access control list or table. Access can be denied based on a specific site, machine, application (port number), the number of simultaneous users, time of day, or day of week. Packet filter firewalls are the least expensive type of implementation.

Table 3.2 Web Firewall Server Software Survey

Product Name	Vendor	Platforms Supported	Operating Systems Supported	Source	Cost
ANS InterLock Service	ANS CO+RE	UNIX	UNIX	www.ans.net	Commercial
BDT Internet Firewall	Beckemeyer Development	UNIX	UNIX	www.bdt.com	Commercial
Black Hole	Milkyway Networks Corp.	UNIX	UNIX	www.milkyway.com	Commercial
BorderWare	NetPartners	PC, UNIX	DOS, Win, UNIX	www.netpart com	Commercial
Brimstone	SOS Corp.	PC, UNIX	UNIX	www.soscorp.com 800.SOS.UNIX	Commercial
Centri	Cohesive	UNIX	UNIX	www.cohesive.com 415.574.3500	Commercial
CONNECT	Sterling Software	UNIX	UNIX	connect@sterling.com 800.700.5579	Commercial
CyberGuard Firewall	Harris Computer Systems	PC, UNIX	UNIX	www.hcsc.com	Commercial
Dialock Boot	Celestin Company	PC	DOS, Win	www.com-dia.com	Commercial
Digital Firewall for UNIX	Digital Equipment Corp.	Alpha	UNIX	www.digital.com	Commercial
Drawbridge	Texas A&M University	PC	UNIX	ftp://net.tamu.edu	Free
Eagle Enterprise	Raptor Systems	PC, UNIX	UNIX	www.raptor.com	Commercial
Eagle Lite	Raptor Systems	PC, UNIX	UNIX	www.raptor.com	Commercial
ExFilter	ExNet	UNIX	UNIX	www.exnet.com	Commercial
Firewall IRX Router	Livingtson Enterprises	Firmware	Proprietary	www.livingtson.com	Commercial

Continued

Table 3.2 Web Firewall Server Software Survey (continued)

Product Name	Vendor	Platforms Supported	Operating Systems Supported	Source	Cost
Firewall-1	CheckPoint Software Technologies	PC, Sun SPARC	UNIX	www.checkpoint.com	Commercial
Freestone	SOS Corporation	PC, UNIX	UNIX	www.soscorp.com	Free
Firewall/Plus	Network-1	PC	DOS	www.iu.net/n1	Commercial
GateKeeper	Herve Schauer Consultants	UNIX	UNIX	www.freenix.fr/~schauer/hsc	Commercial
Gauntlet Internet Firewall	Trusted Information Systems	Firmware	UNIX	www.tis.com	Commercial
GFX-94	Global Technology Associates	Firmware	Proprietary	www.gta.com	Commercial
IBM Secured Network Gateway	IBM	PC	AIX, OS/2, OS/400	www.ibm.com	Commercial
Interceptor	Technologic	PC, Sun	UNIX	www.tlogic.com	Commercial
Mazama Packet Filter	Mazama Software Labs	PC/Linux	UNIX	www.mazama.com	Commercial
NetGate Software Firewall	SmallWorks	UNIX	UNIX	www.smallworks.com	Commercial
Netscape Proxy Server	Netscape	PC, UNIX	UNIX	home.netscape.com	Commercial
NetSeer and NetSeer Light	Telos	PC, UNIX	UNIX	www.telos.com	Commercial
Norman Internet Firewall	Norman Data Defense Systems	PC	UNIX	www.norman.no	Commercial

Continued

Table 3.2 Web Firewall Server Software Survey *(continued)*

Product Name	Vendor	Platforms Supported	Operating Systems Supported	Source	Cost
PORTUS	Livermore Software Labs	PowerPC, UNIX	AIX	www.lsli.com	Commercial
Private Internet Exchange	Cisco/NTI	Firmware	Proprietary	www.translation.com	Commercial
SecureConnect	Morning Star Technologies	UNIX	UNIX	www.Morningstar.com	Commercial
SecurIt	MIDnet	PC, UNIX	UNIX	www.mid.net	Commercial
Sidewinder	Secure Computing Corporation	UNIX	UNIX	www.sctc.com	Commercial
Site Patrol	BBN Planet Corp.	Firmware	UNIX	www.bbnplanet.com	Commercial
SmartWall	V-ONE	PC	UNIX	www.v-one.com	Commercial
SOCKS	David Koplas and Ying Da Lee	UNIX	UNIX	ftp.nec.com	Free
Solstice SunScreen	Sun Microsystems	PC, UNIX	UNIX	www.incog.com	Commercial
TIS Firewall Toolkit	Trusted Information Systems	UNIX	UNIX	ftp.tis.com	Free
Turnstile Firewall System	Atlantic Systems Group	UNIX	UNIX	www.ASG.unb.ca	Commercial

Proxies allow a user to have direct Internet access from behind an organization's firewall. This type of firewall offers the organization out-bound traffic protection. Proxy services available for outbound requests generally include PING, Archie, Telnet, Finger, FTP, gopher, WAIS, WHOIS, and, in some products, access to online services such as America Online or CompuServe.

Circuit-level firewalls provide relay services just between the transport layers of the two participating machines. The transport layer is responsible for end-to-end reliable transmission of the data packets.

Application level firewalls also examine the data packets for IP source and destination addresses but go further, requiring users to have a user ID and password and, in some cases, a smart card. This type of firewall provides in-bound protection and actively relays messages back and forth between the applications on the two machines. This way the application can also be protected and the organization's network can be made virtually invisible to the Internet.

The better solution for a fully-functional firewall is to select one that offers the essential features of all four types. Several vendors offering commercial firewall products are using this approach.

Firewall Server Software Features

Several features are of key importance in selecting firewall server software to adequately protect the organization's network from security breaches. They include access control, authentication, encryption, logging, and administration, among others.

Access Control
Access control is one of the central features offered by all firewall server software. Users are authorized to gain entry to the network based on parameters established by the customer. Typically, the firewall software will contain an access control list in which information on the user, group, service time of day, service day of week, and source and destination addresses are maintained. The firewall examines the TCP/IP header information and matches it to the contents of the access control list. The firewall then either permits or denies access to the organization's network based on the outcome of the comparison.

Authentication

How do you know that the user requesting entry to your system is really that particular user? Users must have a secure and valid manner to prove to the firewall software that they are who they say they are. Firewall software should provide user-level authentication for both incoming and outgoing traffic. Various schemes are available today and include one-time password schemes and cardkey authentication.

Firewalls also may offer remote user authentication for mobile users, trading partners, and customers that require access to the organization's internal network.

Encryption

Encryption may be offered as either a software or hardware solution. Firewalls should offer multiple encryption schemes such as DES and RSA or Diffie Hellman public/private key pair schemes. The firewall should have the capability of simultaneously deploying these schemes so that the user may select the more suitable scheme for the particular transmission. Within a virtual private network, firewall-to-firewall encryption is a consideration.

Logging

The firewall software should provide a variety of logs running 24 hours per day so that an **audit trail** may be established for all connection requests and server activity. The logs should also show **intruder attempts, trusted host spoofing,** and compile **traffic statistics.** Significant security events should be logged on a protected host, also referred to as **drop safe logging.**

Administration and User Interface

At a minimum, a **graphical user interface** should be provided with the firewall software. Point-and-click mouse usage, along with menus, pull-down boxes, and forms, make the software easier to configure initially and maintain thereafter. The software should also offer **backup and restore utilities** to archive data and regenerate the system in the event of a failure.

The firewall software should provide the capability of launching **alarms, alerts, and notifications.** The interface outputs the pertinent data relating to the alarm condition to e-mail, a pocket pager, a pop-up window, a printer, or an audible alarm.

Protocol and Application Support

The firewall software should offer support for various Internet protocols and applications, such as FTP, SMTP, HTTP, NNTP, NTP, Telnet, and gopher.

Address Translation

The firewall software should have the capability to extend the IP address capacity. In most cases, the firewall dynamically assigns addresses from a collection of globally-unique IP numbers so as to provide Internet access to many times the number of hosts allowed by the current IP address allocation methods.

The firewall should also be able to translate all internal addresses into a single address so that the traffic appears to originate from a single source. In this manner, the firewall hides the domain and conceals the design of the organization's internal private network from the external world.

Transparency

Users behind the firewall should not have to enter any commands specifically required by the firewall in order to enact its protective services. In other words, the existence of the firewall should be unknown or transparent to the end users.

Other Firewall Features

The firewall software may also offer a **virus detector** and a **hot word detector**.

Some more advanced firewalls offer the capability of operating in a **client/server mode** to accommodate the geographically-dispersed organization's networks.

MISCELLANEOUS WEB SERVER SOFTWARE

An organization may have a requirement to separate server applications and services that would normally reside within the same Web server. An enterprise may want to maintain separate control over each of the more frequently-used Web server applications. Or Web traffic may be so heavy that bundling all the various applications into one server would impede system performance. For whatever reason, the various Web server software applications in Table 3.3 lend themselves quite well to standalone server environments, depending on the requirements of the particular enterprise.

The electronic commerce server software generally enables an organization to establish a storefront on the Internet, much as a company would open a store physically in a shopping mall. The servers typically provide the Web pages as well as software to handle credit card and third party billing arrangements, electronic messaging, electronic data interchange, form completion, security, and database access.

Database server software provides access to corporate databases by means of a Web interface.

SELECTING WEB CLIENT SOFTWARE

The most critical interface to the World Wide Web from the user's perspective is, of course, their Web browser software application. The browser is a user's portal to the universe of information that is the Internet. Browsers have evolved from simple, text-based versions to those which offer slick graphical user interfaces handling 3-D graphics and virtual reality. All this in just three short years!

Undeniably, the most popular browser in use today is Netscape Navigator. The product sports a robust feature set and is available at a low cost. There are many, many other free, shareware, and commercial browsers that offer similar features and functionality, as shown in Table 3.4.

Web Client Software Features

The Web browser selected must offer a basic set of features and functions as well as several more advanced features that are becoming more useful as the various Web sites are upgraded to include them. While the browser software features described in this section include both basic and advanced features, an organization will need to tailor this feature list to suit its budget, support, and other constraints when selecting the appropriate product. Features discussed include the user interface, performance, interactive user features, HTML, networking, and security, as well as several other frequently required or requested features.

Table 3.3 Miscellaneous Web Server Software

Product Name	Vendor	Platforms Supported	Operating Systems Supported	Source	Cost
CHAT SERVERS					
Global Stage Chat Server	Prospero	UNIX	UNIX	www.prospero.com	Free
IIC Internet Relay Chat Server	Intermountain Internet Corp.	PC, Mac	Win, Mac OS	www.initco.net	Free
CUSTOMER SUPPORT SERVERS					
ARWeb	Remedy Corp.	UNIX	UNIX	415.903.5200	Commercial $1,000/server
CasePoint Web Server	Inference Corp	UNIX	UNIX	www.inference.com	Commercial
ESPLi@aison	Tuebner & Assoc.	PC	Win 95, Win NT	www.teubner.com	Commercial $4,994
DATABASE SERVERS					
d.b.Express	Computer Concepts	PC	DOS, Win	www.pb.net	Commercial
dbWeb	Aspect	PC	Win	www.axone.ch	Free
Webbase	ExperTelligence	PC	Win	www.expertelligence.com	Commercial
Web DataBlade	Illustra	PC, UNIX	Win NT, UNIX	www.illustra.com	Commercial
WebDBC	Nomad Development	PC, Mac, UNIX	Win NT, Win 95, Mac OS, UNIX	www.ndev.com	Commercial
ELECTRONIC COMMERCE SERVERS					
Commerce Builder	The Internet Factory	PC	Win NT, Win 95	www.aristosoft.com	Commercial

Continued

Table 3.3 Miscellaneous Web Server Software (*continued*)

Product Name	Vendor	Platforms Supported	Operating Systems Supported	Source	Cost
ELECTRONIC COMMERCE SERVERS (CONTINUED)					
One-to-One	BroadVision	PC, UNIX	Win, UNIX	www.broadvision.com	Commercial
I Store	Netscape	UNIX	UNIX	home.netscape.com	Commercial
Merchant Solution	OpenMarket	UNIX	UNIX	www.openmarket.com	Commercial
Netscape Commerce Server	Netscape	PC, UNIX	Win NT, UNIX	home.netscape.com	Commercial
OpenMarket Secure WebServer	OpenMarket	UNIX	UNIX	www.openmarket.com	Commercial
TradeWave VPI Products	TradeWave	PC, Mac	Win, Mac OS	galaxy.einet.net	Commercial
E-MAIL SERVERS					
3K POP Server	3K Associates	HP3000	UNIX	www.3k.com	Commercial
Apple Internet Mail Server	Apple	Mac	Mac OS	www.apple.com	Commercial
Mail*Link	StarNine Technologies	Mac	Mac OS	www.starnine.com	Commercial
FAX SERVERS					
Faximum WWW Fax Server	Faximum Software	PC, UNIX	Win, UNIX	www.faximum.com	Commercial
WebFaX Server	Internet One	UNIX	UNIX	www.internetone.com/	Commercial

Continued

Table 3.3 Miscellaneous Web Server Software *(continued)*

Product Name	Vendor	Platforms Supported	Operating Systems Supported	Source	Cost
GOPHER SERVERS					
3K Gopher Server	3K Associates	HP3000	UNIX	www.3k.com	Commercial
LIST SERVERS					
ListServ	L-Soft International	PC, UNIX	Win NT, UNIX, VM, VMS		
ListSTAR	StarNine Technologies	Mac	Mac OS	www.starnine.com	Commercial
NTList	Internet Shopper	PC	Win NT	www.net-shopper.co.uk	Commercial
NEWS SERVERS					
DNEWS	Internet Shopper	PC	Win NT	www.net-shopper.co.uk	Commercial
InterNotes News	Lotus	UNIX	UNIX	www.lotus.com	Commercial
Netscape News Server	Netscape	PC, Mac, UNIX	Win, Mac OS, UNIX	home.netscape.com	Commercial
Topic News Server	Verity	PC, UNIX	UNIX, Win NT, Win	www.verity.com	Commercial
PPP SERVERS					
Foray PPP Server	TechSmith	PC	DOS	ftp.techsmith.com	Free
SGML SERVERS					
BASIS SGMLserver	Information Dimensions	UNIX	UNIX	www.idi.oclc.org	Commercial
DynaWeb	Electronic Book Technologies	UNIX	UNIX	www.ebt.com`	Commercial
SoftQuad Explorer	SoftQuad	PC	Win	www.ptgs.com	Commercial

Table 3.4 Survey of Current Web Browsers

Browser	Company	Platforms Supported	Operating Systems Supported	Source	Cost
Accent on Internet	Accent Software International, Ltd.	PC	Win 3.X, Win 95	800.535.5257	Commercial $129
Air Mosaic Express	Spry	PC	Win	800.SPRY.COM	Commercial
Alis Multilingual Browser	Alis	UNIX, Mac, PC	UNIX, Mac OS, Win	www.alis.com	Commercial $40
AmberGL	DIVE Laboratories	PC, UNIX	Win 3.X, Win NT, UNIX	www.divelabs.com	Commercial $40
Cello	Cornell Law School	PC	Win	ftp.ncsa.uiuc.edu	Free
Chameleon	NetManage	PC	Win 3.X.	www.netmanage.com	Commercial $400
Columbus	Hummingbird Communication Ltd.	PC	Win 3.X	416.496.2200	Commercial
CyberSuite	Ipswitch	PC	Win 3.X, Win NT	617.246.1150	Commercial $95
Emissary	Wollengong			www.twg.com/	$99
Enhanced Mosaic	Spyglass	PC, Mac, UNIX	Win, Mac OS, UNIX	708.505.1010	Commercial
enReality	Online Environs	PC	Win 95	www.environs.com/	Commercial
Explore Anywhere	FTP Software	PC	Win 3.X	800.282.4FTP	Commercial $199
Fetch	Dartmouth College	Mac	Mac OS	www.dartmouth.edu	Shareware

Continued

Table 3.4 Survey of Current Web Browsers (continued)

Browser	Company	Platforms Supported	Operating Systems Supported	Source	Cost
HotJava	Sun Microsystems	UNIX	UNIX	java.sun.com	Commercial
I-Comm	Talent Communications	PC	Win 3.X, Win NT, Win 95, OS/2 Win	www.talentcom.com	Shareware $39
Internet Explorer	Microsoft	PC, Mac	Win, Mac OS	www.microsoft.com	Commercial
Internet in a Box	CompuServe	PC	Win 3.X	800.SPRY.NET	Commercial
Internet Membership Kit	Ventana Media	PC, Mac	Win 3.X, Mac OS	800.743.5369	Commercial $70
InternetPak	Ready-to-Run Software	UNIX	UNIX	800.743.1723	Commercial $280
InterNotes Web Navigator	Lotus	PC	Win NT, OS/2	www.lotus.com	Commercial
Internet Works	NaviSoft	PC	Win, Win NT	800.453.7873	Commercial $129
Lynx		PC, UNIX	Win, UNIX	ftp2.cc.ukans.edu	Free
Mariner	Network Computing Devices	PC, UNIX	Win, UNIX	www.ncd.com	Commercial
MKS Internet Anywhere	Mortice Kern Systems	PC	Win 3.X, DOS	800.265.2797	Commercial $99
MacWeb	EINet	Mac	Mac OS	ftp.einet.net/	Free
Mosaic	NCSA	PC, Mac, UNIX	Win, Mac OS, UNIX	ftp.ncsa.uiuc.edu	Free

Continued

Table 3.4 Survey of Current Web Browsers (continued)

Browser	Company	Platforms Supported	Operating Systems Supported	Source	Cost
Mosaic in a Box	CompuServe	PC	Win 3.X, Win 95	800.557.9614	Commercial $15
MultiNet for Windows	TGV, Inc.	PC	Win 3.X	800.TGV.3440	Commercial $400
Nautilus Internet Explorer	ElectricMail	PC, Mac, UNIX	Win 3.X, Mac OS, UNIX	www.elmail.co.uk	Commercial
NetCruiser Plus	Netcom	PC, Mac	Win, Mac OS	800.353.6600	Commercial $45
Netscape Navigator	Netscape	PC, Mac, UNIX,	Win, Mac OS, UNIX	home.netscape.com	Commercial $49
NetShark	Intercon Systems Corporation	PC, Mac	Win 95, Win NT, Mac OS	800.INTRCON	Commercial $40
NetSurfer	Netsurfer	UNIX	UNIX	www.netsurf.com	Commercial
OmniWeb	Lighthouse Design	UNIX	UNIX	omniweb@lighthouse.com	Commercial
Oracle Power Browser	Oracle	PC	Win 3.X	www.oracle.com	Commercial
Pathway Access	Wollongong Group	PC, Mac, Power Mac	Win 3.X, Mac OS, VMS	www.twg.com	Commercial $350
PC/TCP OnNet	ftp software	PC	Win	800.282.4FTP	Commercial
Prodigy	Prodigy Services	PC	Win	www.prodigy.com	Commercial
Quarterdeck Mosaic	Quarterdeck	PC	Win	www.quarterdeck.com	Commercial $30

Continued

Table 3.4 Survey of Current Web Browsers (continued)

Browser	Company	Platforms Supported	Operating Systems Supported	Source	Cost
SlipKnot	MicroMind	UNIX	UNIX	plaza.interport.net	Shareware $30
Super Mosaic	Luckman Interactive	PC	Win	213.468.8881	Commercial
Turbo Gopher	University of Minnesota	Mac	Mac OS	ftp.204.29.20.101/pub	Free
Virtus Voyager	Virtus	PC, Mac	Win95, Mac OS	www.virtus.com	Commercial
VOL Internet Browser	VOL—Video On Line	PC	EWin	www.vol.it	Commercial
Web Explorer	IBM	PC	OS/2	www.ibm.com	Commercial
WebRouser	Eolas Technologies	UNIX	UNIX	312.337.8740	Commercial
WebShark	InterCon Systems	PC, Mac	Win, Mac OS	www.intercon.com	Commercial
WebSpace	Template Graphics Software	PC, Mac, Power Mac	Win 3.X, Win NT, Mac OS	800.541.4847	Commercial
WebSurfer	NetManage	PC	Win	408.973.7171	Commercial
WinTapestry	Frontier Technologies Corporation	PC	Win 3.X	www.frontiertech.com	Commercial $125
WinWeb	Microelectronics Computer Technology	Win	Win	ftp.einet.net/einet/pc	Free
WordPerfect Internet Publishing System	Novell	PC	Win 3.X	800.453.2617	Commercial

User Interface

This is the pivotal feature when selecting a Web client browser. The user interface should be graphical, colorful, intuitive, and easy to use. It should offer text boxes to fill in URLs, hot list and history list buttons or icons, pull-down menus, and buttons for frequently-used features such as back, home, stop, forward, print, search, copy, reload, etc. The browser should support image maps, forms, scripts, and CGI.

When downloading pages, images, or files, the browser should show the progress of the transaction by means of a percent-complete notation, the number of bytes remaining, or a status bar. Another good progress feature is for the browser to keep track of number of minutes of connection time during the user's Internet session.

The browser should permit a user to both leave and interact with a page before all the contents are displayed.

It is very beneficial if the browser enables a user to display more than one page in adjacent windows.

The browser should be easy to install and configure by using forms or scripts to automate the implementation process. Installing and configuring the TCP/IP desktop connection and the connection to the Internet service provider should be facilitated by an intuitive user interface developed for this purpose.

The browser should offer a remote access facility to enable mobile or off-site users to access the system.

Performance

Users expect their browser to respond to their requests in a timely manner. Even though the browser's speed of access is determined by many external factors, such as network traffic or server speed of the destination Web site, a browser can offer several ways to maximize its own speed of information retrieval and delivery.

The most basic way to increase the speed of retrieval is to enable the user to turn off the receipt of graphics and opt for a text-only display. If the user subsequently wants to view an imbedded graphic, the browser should permit this action as well.

Next, the browser should paint the page in waves, showing the text portion first, reserving a space for any images, and then filling in the images. Some browsers will hold the transmission until the entire page has been received before displaying it to the user. This makes the performance of the browser seem inordinately slow to the user.

The browser should have the capability of loading multiple pages, and it should permit caching of visited Web pages to enable the user to quickly return to them. A nice feature here is for the users to be able to select the maximum number of pages they want to have cached during any one session.

Interactive User Features

During the course of locating and retrieving information from the Internet and other Web sites, users will have a need for a number of interactive features. The browser may offer several of these, such as the following:

- search engine
- electronic mail
- bulletin board systems
- chat services
- gopher
- Telnet
- FTP
- Usenet
- news readers
- Archie
- WAIS

HTML Features

The browser should support the basic HTML 1.0 feature set, such as hypertext links. In addition, as the new HTML 3.0 anchor tags are becoming widely used in Web sites, support for this is highly desirable. HTML 3.0 enables the use of tables, background images, centering, etc. The browser may also offer an HTML authoring capability for the users to create Web pages of their own.

Networking Options

At a minimum, the browser selected should offer TCP/IP connectivity. In addition, the organization may require support for other networking options, including token ring, Ethernet, Novell NetWare, NetBIOS, NetBEUI, AppleTalk, IPX/SPX, Banyan, 3-Com, and Windows for Workgroups. Also, determine whether the browser requires a SLIP or PPP connection.

Security

Increasingly, browsers are being used to transmit sensitive information, such as a person's recent purchases, credit card numbers, or a company's proprietary information. For this reason, browsers need to be secure. They need to support passwords and user IDs, S-HTTP, and SSL, at a minimum. It is also desirable that the browser display a warning message to the user when he or she attempts to transmit information (typically as filled in on an electronic form) across the Internet. As more progress is made in the area of public key cryptography, the use of RSA encryption or its equivalent will also become a requested feature.

Proxy Services

The browser should offer basic proxy services to permit the users within the organization to send out through a firewall. The browser should also offer status messages, such as when the URL could not be loaded by the proxy service or the URL is forbidden to be accessed by that particular user.

File Format Support

The browser should at least offer support for the following file formats: GIF, JPEG, BMP (Windows bitmap), and TIFF. This feature can be supported by file decompression utilities or image viewers.

Advanced Features

The new Web business service may require the more advanced features available in newer versions of some of the Web browsers. These advanced features include the following:

- Virtual Reality Modeling Language (VRML)—used to create virtual digital worlds for display on the user's browser

- Applets—enable a user to create and add new features to their browser and provide interactive objects within the Web pages
- Group conferencing—provides an electronic whiteboard feature for group review and annotation of shared documents
- Document management—provides version control, history, check in/out, etc., of an organization's documents
- Electronic publishing—permits HTML documents to be generated from existing documents created in different file formats
- Calendaring and scheduling—provides users with a desktop calendar and meeting or conference room scheduling tool

Terminal Emulators

Some companies require that the browser software support terminal emulation. Typical terminal emulations found in browsers include VT100, VT200, VT220, VT320, and TN 3270.

SELECTING TCP/IP NETWORKING SOFTWARE

To provide World Wide Web services over a Local Area Network to users within the enterprise, a TCP/IP networking product will be used to bring IP to the desktop. Several products, as shown in Table 3.5, currently offer a wide range of features, enabling various clients to communicate with TCP/IP hosts. The organization will typically select the TCP/IP package that supports their in-place hardware platforms and operating systems. The most common features to request in a TCP/IP networking product are discussed in the following section.

TCP/IP Networking Software Features

Most TCP/IP software applications support such features as a graphical user interface, file and directory sharing, file caching, network drives as local drives, data transfer between desktops and other network devices, and printer sharing. The products differ widely in the network protocols and operating systems supported, applications available, and in their advanced features.

User Interface

The TCP/IP product should offer a graphical user interface that supports, at a minimum, pull-down menus, icons and buttons, cut-and-

Table 3.5 TCP/IP Networking Software

Product	Vendor	Platforms Supported	Operating Systems Supported	Source	Cost
Acadia/VxD	Ipswitch	PC	Win, Win95	www.ipswitch.com	Commercial $395
BW-Connect NFS	Hummingbird Communication Ltd.	PC	DOS, Win 3.X, Win 95, Win NT	www.hummingbird.com	Commercial
ChameleonNFS	NetManage	PC	Win	www.netmanage.com	Commercial $495
ICE.TCP	James River Group	PC	DOS, Win, Win NT	www.jriver.com	Commercial $695
MacTCP	Apple	Mac	Mac OS	www.apple.com	Commercial
Multinet for Windows	TGV	PC	Win	www.tgv.com	Commercial
NOV*IX	FireFox	PC	NetWare	www.firefox.com/	Commercial
OS/2 Warp	IBM	PC	OS/2	www.ibm.com/	Commercial
PC-interface	Locus Computing	PC, Mac	DOS, Win, Mac OS	www.locus.com	Commercial $239
PC/TCP Network Software for OS/2	ftp Software	PC	OS/2	www.ftp.com	Commercial $400
PC/TCP OnNet 1.2	ftp Software	PC,	DOS, Win	www.ftp.com	Commercial $450
SuperTCP Pro	Frontier Technologies	PC	Win 3.X, Win 95, Win NT	www.frontiertech.com	Commercial
TCP/Connect II	InterCon Systems	Mac	Mac OS	www. intercon.com	Commercial
Vantage/IP	Ipswitch	PC	OS/2	www.ipswitch.com	Commercial $395
Windows 95 and Windows NT	Microsoft	PC	Win 95, Win NT	www.microsoft.com	Built-in
Winsock	Trumpet Software International	PC	Win	www.trumpet.com	Shareware

paste to other applications, and point-and-click access. The interface should also support keyboard mapping.

Network Protocols
The TCP/IP networking product should have the capability to coexist with a variety of other network protocols. These may include UNIX, SPX/IPX, NetWare 3.X and 4.X, AppleShare, NetBIOS, VINES, NetWare/IP, LAN Manager, and Windows for Workgroups.

Hardware Platforms
The enterprise will select a TCP/IP product that supports their installed base of computer platforms. Such hardware platforms include UNIX, DEC, IBM, Mac, and Intel-based PCs.

Operating Systems
Operating systems supported by the TCP/IP product typically include DOS, Windows, Windows 95, Windows NT, Mac OS, UNIX, and OS/2.

Terminal Emulation
The TCP/IP package may support one or more of the following terminal emulations: VT100, VT102, VT220, VT320, VT340, IBM 3278, TN3270, WN3270, Int14, TN5250, and TV1955.

Applications
Application support is critical to furnishing the end users with a full suite of Internet services. The TCP/IP software package may support one or more of the following applications:

- NFS (Network File System)
- electronic mail (SMTP/MIME, POP2, POP3)
- FTP and trusted FTP
- Telnet
- News, INews, NewsReader
- gopher, WHOIS, Archie, Veronica, Finger
- Bind, Ping
- World Wide Web
- Phone Tag

Management

The software package may offer management utilities, such as those based on the Simple Network Management Protocol (SNMP) or Remote Network Monitoring (RMON). Management information will be gathered from the workstations and consolidated into a Management Information Base, which can then be mined for statistical and trending information.

Security

Most TCP/IP packages offer fairly minimal security features. Passwords, user IDs, and restricting server access are the most prevalent features.

Advanced Features

The TCP/IP networking software may offer one or more of the following advanced features:

- network whiteboard
- conferencing
- scanner
- calendaring and scheduling
- desktop management
- collaborative tools

SELECTING A TURN-KEY WEB SERVER SOLUTION

Several computer manufacturers have bundled their hardware with Web server software and other application programs to provide consumers with turn-key Web server solutions. These servers are generally on the higher end of the hardware performance scale, using RISC-based systems around the 100MHz mark. The Web server systems typically include the operating system, communications software, and TCP/IP, as well as the Web server and browser software, CGI, E-Mail, WAIS, Telnet, DNS, FTP, proxy services, and HTML authoring. Some servers offer a more advanced feature set, including a VRML authoring tool and browser, and graphics or word processing applications. Most servers provide some level of administration, configuration, and maintenance utilities.

In situations where the organization wants to jump on the Internet rapidly and a long acquisition process could not be justified, a turn-key implementation is a very viable option. Table 3.6 depicts a selection of turn-key Web servers.

An example of all the software, hardware, and services that may be bundled in a turn key solution can be seen from HLC Internet's internet.now offering:

Internet Service

— 3-year Internet access

— Dedicated high-speed 56Kbps connection

— All local telephone company (telco) costs

— Domain name registration

Hardware

— Internet Alpha Server

— CSU/DSU

— Fast Router

— On-site warranty

— 15-inch monitor

— Cables

Pre-installed Software

— Windows NT

— Purveyor WebServer

— TCP/IP

— MS Word

— MS Internet Assistant

— Eudora Mail

— Digital Roadmap (includes over 70 Internet utilities)

SELECTING WEB SERVER HARDWARE

The Web server uses a totally different configuration paradigm than that of the traditional LAN server. In the LAN environment, a count would easily be made of all the users designated for that particular

Table 3.6 Turn-Key Web Server Solutions

Product Name	Vendor	Platforms Supported	Operating Systems Supported	Source	Cost (as of 1/96)
Internet/4XX	Financial Technologies	PC	OS/400, UNIX	516.569.5767	$18,500
Instant Internet	Performance Technology	PC	NetWare, PowerLANs	800.327.8526	$3,500
Internet Alpha Station 200	Digital Equipment Corp.	DEC Alpha	UNIX	www.digital.com	$7,500
Internet.now	HLC Internet	DEC Alpha	Win NT	www.hlc.net	56K: $999/Mo. T1: $2596/Mo.
LANLink	Internet Connection	PC	Win NT	www.tic.net	$3,500–5,500
Netra i5	Sun Microsystems	UNIX	Solaris	www.sun.com	$8,500
OneWorld Internet	Global Village	PC, Mac	Win, Mac OS	www.globalvillage.com	S1,999
PowerEdge Web Server	Dell	PC	Win NT	www.dell.com	$6,500
Powersolutions	IBM	PowerPC	AIX	www.ibm.com	$10,000
WebBox	Webtronics (Corporate Source)	Firmware	Tcl Source Code (ftp.cs.berkeley.edu.)	www.wtnx.com 714.582.1946	$990
WebForce°Indy	Silicon Graphics	UNIX	UNIX	www.sgi.com/	$11,000
WebServer	Hewlett Packard	UNIX (HP 9000)	UNIX	www.hp.com	$8,500
Web Server 10	Intergraph	PC	Win NT	800.345.4856	$4,000
Workgroup Server 8150	Apple	Power Mac	Mac OS	www.apple.com	$5,000

server and a calculation performed to reach the maximum number of concurrent users during the busy hours. This information would then be combined with the number and type of applications the server would be running, and the LAN administrator or computer system engineer would size the system accordingly. The choice of the hardware manufacturer would generally be the same as that currently deployed within the enterprise.

In the Web arena none of this works. No one within the organization will be able to predict—with any degree of certainty—exactly how many users will access the system at any one time. Also, since the Web is worldwide, our busy hours will not be the same as those in Frankfurt. The Internet virtually never sleeps and people will be accessing the organization's home page 24 hours a day, everyday. The organization will not be able to predict which documents or applications, such as FTP, e-mail, or news, will be accessed by the users, either. And, since the Web business server will be somewhat isolated from the rest of the organization's network, choosing the same hardware platform as that currently deployed becomes a moot point.

The only thing the organization will know with certainty is how many documents will be available from its own Web site and their file sizes. This knowledge affects the amount of hard drive space and the throughput of the server. Web applications such as e-mail are very demanding, even today. In the very near future, the Web will shift into high gear as multimedia messaging and file transfers, 3-D modeling, and database access become commonplace.

The better solution to this configuration chaos is to "think active." Be assured that your site will be popular and receive many thousands of accesses per day. For this reason, select a Web server hardware platform that is scalable and expandable without going through the burden in time, labor, and cost of upgrading to an entirely new system. A server that offers incremental growth in RAM and hard disk space is preferred. Separating the major services offered, such as e-mail, FTP, or the most frequently-accessed documents, and placing them on their own linked servers will enable the organization to better manage network traffic, offer users better response times, and obviate the need for one massive and very expensive server.

Table 3.7   Optimal Web Server Hardware Configurations

Hardware Configuration	Small Enterprise Server 30,000 hits/day	Medium Enterprise Server 150,000 hits/day	Large Enterprise Server 300,000 + hits/day
Processor	75MHz	100MHz	133–166+ MHz
RAM	16MB	32MB	64+ MB
Hard Disk	1GB	2GB	4GB
Back up Disk	500K	1GB	2GB
Cache	256K	512K	1MB
Monitor*	15"	15"	15"

* Save on the monitor and keyboard (or administer the server remotely), since the system will be used as a server and not as an end user's computer.

Optimal Web server hardware configurations are depicted by the size of the enterprise and the anticipated number of hits (user accesses) per day in Table 3.7. The major hardware vendors listed in the Turn-Key Solutions section earlier also offer server hardware in a range of sizes and configurations. The UNIX-based machines will be quite a bit more expensive, but generally offer better throughput in sustained I/O per second and more software options.

Summary

In this chapter the software and hardware acquisition process was examined to reduce the time and costs required to select appropriate technology for the new Web business service. By taking a thorough look at the both the process and the technology, the organization will dramatically improve the manner in which hardware and software are procured for the entire enterprise.

The task of sorting through the myriad Internet and Web software and hardware products can be daunting to those deploying a Web business service. Fortunately, the Internet itself offers many sources of free and inexpensive software products to use that will run on all the hardware platforms currently in the computing environment of most organizations. Or the enterprise may turn to commercial, off-the-shelf products for their rich feature set and higher levels of technical support and maintenance.

The only remaining key piece of technology to select for the Web business service is an Internet or Web service provider. The salient points to consider and sources are featured in the next chapter.

CHAPTER 4

Selecting Internet and Web Service Providers

"Put us on the Web! Please, we wanna be on the Web!" Rather than getting Jason's 12-year-old son, the little computer genius, to put all this together, the Fremont office decided to launch a comprehensive seek-and-select effort to locate a suitable provider of Internet and Web services. As the selection team delved further into the task, they became overwhelmed with the sheer number of providers and options available. The office simultaneously launched an effort for a "make or buy" decision regarding the development of a Web site. There were Internet Service Providers, Internet Access Providers, IP Service Suppliers, Web Presence Providers, Web Service Providers, Web page designers, and lots of consultants. What to do? Who to select? Should the office create and maintain their own Web site or leave this to the expert Web Service Providers? Should the office maintain its own internal Web server and have the external server managed by a third party?

To enable the Fremont office to make a good decision, the selection team developed a set of requirements for evaluating the ideal Internet and Web Service Providers. This list facilitated the selection of reliable and forward-thinking providers, and significantly reduced both time and cost. The details of this requirement's generation exercise are discussed in the Services Provided sections in this chapter.

Internet Service Providers

Internet Service Providers (ISPs) funnel traffic between the customer and the Internet. The customer selects the network access, speed, and service mix, and the ISP establishes and maintains the connectivity. ISPs are also called Internet Connectivity Providers, IP Service Suppliers, and Internet Access Providers.

Selecting an Internet Service Provider is similar to ordering service from a long distance carrier or data communications services from a Value Added Network such as MCI or Sprint. Reliability at an affordable cost are primary considerations.

The good news is that prices are dropping and the range of product and service offerings are dramatically increasing as more and more providers come online. Software is becoming easier to use and many providers have developed more of a customer focus, seeking to provide added value and distinguish themselves from the masses of other providers.

Basically, an organization is looking for the most robust service offering and the most reliable and consistent access for the least cost per connect hour. Also, establishing a working relationship with the ISP is beneficial, as the organization will need customer support and technical advice in order to provide their own reliable Web service. The organization must determine which services will be extended to their Web site users, whether internal or external. For example, electronic mail may be extended to both internal and external users, but database search and newsgroup access may just be offered to internal users.

Today, there are three options for connecting to the Internet:

- Commercial online service provider
- National Internet service provider
- Local Internet service provider

COMMERCIAL ONLINE SERVICE

Commercial online services predate most of the traditional ISPs and, as such, have name recognition. Lately, all of these services have Web and Internet access offerings in an effort to fully compete with the ISPs. Commercial online services include such companies as CompuServe, Prodigy, Microsoft Network, Delphi, and America Online. The advantages and disadvantages of using a commercial online service to connect to the Internet are as follows:

- Pros
  — Easy to install
  — Good user interface
  — Value-added content and features
- Cons
  — Per-hour connect time charges are expensive
  — May not offer all the Internet services
  — Slow performance
  — Proprietary content

NATIONAL INTERNET SERVICE PROVIDER

National Internet Service Providers offer connectivity and value-added services from offices located across the country, and include such companies as PSINet, UUNET, NetCom, AT&T, MCI, and Sprint. The advantages and disadvantages of using a national Internet service provider to connect to the Internet are as follows:

- Pros
  — High reliability
  — High-performance backbones
  — Competitive pricing
- Cons
  — Lack of customized services
  — Reduced customer support levels
  — Lack of "personal touch"

LOCAL INTERNET SERVICE PROVIDER

Local Internet Service Providers are those firms with only one location, one company in your geographic area. Local ISPs allow access to the domestic and international Internet and offer competitive pricing and service offerings to those of the national ISPs. They are local and are interested in establishing a close relationship with their customers. They will offer more customized services and software than the larger, national firms. The advantages and disadvantages of using a local Internet service provider to connect to the Internet are as follows:

- Pros
  - Good customer support levels
  - Competitive pricing
  - Customizable software and configurations
- Cons
  - Access to service
  - Availability (modem sharing)
  - Limited service offerings

SERVICES PROVIDED

The following sections discuss the service and support levels, the many features and functions available, performance, applications offered, financial considerations, and several more topics of interest to the prospective customer of an Internet Service Provider. Again, the organization must match its needs and budget constraints to the feature set provided.

Service Levels

It is of paramount importance to establish exactly what level of service you can expect from the prospective ISP. To gather this information, ask for their busy-hour statistics and peak connect times (for example, normal business hours, evenings, or on weekends). Determine how many customers share the same facilities and which services are located on the same server. Find out if the high-volume, popular sites are on dedicated servers or if all customers run on the same server.

Conduct preliminary testing to evaluate the availability and access to the service provider's facilities. Dial up the ISPs facilities at different times of the day and night to determine the number of busy signals.

Ask the provider if it is possible to change or upgrade the initial level of service selected. For example, you may launch the service with a 56K leased line and realize immediately you need a T1 connection. Determine the additional installation and upgrade charges for this change.

Determine if the ISP has scheduled outages and when they will occur. This information is useful when your organization is located in a different timezone than the provider.

Find out if the provider's software can be customized for a particular customer's needs. This is a value-added service that acts as a discriminator among the various ISPs.

Support Levels

The most basic support an ISP can offer is either allowing an e-mail message to the system administrator or providing online help. But there is simply no substitute for a fully-staffed Help Desk facility.

Most of the larger ISPs will have a Network Operations Center or Help Desk established to provide assistance to customers. Determine if this facility is always staffed (7 days, 24 hours per day). At the very least, it is imperative that trained personnel be available to resolve problems during normal business hours in your timezone. There is a difference between being always available and always on call. Just having an answering service or beeper access to personnel won't suffice if you have placed business-critical applications such as electronic catalog ordering on the Web server.

Ask the ISP how many technicians and support people are available for problem resolution. Where are they located? Determine the technical competency of the support staff. They must be highly experienced in TCP/IP networking and in systems engineering. Also, check to see what turnover rate the ISP is experiencing in the support staff. This may be an indicator of financial or organizational problems.

The ISP must provide you with toll-free support telephone numbers or local access telephone numbers. You will need these numbers in case your Internet connection cannot be accessed, effectively eliminating the online help. Prior to signing up with the ISP, call the support numbers to check on busy signals and how long you're on hold waiting for someone to assist you.

Determine the ISP's response time to problems. Most should guarantee at least a two-hour response time. Also find out on what equipment support is offered; i.e., modems, communications software and hardware, non-connection-related problems like computer hardware and software, and third-party support for software and hardware.

Find out how to expedite a problem from the first level support of the Help Desk to that of a highly-trained network or system engineer. Also determine if it is possible to have a technician arrive on-site to resolve a problem, if required, and how much this service would cost. Is there an option to bring your equipment to the ISP's site to resolve a problem?

Determine what additional services the ISP is willing, for a fee, to provide. Such services would include consulting, planning, setup services, documentation, training, and online tutorials.

Vendor Viability

The ISP will have a vision, a mission for their company, along with goals and objectives to achieve that vision. Discuss these items with the ISP to determine if there is a match between their vision and goals and that of your own organization. Find out where the ISP is physically located. Check out their home page for access and availability.

ISPs, taken as a whole, have not been in business for the eons the long distance carriers and data communications companies have been. This is a fairly recent business opportunity that ISPs have capitalized on. So, when the ISP says that they have only been in business for one year, this may not be as much of a determining factor as it would be for a hardware vendor. It's a good idea, though, to get as much information on the ISP as possible to form an impression of the long-range viability of the firm. If Dun and Bradstreet ratings are available, use them. If the company is a member of the Commercial Internet Exchange (CIX), this is a good sign. CIX is an international organization open to providers offering TCP/IP networking services to the public.

Ask for an organization chart and determine if the ISP is a subsidiary of a larger organization. Does the ISP have a positive cash flow? Is the ISP growing? How many employees do they have?

Ask for a full customer list to determine how many customers the ISP currently has. What proportion of these accounts are commercial, institutional, or for individuals? Do they have any major accounts on which they are totally dependent? If so, the loss of these accounts could adversely impact the ISP's capability to stay in business and service your account.

Ask for three references from customers of a similar size and configuration as your own organization. Call these references; don't just look at their home pages. It is very simple to fake the existence of a home page. Ask the references how long they have been a customer of the ISP and what service levels have they been experiencing. Find out how often their connection goes down and how long the ISP takes to resolve problems. Ask about their billing; is it accurate and what has the ISP done to correct any discrepancies.

Performance and Network Design

The manner in which the ISP's network is configured and the performance of that network are primary considerations in selecting a highly reliable and available service.

First and foremost, you need to determine what hardware and software the ISP is using and why. You are looking for leading-edge technology, not reconfigured surplus equipment that was just lying around. Inquire as to the servers, workstations, terminal servers, hub/router equipment, and telco communications equipment they are using. Also, check into the server and client software, security package, and billing and accounting software the ISP is using.

The ISP's network topology or physical and logical network design is also a primary concern in the selection process. Ask for a network map showing physical hardware and lines, not virtual connections or "clouds." Find out what backbone technology are they using—frame relay, ATM, T3—and how fast their connection is to the Internet. Determine which links are operational and which are planned. Often ISPs will display lines that are merely planned and not installed and working. This is deceptive and can give the potential customer a false sense of the true backbone speed and connectivity of the ISP. Notice the speed bottlenecks between you and the provider and to other locations. If your connection is a 128Kbps ISDN link, but a frequently-called location is only a 28.8Kbps dial-up link, then your data will literally go nowhere fast.

Determine the number of phone lines and modems (what speeds) are installed and working at the ISP's site. This should give you a good idea of the level of modem availability the ISP is capable of sustaining. What is their customer to line ratio? A 10:1 ratio is a good indicator. Find out how many lines are installed in each of the ISP's calling areas. What is the ISP's bandwidth to customer allocation? What upgrade plans do they have for their communications facilities? How many lines are on order and when are their approximate installation due dates?

Find out how the ISP performs network management on their backbone network. What tools do they use? Who in the organization performs network management? Are they constantly conducting performance and tuning exercises? Are they satisfied with the time it takes for a problem to be noticed and worked through to completion?

Look at the relationships the ISP has with their local telephone company and Interexchange Carriers. The telco network is really the ISP's backbone and the ISP must be on good terms with the telco to get good service. Determine how many other Internet service providers they are connected to. If there is only one other connection, how often does it fail?

Where are the ISP's Points of Presence (POPs)? How far away is the closest one to your facility? Is the customer required to purchase the local loop segment from the telco to the provider's POP?

Explore the ISP's plans for disaster recovery. Are the plans comprehensive for the geographical area? Have these plans ever been tested? What are the hardware and software fault tolerance and redundancy levels? Find out if the hardware and software are fully redundant, if hot swapping and mirroring are used. Is the site on a Universal Power Supply system?

Determine what maintenance and repair services the ISP has for its own network. Who do they call in the event of a failure or disaster? What is their mean time between failures for their backbone network?

Area Served

Determine the geographical area (towns, cities, regions, etc.) served by the ISP, the fee structure for each area, and the free calling radius. Establish whether the Internet coverage is limited to North America, instead of being open and international. Find out if there are any additional charges for international access. Ask for a list of local access number in all locations served by the ISP.

Network Connectivity

There are basically four types of network connectivity offered by an ISP.

UNIX Shell Account

This is the most basic and inexpensive service available. The customer uses their own modem and communications software to dial up the service provider. Once the user logs into the system, the user operates as a UNIX terminal on the ISP's computer. The shell account provides a command-line interface and the user must know UNIX in order to effectively use this connection.

SLIP/PPP

This is also a very basic dial-up service that provides a graphical interface. PPP is preferred as it is a more reliable protocol. Make certain that the ISP is offering a "true" PPP connection using standard protocols; some of the Internet applications, videoconferencing and CU SeeMe, for example, will not run under a purported SLIP/PPP connection such as The Internet Adapter or TIA. Also, security issues must be addressed with this option.

ISDN

This option significantly upgrades the network speed available to 128Kbps and is offered in most larger metropolitan areas. The service is highly reliable, but the hardware required—an ISDN modem—is relatively expensive.

Leased Line

This is a dedicated line that connects the customer directly with the ISP using telco facilities. Several higher network speeds are available, including 56K, T1, fractional T1, and T3. The advantage is that the connection is solely for the use of the organization, which improves the availability and access of the service.

Network Speeds

The ISP may offer a variety of network speeds for Internet connectivity. Your organization needs to determine requirements for both incoming and outgoing bandwidth. For example, your organization may plan on receiving a very large number of hits on the Web server per day, but not provide much in the way of file transfers out.

The most common network speed for the smaller ISPs is a 28.8Kbps dial-up modem. Check which cities or areas have which speed modems, as this may represent a bottleneck between your organization and a frequently-called location.

Larger ISPs will offer higher network speed capability, such as 56K, T1, fractional or shared T1, or, in some instances for extremely large and active sites, a T3 connection. Other ISPs may have the capability of offering ISDN (128K) service. Check to see what is available and what the ISP's plans are to upgrade their facilities to higher network speeds.

The minimum recommended speed to launch a moderately active Web service would be a T1 connection to the ISP.

Domain Name Registration

The ISP will register your domain name with the appropriate Internet authority (InterNIC Registration Services http://www.internic.net). This could take as long as one month, so getting started with the service provider may not be as instantaneous as one might think. This Internet domain name is unique in all the world. It represents your organization to the global Internet community. The name should reflect your organization's name as completely as possible in 24 characters or less. The domain name is the name to the right of the "@" sign in the Internet address and takes the form of *username@domainname.type*. For example, Andy Rooney's address at the Columbia Broadcasting Company might be *arooney@cbs.com*. It is important to have this domain name as your very own so that, if you must change ISPs, the name will go with you.

Applications Supported

The ISP should support a variety of the traditional Internet applications and services from which the organization may choose. Applications supported should include most of the following:

- FTP—full, unrestricted
- Telnet—full, unrestricted
- World Wide Web—Check to see if many of their pages are under construction. Also, look at the layout and content of the pages. Check the disk space allocated for user accounts (5MB is good). Determine what limitations exist on content— no commercial content, no indecent content, etc. Will an increased traffic volume prompt extra charges? Can you create and publish your own pages? Which browser is included?
- Gopher
- WAIS
- E-mail—Determine the charges and constraints, such as the number or size of messages or when to send a very large message. What package is provided—Pine, Eudora?
- News Usenet—Determine how many newsfeeds the ISP carries. Are they sorted or classified in any way? Can the newsfeed be customized?
- IRC (Internet Relay Chat)—You'll need both local and international channels
- Archie
- Finger—to determine who is online at remote systems
- Credit card authorization—an advanced service required for electronic commerce
- Bulletin board systems, chat rooms, and forums

- Commerce server
- List server

Security

The security measures taken by the ISP and offered to their customers are definitely a concern. Determine the physical security of the ISP's servers and communications hardware. Is it in an access-controlled area? Who has access? Regarding logical security, find out who has access to the customer's files, how the passwords are set up and maintained. If the ISP offers firewall and proxy services, what encryption schemes are available and can the ISP set up a unique access group to share files between your organization and other trusted customers on their service? What security measures are in place for the handling of credit card authorizations and other financial transactions?

Usage

The manner in which the ISP charges for Internet connectivity can vary considerably. Some companies offer a flat rate with an unlimited number of connect hours. Others offer a metered service in which the first 10 or so hours are charged at one fee and additional hours are charged at another fee. The best usage arrangement for your organization depends on how many employees will be accessing the service, what Internet services (such as FTP, Telnet, and gopher) will be accessed, how many external users will be accessing the Web server (number of hits), how large the data files are that will be transferred to the external users, how much e-mail will be sent and received, and when the most traffic will be generated.

An analysis of the organization's predicted usage should lead to a matching rate schedule. A comparison of costs across several of the ISPs—using 300 hours per month or unlimited access as sample price points—will result in a good usage analysis.

Financials

The financial aspects of selecting an ISP generally fall into two categories: fees and methods of payment. How much does it cost and how does the organization render payment?

Fees

The ISP will explain their fee structure to you. Typically, the following fees are applicable to most of the ISPs. If some of them are not mentioned, ask if they are included with the standard billing rate or if special charges apply.

- Disk space—How much disk space is allocated per user account? What additional charges are incurred for more disk space? What are the increments?

- Usage—Flat rate, unlimited, or combination. Find out about weekend, holiday, and evening rates. Is it possible to bank any unused monthly hours? What are the hourly billing increments (12-minute increments, for example)?

- Port charge—Installation and monthly

- Set up—Non-recurring installation charges

- Domain Name Registration—Fees over and above InterNIC's $100 per domain name and $50 annual fee

- UUCP mail and NNTP newsfeed registration

- Anonymous FTP

- Web space—Home page and subsequent pages for user accounts

- POP accounts

- Telco line—Monthly fees and setup charges for local loop, ISDN lines

- Cancellation charges

- Upgrade/downgrade service level

Methods of Payment

The ISP will specify the methods of payment within the Service Agreement. Payment policies may have the monthly payment due on receipt or within 30 days. Do they support electronic funds transfer or accept credit card payments? Late payment policies and cancellation of service policies will also be specified here. Find out if there are any free hours, discounts for pre-payment for up to six months service, or one month's free service at the end of a full year.

Service Agreement

Ask for the ISP's Service Agreement, which will specify the Terms and Conditions that the service provider mandates in order to extend

Internet connectivity to your organization. Items covered will be the specific service configuration (T1 line with unlimited usage, for example), service term (30 days is typical), the payment policies (bills due on receipt, late payment fees, etc.), termination policies, and so on. Review this document carefully, as it will become a legally binding document if the ISP is selected. If the language is fairly obtuse, consult with your attorney.

Appropriate Use Policy

Some ISPs have an Appropriate Use Policy specifying what types of content and transactions can and cannot be made over their facilities. Review this AUP carefully, especially if your business is one that may involve some of the areas that may be considered indecent. There have been a number of court cases to date in this area and it's best to know up front what the ISP expects to carry over its facilities.

Hardware Required

To establish a connection with an ISP, a few pieces of hardware will be required. If the connection is a dial-up line, a modem will be necessary. Select one that has a speed of 28.8Kbps. Anything less will be too slow and adversely affect the amount of connect time you will have on your Internet connection.

A leased line connection will require a CSU/DSU (Channel Service Unit/Digital Service Unit) and a router. These two pieces of hardware properly format the data and transmit it across the leased line to the Wide Area Network that is the Internet.

You may wish to purchase the CSU/DSU and router or you may lease them from the ISP, if it is an option.

Software Required

The ISP should provide you with a list of software that is required for your Internet connection. This could be public domain software, shareware, or commercial packages. You can count on a TCP/IP stack being required. Are any software packages specifically recommended by the vendor? These may offer greater compatibility and interoperability with the ISP's system than other packages on the market.

Getting Started

An essential part of the ISP selection process is determining how to actually get started with the service. Will you simply download their software using your credit card to guarantee the sale? Will you receive a package in the mail containing diskettes and a service agreement? Will a technician make a site visit to conduct the installation and complete the paperwork?

Find out how long it will take to install the connectivity and be up and running. If Domain Name Registration is required, the whole process could take up to one month, assuming that all of the required hardware and software is available.

Locating Internet Service Providers

Internet Service Providers can be located using a variety of Internet and non-Internet sources.

INTERNET SOURCES

Table 4.1 offers a collection of URLs that contain lists of ISPs. The table presents the URLs by city, state, geographical area, or country, along with several international lists containing more than one country.

National Internet Service Providers include all the major online service companies (Prodigy, CompuServe, America Online, Delphi, Microsoft Network, and Genie), PSINet (www.psi.net/), NetCom (www.netcom. com/), InternetMCI (www.internetmci.com/), and BBNPlanet (www.bbnplanet.com), plus many more.

The most useful source for Internet Service Providers worldwide today is The List (http://www.thelist.com), shown in Figure 4.1, which features over 2,000 companies. The List enables the user to search by provider name or domain name in the U.S., Canada, in the CompuServe and SprintNet Networks, by state or province, by area code, or by country or country code. As can be seen from Figure 4.2, the information gathered on each Internet Service Provider is quite extensive,

Table 4.1   Locating Internet Service Providers

Internet Service Provider Lists	Source
MAJOR CITIES	
Atlanta	ftp://ftp.netcom.com/pub/be/beh/atlanta.html
Baltimore and Washington, DC	http://www.cris.com/~raydaly/plexacce.html
Boston	http://www.astro.phast.umass.edu/misc/boston.html#isp
Chicago	http://www.mcs.com/~wsmith/providers.html
Dallas/Ft. Worth	http://www.webfeats.com/dfwisp/
Denver	http://www.rmiug.org/rmiug/providers/
Kansas City	http://www.sky.net/~eml/kcproviders.html
New Orleans	http://www.lib.lsu.edu/general/isp.html#new
St. Louis	http://ibc.wustl.edu/stlouis_clones.html
Philadelphia	http://www.cis.temple.edu/~mandviwa/intprov.html
Pittsburgh	http://www.telerama.com/~soup/provider.html
Reno	http://pogonip.scs.unr.edu/cs/provider.html
STATES	
Alabama	http://www.hal.com:80/users/rlr/Alabama.html
Arkansas	http://www.acumug.org/acumug/arkansas/city.html
California	http://www.research.digital.com/src/virtual-tourist/final/CaliforniaNet-providers.html
Colorado	http://www.rmsd.com/internet.html
Connecticut	http://www.fcc.com/ctisp.html
Delaware	http://www.udel.edu/educ/prov.html http://www.tju.edu/~theall1/csp/
Florida	http://www.sundial.net/~atruex/isps.html
Hawaii	http://www.hinet.com/inetprovide.html
Illinois	http://www.outfitters.com/infobahn/localprov.html
Iowa	http://www.scl.ameslab.gov/links/www-iowa.html#service
Kansas	http://history.cc.ukans.edu/heritage/iap.html
Kentucky	http://www.iglou.com/gizweb/locals.htm#KY16
Louisiana	http://www.lib.lsu.edu/general/isp.html
New Jersey	http://www.iserver.com/web/states/newjersey.html

Continued

Table 4.1   Locating Internet Service Providers *(continued)*

Internet Service Provider Lists	Source
Maine	http://www.netmaine.com/providers/providers.html
Maryland	http://www.clark.net/pub/journalism/iaptable.html
Massachusetts	http://www.astro.phast.umass.edu/misc/mass.html#isp
Michigan	http://detnews.com/cyberia/mich/isps/index.html
Minnesota	http://www.mr.net/providers.html
Mississippi	http://www.ces.msstate.edu:80/homepages/cas/pubinet.html
Montana	http://www.ism.net/montana/isp.html
Nebraska	http://www.novia.net/~rfulk/web/nenet.html
New Hampshire	http://www.state.nh.us/subject/computer.html
New Jersey	http://njnie.dl.stevens-tech.edu/connect/isp.html
New Mexico	http://www.swcp.com/~dmckeon/nm-isp.html
New York (ISDN)	http://www.users.interport.net/~digital/isps.html
Ohio	http://www.infinet.com/~dionisio/Connections.html
Oklahoma	http://www.educ.ucok.edu/colleges/coba/okc_slip.html
Oregon	http://www.or.gov/provider.htm
South Dakota	http://www.dsu.edu/sodapop/
Texas	http://www.iserver.com/web/states/texas.html http://www.hal.com/~rlr/Texas.html
Utah	http://www.state.lib.ut.us/provider.htm
Vermont	http://www.cit.state.vt.us/vtne.htm#iap
Washington	http://www.iserver.com/web/states/washinton.html
Wisconsin	http://www.inmarket.com/wisconsin/internet.htm
Wyoming	http://159.238.106.10/wyld/wyoisps.htm
US REGIONS	
New England	http://www.pn.com/neci/providers.html http://www.homesmag.odc.com/providers.html
SF Bay Area	http://www.best.com/~ophelia/isp.html
United States	http://www.primus.com/providers/ http://www.thelist.com
Western States	http://www.cybertoday.com/cybertoday/ISPs/

Continued

Table 4.1 Locating Internet Service Providers *(continued)*	
Internet Service Provider Lists	**Source**
INTERNATIONAL LISTS	
Africa	http://www.aidat.org/aidat/isplist.html (
Canada	http://www.holstein.ca/inquiry/iap/iap.htm
Finland	http://www.utu.fi/info/yhteydet.html
Switzerland	http://heiwww.unige.ch/switzerland/ internet_access_providers.html
United Kingdom	http://www.ukdirectory.com/computer.html
	http://www.limitless.co.uk/inetuk/table.html
Lists containing several countries	http://www.thelist.com
	http://www.commerce.net/directories/products/isp
	http://www.internic.net/internic/provider.html
	http://www.cix.org/CIXInfo/members.html
	http://www.active.co.za/index-za/isp.html
	http://www.yellow.com
	http://isotropic.com/metro/scope.html
	http://akebono.stanford.edu/yahoo/Business/Corporations/ Internet_Access_Providers/
	http://www.herbison.com/herbison/iap_meta_list.html
	http://ultralist.upx.net/
	http://www.best.be/iap.html
Global ISDN Providers	http://techweb.cmp.com/nwc/isdn/isdnisps.htm

including service areas, contact telephone, e-mail addresses, URL, services offered, and pricing.

Other useful Internet resources include the Commercial Internet Exchange members list (http://www.cix.org/CIXInfo/members.html), and Yahoo's excellent global listings by state (http://www.yahoo.com/ Regional/U_S__States/Mississippi/Internet_Service_Providers/), and by country (http://beta.yahoo.com/Regional/Countries/Germany/ Internet_Service_Providers/). For U.S. Internet Service Providers, a good overall list can be found at (http://www.primus.com/providers/). More "up close and personal" information about ISPs can be found by frequenting the Usenet news group of alt.internet.services.

Figure 4.1   The List Home Page

NON-INTERNET SOURCES

Non-Internet sources to consult to locate an ISP are the local telephone book, local computer magazines, national computer magazines such as Information Week, Communications Week, Internet Now, New Media, and newspapers such as the business section of the local paper, USA Today, or the Wall Street Journal.

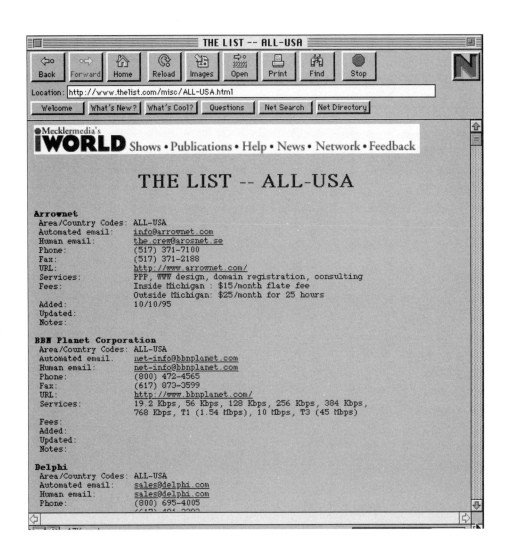

Figure 4.2 The List U.S. Internet Service Provider Detail

Also, networking with other organizations of a similar size may turn up some good information on various providers. Ask around.

Web Service Providers

Web Service Providers (WSPs)—also known as Web or Internet Presence Providers—are companies that will design, create, manage, and host your World Wide Web site on their server for a monthly fee.

These companies are using the Internet and the World Wide Web in ways that fundamentally change the nature of advertising and information distribution, create new markets, and offer new ways of selling. They will design your home and subsequent pages and perform other services, such as publicizing your site. Organizations that do not have the in-house expertise to design and manage their own Web site, or those organizations that have so much traffic that their own network has been adversely impacted, may decide to select a WSP to provide them with a Web presence.

Selecting a Web Service Provider is a little more involved than choosing an Internet Service Provider. The organization must work with the WSP to design and create the Web pages, set up the navigation of those pages, and maintain links to other sites, applications, and services. An organization is looking for an innovative WSP with whom it can build a good working relationship for the long term.

The services typically provided by a WSP are discussed in the following section. Again, the organization should match its needs and budget constraints to the services offered.

SERVICES PROVIDED

Many of the topics that would be appropriate here have already been addressed earlier in the Internet Services Provided section. For example, the WSP may also provide your organization with Internet access, traditional Internet applications and services, and Domain Name Registration. The requirements listed earlier in the Performance and Network Design section also apply to the WSP. The topics discussed below are those unique to the WSP.

Web Site Hosting

The Web Service Provider will "host" your Web site on its own Web server. Hosting means that your Web site will be accessed by external and, perhaps, internal users at the WSP's facilities. Your organization will be renting space—similar to the rental of a storefront in a shopping mall—on the WSP's server. The WSP provides the server hardware and software, communications equipment, Internet connection, Web site, traffic statistics, performance monitoring, and Web site management in exchange for a monthly subscriber's fee.

Large organizations with an extremely active Web site are moving to host facilities to reduce the amount of traffic borne by their own networks and to avoid the expense of upgrading their network to provide more bandwidth. Other candidates are small organizations lacking the technical expertise to develop and manage their own Web site internally.

Web Site Design

Most WSPs will offer pre-built Web pages for the customer who doesn't want or need a customized Web site. These pages would include the basics, such as text, one or two graphics, an e-mail link, links to other pages, and perhaps a guest registry or user feedback form. The alternative is to opt for the customized design, which significantly increases the cost of designing and creating the Web site. In this case, the WSP may act as a general contractor, pulling together the resources required (such as graphic designers, writers, advertising professionals, programmers, etc.) to deliver a customized Web site. With the customized version, several steps must be considered in producing a quality Web site, one which will draw first time and repeat visitors. These steps include Web site planning, Web page creation, navigation, and Web page content.

Web Site Planning

The overall Web site plan is the fundamental, working document created by the WSP, with assistance from the customer. This document is used as a planning tool for the duration of the relationship between the customer and the WSP. The Web site plan typically contains the following information:

- Prototypes of the Web home and subsequent pages
- Navigation and flow of the potential users through the entire site
- Links required to other pages and sites
- Interfaces with existing applications, such as company databases
- Internet connectivity required
- Document conversions required
- Contract elements, such as term of service, fee schedule, payment policies, predicted user accesses (hits), etc.
- Other services provided

Web Page Creation

Of primary importance is the "first impression," the first glimpse the user has of the home page when it initially loads on their browser. The WSP will, through personal contact with the customer, gather information that can be converted into Web page copy. The WSP will ask for marketing brochures, company logos, company annual reports, still photographs, audio files, video tapes, and any other media the customer may want to see on the Web pages. The WSP will then create Web pages that, hopefully, will foster a good first impression and keep the users coming back to the site.

The WSP will then create page layouts using standard and internationally-accepted HTML authoring tools. The WSP will insert the links required, as well as any CGI scripts, e-mail links, icons or buttons, audio clips, etc.

Web pages should be written so that they will look good with ALL browsers, including those that do not support graphics, such as Lynx. A link at the top of the home page stating "For text-only browsers" will enable non-graphical interface users to access the page faster. Netscape Navigator enhancements such as tables and centering may be used, but not so they detract from the appearance of the page when another browser is used. Some Web pages have the capability to detect the client's version of Netscape Navigator or Mosaic and either make adjustments in the page layout or offer to download the proper software for the client.

Content

Services that the WSP will offer in the area of Web content include the following:

- HTML authoring
- Graphic design and illustration
- Scanning and digital imaging
- Logo creation
- CGI programming
- Editorial services
- Multimedia creation
  — Java applets

- — Audio
- — Video
- — Animation
- — 3-D
- — Virtual reality using VRML
- Electronic brochures/catalogs
- Language translation services
- Advertising

Content should have the capability of being dynamic or readily changeable so as to keep the target market returning to the Web site. The content should also include some "giveaways," such as a screen saver or a new Java applet.

Text should be used sparingly and be "pithy;" that is, succinct, concise and easily understood. All content should be grammatically correct, written on a level suitable for the target market, and absolutely spell-checked.

Integration with Existing Applications

The WSP may provide integration with the organization's existing applications. For example, the Web site may include a link that presents a fill-in form to the customer. This form then feeds into a database which captures the customer's information. The database then triggers an order process which eventually sends the requested item (a brochure, CD-ROM, video, etc.) to the customer.

Other applications include integration with the organization's e-mail systems, inventory systems, accounting systems, and credit card verification and authorization systems.

Document Conversion

The WSP may provide the capability to convert the organization's existing documents into HTML format to be placed on the Web site. This conversion process is relatively straightforward, as software applications have recently been released to readily convert several different document formats into HTML. This conversion process may also include language translation services to provide content for international visitors.

Intranet Services

The WSP may provide an intranet service to bring Web technology to full use within the enterprise. The WSP would then work with the various internal departments, gathering content information, planning department or workgroup specific Web pages, and linking these department pages to other pages, sites, or applications.

Consulting Services

The WSP may offer several additional consulting services, including

- Infrastructure management
- Technology direction
- Documentation
- Online tutorials and help screens
- Training
- WWW presence management

Publicity and Marketing Services

The WSP may offer publicity and marketing services. This service places your site in the more common search engines and hot lists on the Web, such as InfoSeek, Yahoo, Lycos, Excite, Alta Vista, Magellan, etc.

The WSP will also make recommendations for extending the reach of your Web site through traditional media—placing your URL on your business cards; in magazine, television, radio, and newspaper advertisements; in the telephone book; on hard copy marketing brochures; in your annual report; or in customer invoices and other notifications.

Support and Maintenance

Support and maintenance services provided by the WSP would include keeping the Internet connection functioning properly, monitoring the site's traffic, changing content and links as required, as well as those services addressed earlier in the Support Levels section.

Security

The WSP should provide the same physical and logical security measures as discussed earlier in the Internet Service Provider's section.

Security is better under the Web hosting arrangement since intruders will enter the WSP's network and facilities instead of the organization's.

Commerce

More and more WSPs are offering electronic commerce services as a way to provide added value to their customers and differentiate themselves from the throngs of other providers. Providers may offer such services as a storefront in an electronic mall, order processing, credit card verification and authorization, electronic funds transfer, and more. Several specialty providers are concentrating their efforts on specific market segments, such as real estate agencies, stock brokerages, music companies, etc. The provider then creates pages and applications that are geared to that market, and the customer benefits from their proven expertise in this area.

Traffic analysis

Increasingly, customers are demanding that their WSP offer traffic analyses detailing the number of hits on their Web site, which domains, and even what was ordered. These statistics will then be used to plan Internet connectivity upgrades to higher-speed networks, offload certain content areas to dedicated servers, change the marketing mix offered on the site, market to different geographical areas or businesses, etc.

Financials

Financial considerations in selecting a WSP include the fee structure for the design, creation, management, and hosting of the Web site and the methods of payment.

Fees

Fees for Web site design and hosting vary widely. Basically, you can pay whatever you want. Some providers are trying to establish themselves in this market and are offering a per-site hosting price of as low as $10 per month. Others are much more experienced with Fortune 500 clients and may offer either a time and materials type of contract or a turn-key arrangement of $5,000 start to finish, plus a monthly subscriber's fee of $100 per month.

The WSP will have a fee structure that includes the following items:

- Home page design
- Subsequent page design
- Application integration
- Set-up and installation
- Disk storage
- Server activity
  - number of hits per day or per month
  - data transferred from server to client
  - percent of gross order activity
- Server on dedicated machine
- Domain Name Registration
- Internet access
- Consulting services
- Publicity and marketing services
- Traffic analysis
- Document conversion
- Variable rates for personal and business accounts

Methods of Payment

Basically, the methods of payment, late fees, cancellation policies, etc., will be the same as that discussed in the Internet Service Provider section above. However, the name recognition of your company may reduce the price somewhat in the case of the WSP, especially if it can be used in their advertising and promotional literature.

Getting Started

Find out from the WSP what is required to bring the Web site online and how long it will take to design, create, and test the new site. Typically, the WSP will provide a quick prototype of the Web site and then, if approved, will deliver the finished product within the agreed-upon timeframe. The customer, if already connected to the Internet, can then access their new Web site's URL and view the finished product before it actually becomes available to the Internet community at large.

Locating Web Service Providers

Locating Web Service Providers is a bit more difficult than finding Internet Service Providers. The various Internet search engines have categories for Web Service Providers, Internet Service Providers, Web Consultants, and Web and Internet Presence Providers. The results of searching these categories are individual WSPs, not lists, as in the Locating Internet Service Providers section earlier. Searching your local newspapers or magazines, as well as networking with other organizations, will be the best way to locate a WSP in your area.

Finding a WSP in your immediate geographical area is most beneficial, due to the close working relationship required. Creating your Web site can be done by means of the post office, electronic mail, or file transfer, but the personal touch is much more conducive to delivering a satisfactory product than the arm's length approach required by a distant WSP.

Table 4.2 lists a sampling of WSPs gleaned from a variety of sources. All of the Web Service Providers included in this table provide Home and Basic Web page serving, HTML authoring and Web application development as well as CGI scripting. The area(s) column depicts the area code or geographic area served by the Web service provider. If the cell is blank, the service provider either offers no dial-in capability or there is no restriction as to the geographical area.

Summary

New Internet service providers and Web presence providers open for business every day. It is no simple task to select a service that not only meets the firm's requirements, but will provide enhanced services and grow with the firm. This chapter provided guidelines on how to find, analyze, and select service providers.

In the next chapter we will discuss staffing or outsourcing part or all of the Web service.

Table 4.2 World Wide Web Service Providers

Provider	Speed	Pre-Built Apps	FTP	E-Mail	Gopher	Source	Area(s)
Atlantic Computing Technology Corporation	56K	X	X	X	X	www.atlantic.com/	
Baynet Company	128K				X	408.720.8892	
BEDROCK Information Solutions, Inc.	T1		X	X	X	www.bedrock.com 703.760.7898	
BizNet Technologies	T1	X		X	X	www.biznet. comblackburg.va.us 703.231.7715	
Branch Information Services	T1	X	X	X	X	branch.com	313
Computer Solutions by Hawkinson	T1	X	X	X	X	www.mhv.net/	NJ
Computing Engineers, Inc.	56K	X	X	X	X	www.wwa.com 312.282.8605	312, 708
Coolware, Inc.	T1		X	X		none.coolware.com/ 415.322.4722	
CTS Network Services	T1	X	X	X	X	www.cts.com	CA (619)
CyberBeach Publishing/CyberGate	T1	X	X	X	X	www.gate.net/ 800.NET.GATE	FL
Data Transfer Group	19.2K	X	X	X	X	mark@thegroup.net	
Demon Internet Ltd.	256K		X	X		www.demon.co.uk +44.181.349.0063	UK
Digital Marketing, Inc.	T1		X	X	X	www.digimark.net/	

Continued

Table 4.2 World Wide Web Service Providers (continued)

Provider	Speed	Pre-Built Apps	FTP	E-Mail	Gopher	Source	Area(s)
Downtown Anywhere, Inc.	T1 (fractional)	X	X	X		www.awa.com/ 617.522.8102	
EarthLink Network, Inc.	T1		X	X		www.earthlink.net 213.644.9500	CA (Southern)
Electric Press, Inc.	T1	X	X	X	X	www.elpress.com 703.742.3308	
Flightpath Communications	28.8K	X	X	X	X	www.flightpath.com/	
Global OnLine	128K	X	X	X	X	tony@cityscape.co.uk	Worldwide
Great Basin Internet Services	T1	X	X	X	X	www.greatbasin.net/ 702.829.9700	
HLC Internet	T1	X	X	X	X	www.hlcnet.net 800.915.5515	
Home Pages, Inc.	128K	X		X		www.homepages.com	
IDS World Network Internet Access Services	T1	X	X	X	X	www.ids.net 800.IDS.1680	
INET Marketing, Inc.	T1	X	X	X	X	www.imarket.com 407.298.1666	
InfoMatch Communications, Inc.	56K–T2	X	X	X	X	infomatch.com 604.421.3230	604
Interlink On-Line Services	56K	X	X	X	X	www.interlink.bc.ca/	BC (604)
Internet Distribution Services	56K–T1	X	X	X	X	www.service.com 415.856.8265	

Continued

Table 4.2 World Wide Web Service Providers (continued)

Provider	Speed	Pre-Built Apps	FTP	E-Mail	Gopher	Source	Area(s)
Internet Information Services, Inc.	T1	X	X	X	X	www.iis.com 800.638.7821	301, 410, 703, 800
Internet Information Systems	T1 (fractional)			X		www.internet-is.com/ 510.793.6142	
Internet Marketing, Inc.	T1		X	X	X	cybersight.com	
Internet Media Services	T1	X				conru@cdr.stanford.edu	
Internet Presence & Publishing, Inc.	T1	X	X	X		www.shopkeeper.com 804.446.9060	VA (S.E.)
Internet Services Corporation	T1	X	X	X	X	www.netservices.com/ 412.321.2912	
InterNex Information Services, Inc.	T1		X	X	X	www.internex.net/ 415.473.3060	CA (510, 415, 408)
Internex Online	14.4K	X	X	X	X	www.io.org/	Toronto
Kaleidoscope Communications	256K	X	X	X	X	www@kaleidos	
MicroSystems Internet Services	T1		X	X	X	www.comnet.com/	801
Net+Effects	14.4K	X	X	X	X	www.net.effects.com	
NSTN, Inc.	T1	X	X	X	X	www.nstn.ca 902.468.3679	902, 506, 613, 416, 905
Oslonett, Inc.	128K	X	X	X	X	www.oslonett.no	

Continued

Table 4.2 World Wide Web Service Providers (continued)

Provider	Speed	Pre-Built Apps	FTP	E-Mail	Gopher	Source	Area(s)
Primenet	T1	X	X	X	X	www.primenet.com/ 602.870.1010	AZ
Quadralay Corporation	T1	X		X		www.quadralay.com 512.346.9199	
Quantum Networking Solutions	T1		X	X	X	www.gcr.com	
SSNet, Inc.	56K	X	X	X	X	ssnet.com:8010/ssnet/ ssnhome.html	302, 610, 215
STD Systems & Networking, Inc.	T1	X	X	X	X	www.rtd.com/ 602.318.0696	AZ (602, 668)
Stelcom, Inc.	T1 (fractional)`		X	X	X	www.webscope.com 516.897.8168	
TAG Systems, Inc.	56K					www.tagsys.com/ 800.TAG.8281	
Teleport, Inc.	28.8K		X	X	X	www.teleport.com	OR, WA
Telerama Public Access Internet	T1 (SMDS)	X	X	X	X	www.lm.com	PA
TeleVisions, Inc.	T1		X	X	X	www.tvisions.com 508.263.0430	
The Computing Support Team, Inc.	T1	X	X	X	X	www.gems.com/ 800.493.GEMS	
The Innovation Group/Metro.net	10M	X	X	X	X	postmaster@igdell.mk.slip	
The Internet Group	T1		X	X	X	www.tig.com/ 412.661.4247	

Continued

Table 4.2 World Wide Web Service Providers *(continued)*

Provider	Speed	Pre-Built Apps	FTP	E-Mail	Gopher	Source	Area(s)
The New York Web	T1	X	X	X	X	mosco@mailhost. nyweb.com	
The Sphere Information Services	56K		X	X		www.thesphere.com 408.369.9105	
TLsoft	28.8K		X	X		info@tlsoft.com	
Winsey Information Services, Inc.	28.8K	X	X	X	X	www.winsey.com/ 604.421.4741	Vancouver 604
XOR Network Engineering	T1		X	X	X	plaza.xor.com/ 303.440.6093	
zNet	T1		X	X		info@znet 408.477.9NET	CA (Santa Cruz, San Jose)

CHAPTER 5

Staffing
and Outsourcing

"Chris, one of our clients wants to set up their own Web site and is looking for some advice. Remember all the fun we had looking for Web expertise?" said Jason, thinking that this might be an excellent opportunity to offer a value-added service to one of the Fremont office's major accounts.

"Yes, I remember. We were really lucky to have most of the talent we needed in-house. Firms that don't have that luxury surely must be either desperately seeking WebMasters or are seriously considering outsourcing the site. The technology is just so new that finding Web professionals who aren't already snapped up is difficult at best."

The Fremont office's Web site had only been in production for a short time, but all those involved had learned volumes about how to staff and manage the service. As Chris pointed out, finding people with solid Web expertise is a daunting task, especially when management knows only the information delivery and marketing potential of the Web, with the nitty gritty technical details to surface later. This chapter details the services typically provided in a Web service, along with the expertise and skill levels required of the personnel to create and manage the site(s). The chapter also entertains the notion of outsourcing all or part of the Web service and provides a sample outsourcing Request for Proposal on page 178.

Staffing

Staffing the Web service requires far more than just matching the services to be provided with the skill set required to deliver those services. Just finding Web professionals in this very new industry is a chaotic process. Building the support organization—whether the enterprise is very small or a global conglomerate—takes considerable planning and an innovative, less rigidly-structured approach.

Forget everything you learned in Management 101! This is the cyberscene and organizations ("cyborgs") will never be the same again. Ready access to the current of information flowing through an organization equalizes all employees, empowering them and giving the lowest-ranking clerk the same sources of knowledge as the CEO. Management structures are fast becoming virtual, in which far-flung groups of people with specific skills band together to complete a specified task, break apart, then form new task groups. The hierarchical structure of most organizations does not fit the model of the flat, distributed, and homogeneous nature of the Web.

MATCHING WEB SERVICES AND EMPLOYEE EXPERTISE

A skill set is suggested for each of the Web services provided in Table 5.1. Not all sites will be offering every service illustrated in the table, but the core services of Web server installation and administration, Web site management, Web page design, and Internet access will be found within each Web business service. Not all skills and expertise levels suggested within the table will be found in each candidate Web employee. Here again, the expertise to look for in a Web professional would be taken from the following core skills:

- Programming
- Hardware, software, operating systems
- File conversions and compression
- Network communications
- Internet
- Graphics and multimedia
- Writing

Table 5.1 Services Provided and the Skills Required to Deliver Them	
Web Services Provided	**Required Skills and Expertise**

Server installation and administration	Server hardware
	  • UNIX, PC, Mac
	Server software
	  • Web server software
	  • Operating systems—UNIX, Windows, Mac OS
	Networking
	  • TCP/IP, IPX, NetWare
	Performance analysis
	Disaster recovery
	System monitoring
	Problem isolation and resolution

LAN/WAN connectivity	Network configuration Network engineering TCP/IP Wiring schemes—Ethernet, token ring, fiber optics, twisted pair Networking technologies—T1, 56K, ATM, Frame Relay, ISDN Traffic analysis and capacity planning Problem isolation and resolution
Security	Firewall server installation/administration Proxy services Encryption products and standards Password maintenance Physical security
Internet access	Data communications hardware/software Routers CSU/DSU Domain name services Interface with Internet Service Provider
Internet applications	FTP, Telnet Gopher Finger, WHOIS, WAIS, Archie, Veronica IRC, Chat, BBS, listserv, Usenet Search engines Web indexing

Continued

Table 5.1   Services Provided and the Skills Required to Deliver Them *(continued)*

Web Services Provided	Required Skills and Expertise
Internet applications *(continued)*	Web crawlers
Web page development	User interface HTML authoring Page layout and design Programming—C, C++, Perl CGI scripts Multimedia—Java Applets, Audio, Video, Animation, 2-D and 3-D rendering, VRML File compression technologies—JPEG, GIF, MPEG Graphic design and illustration Navigation and page flow
Web service management	General knowledge of the Web, Windows, Netscape (or other browser), HTML, graphics Customer interface Project planning and management Budgeting and forecasting Statistical analysis Requirements analysis Standardization of common tools
Web content and page management	Requirements analysis Navigation and page flow Change control Customer interface Directory management
E-mail	Simple Mail Transport Protocol—SMTP Directories Directory synchronization Application program interfaces (CMC 2.0, VIM, MAPI)
Links to other applications	Database systems—Oracle, Sybase, SQL, Microsoft Access, FoxPro, DB2 E-mail—same as above Application program interfaces
Electronic software distribution	File transfers System configurations

Continued

Table 5.1	Services Provided and the Skills Required to Deliver Them *(continued)*
Web Services Provided	**Required Skills and Expertise**
Electronic software distribution *(continued)*	Script writing
Help Desk, customer support	Telephone skills Business communications—telephone, writing (responding to e-mail) Customer interface Working knowledge of browser, network connectivity, Web tools and functions, servers
Education and training	Presentation skills Tutoring skills Curriculum design Materials preparation (hard copy or online)
Documentation, procedures and practices	Technical writing Publishing software packages
Financial-business management	Accounting and chargeback methodologies Budgeting Forecasting Cost justifying new applications
Site marketing and public relations	Demonstration and product presentation skills Customer needs/requirements analysis Application of technology to business problems Outgoing and energetic personality
Legal services	Legal counsel experienced in the copyrights, trademarks, service marks, patents and royalties of multimedia data types and programs

- Group as well as individual contributor
- Creative, innovative, keeps up with emerging technologies
- Application of technology to solve business problems
- Analytical

THE WEB SERVICES ORGANIZATION

Providing consistently high-quality and innovative Web services requires a slim and flexible organization, whether the enterprise is small, medium, or large in terms of the number of desktops with Web browsers and Internet access. This section focuses on who manages the WebMaster and how Web service organizations are structured today, and offers typical organization charts for the various sizes of enterprises.

Who Manages the WebMaster?

At this point, WebMasters are reporting to a wide variety of positions within the management chain. This is due to the newness of the technology and the fact that the Web service has broad applicability to all facets of the organization. It is an information delivery tool, a new publishing medium, a marketing mechanism, and a creative outlet for all divisions within the enterprise. The WebMaster may report on paper through one functional division, but may, in actuality, get more direction and work from many other entities within the organization.

Today's WebMasters are reporting to the following management positions. This list is, of course, not all inclusive.

- Managing Director of Corporate Communications
- Director of Information Services
- Vice President of Marketing Communications
- Director of Applications or Publications
- Manager of Internet Operations
- Chief Information Officer
- Director of Art

Sample Organizational Charts

Sample organizational charts are included here as a guide for determining the number and structure of the Web service personnel. The organizations have been categorized by the number of their Web browser-equipped desktops and other factors. Entities may have a huge number of employees but fewer desktop computer systems. The key factors are not the number of employees, but the number of desktops that will be using the Web service, the amount of support required for the users, the amount of traffic and content on the Web site(s), and whether the Web site(s) will be internal, external, or both. These determining factors are detailed in Table 5.2.

Table 5.2 Sizing the Web Services Organization			
Determining Factors	Small Organization	Medium Organization	Large Organization
Number of desktops	to 300	to 2,000	to 50,000+
Company locations	1	2	Many
Web site traffic	30,000 hits/day	150,000 hits/day	300,000 + hits/day
Web site content	1GB	2GB	4GB
Internal Web site(s)	1	3	Many
External Web site(s)	1	1	1
Dedicated, full-time web employees	1	3	6 or more

Small Organization

A small, single-location organization with up to 300 Web browser-equipped desktops would typically require only one full-time Web employee. This person would be the entire company's WebMaster, performing all the daily duties described in the WebMaster job description in the next section. The WebMaster would administer the organization's low-traffic, small-content internal and external Web sites and conduct all customer interface and marketing activities. The WebMaster would typically report to the Vice President in charge of Operations or Marketing. Figure 5.1 illustrates a sample organization chart for a small enterprise.

Figure 5.1   Web Services Organization Chart for a Small Enterprise

A very small organization of under 25 desktops would likely find it expedient to outsource their Web site to a provider.

Medium Organization

A dual-location, medium-sized organization with up to 2,000 Web accessible desktops would benefit from three full-time dedicated Web professionals. The organization would have one WebMaster and two Web page designers, performing the duties as outlined in the next section. Due to the small size of this department, the individuals would most likely overlap in expertise and be able to perform each other's duties as required. For example, the Web page designer would perform Web site administration, as well as interface with the Internet Service Provider. The group would tap additional resources as required, such as an applications developer for links into databases, or an electronic mail administrator to provide an automatic response to a Web user from the e-mail system. This group would manage Web sites with up to 150,000 hits per day and at least 2GB of content. This small department would typically report to a Manager of Information Services, Marketing, or Corporate Communications. A sample organization chart for the medium-sized enterprise can be found in Figure 5.2.

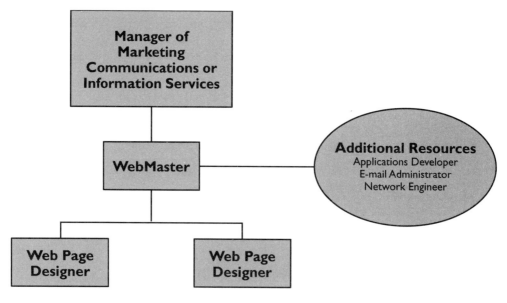

Figure 5.2   Web Services Organization Chart for a Medium Enterprise

Large Organization

A large multi-geographic enterprise with at least 50,000 Web browser-equipped desktops would have a sizable Web team. The flattened nature of Web technology and the movement toward the virtual enterprise lend themselves to establishing a virtual Web services organization consisting of a Web services manager, a senior WebMaster (technical lead), and virtual teams of Web experts loosely organized into geographic or functional service centers. Each team would be headed by a regional or functional WebMaster and would include Web page designers, graphic artists, application developers, and network gurus, as required. The teams would also draw on additional expertise as needed within the organization, such as database integrators, e-mail administrators, legal advisors, business managers, or public relations. A sample organization chart for a large enterprise is shown in Figure 5.3.

The organization would also benefit from having an advisory board to ensure the quality and consistency of all content and page design, establish policy, and to set the technical and marketing direction and standards of the service. Advisory board members would be drawn, at minimum, from the following areas within the enterprise:

- Corporate Headquarters
- Corporate Communications
- Corporate Public Relations
- Corporate Finance
- Marketing and Sales
- Information Systems
- Telecommunications

Another ad hoc organization that proves most beneficial for a large enterprise's Web business service is the Web Forum. This group is composed of the Internet and Web pioneers within the enterprise. The forum meets to share innovative ideas, competitive strategies, technologies, shortcuts, and lessons learned. This group provides technical guidance to the advisory board and Web personnel.

SAMPLE JOB DESCRIPTIONS

The following sample job descriptions are for the most common positions required to design, create, and manage a Web business service.

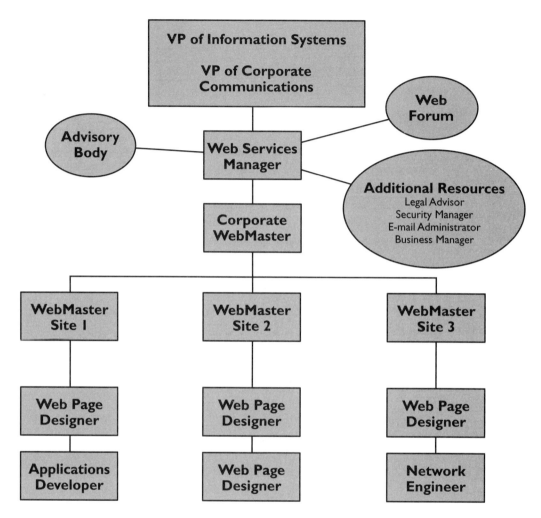

Figure 5.3 Web Services Organization Chart for a Large Enterprise

These descriptions contain more than would typically be specified in most recruitment notices. The organization is encouraged to select those aspects that most closely match the Web services planned, the computing environment, and the network of the enterprise.

The Web Services Manager

In medium- to large-sized organizations, the Web Services Manager would be the individual responsible for the overall management of the Web business service. This person would supervise a staff consisting of one or more WebMasters, Web Page Designers, and Network Engineers, etc., and would interface with the customers, legal counsel, business management, and other corporate personnel.

The Web Services Manager will need to strike a balance between having a creative vision and being able to develop and manage the Web service. This skill is sometimes lacking in those very proficient in computer programming; this is why an individual with a media or marketing communications background and with experience in applications development or systems administration would be worth a closer look.

Job Description
The Web Services Manager is responsible for establishing and managing an active Web business service and for working with corporate clients in designing and implementing Web pages. This position requires a self-directed individual proficient in the implementation, maintenance, and support of a service-oriented application. The Web Services Manager will work with corporate teams to design Web publishing standards and will evaluate new technologies and applications for the Web service.

Candidate Profile
- Over three years experience in business development, marketing communications, or applications development and delivery
- In-depth knowledge of the Internet and the World Wide Web technology and applications
- Solid project management and presentation skills
- Solid customer interface skills
- MBA or similar degree preferred

The WebMaster

The WebMaster must be skilled in assessing the information needs of the organization, identifying the resources that fill them, and making those resources easily accessible by using Web technology.

Job Description
The WebMaster is responsible for the design and creation of the Web site and for its ongoing administration and maintenance. This position

requires a self-directed and motivated individual to develop and maintain Web sites and content. The individual will also design, develop, and maintain network connections and Web server hardware and software, as well as recommending and integrating computer technology with Web services.

Candidate Profile
- 2 years related experience
- TCP/IP networking
- C, C++, Perl, and CGI programming, UNIX
- HTML/database integration (CGI's to database interfaces)
- HTML forms functionality
- WAN configurations (routing knowledge a plus)
- Systems analysis, integration, and administration
- Firewalls and network security (RSA, DES, S-HTTP, digital signatures)
- Excellent communications skills
- BS in Computer Science or equivalent preferred

The Web Page Designer

The Web Page Designer combines graphic illustration skills with writing ability and computer technology to design and develop the content of the Web site. The Web Page Designer must also be able to design the navigation and flow of the pages. This individual must have a creative flair as well as good written communication skills.

Job Description
The Web Page Designer will work closely with management and customers for the production and implementation of Web pages. The position requires proficiency in writing and graphic design. The individual must be detail-oriented and organized with excellent communication skills.

Candidate Profile
- 2 years related experience
- Web page design, layout, and flow
- Use of HTML 3.0 commands

- CGI scripting
- Computer graphics design
- Multimedia development—audio, video, animation, 2-D and 3-D graphics, VRML
- File compression and conversion utilities—JPEG, GIF, MPEG
- Prototyping skills
- Java and API experience
- Magazine or newspaper publishing experience
- BA in Fine Arts, BS in Computer Science, or equivalent preferred

The Web Network Engineer

In a large organization, the Web Network Engineer provides the infrastructure support for the delivery of Web services to customers by means of the LAN or WAN. This individual also develops specifications, performs troubleshooting and problem resolution, and investigates the application of emerging networking technologies to the Web service.

Job Description

The Web Network Engineer provides installation services for Internet connectivity, security, and World Wide Web services. The individual will work closely with the Web team to optimize customer delivery of the Web service using architecture as well as implementation skills.

Candidate Profile

- 2–5 years related experience
- LAN/WAN inter-networking—TCP/IP, Ethernet, NetWare, ISDN
- Circuit provisioning, protocols, and network connectivity
- Firewalls and network security (RSA, DES, S-HTTP, digital signatures)
- Installation and configuration of networks
- Workstation and operating system configuration and support
- Troubleshooting and problem resolution
- Customer interaction skills
- BS or equivalent preferred

DESPERATELY SEEKING WEBMASTERS

Where do you find the perfect WebMaster or other Web service personnel? Even though this technology is so very new, savvy computing, authoring, graphics, and communications people are adapting their skills base to that of the Web. The number of people with the skills set applicable to the Web is growing exponentially. They can be found by looking within the enterprise, at other organizations, or through traditional and emerging means and media.

Grow Your Own

Organizations may mine their own employees for in-house expertise that either directly applies to Web technology or can be adapted to it. Look for people with communications, media relations, computer programming, applications development, system administration, system analysis, or graphic design experience. Look for creative people that enjoy working with new technologies and working with other people. Those who are outgoing, enjoy applying technology to solve business problems, and know the organization's structure and culture will be more readily able to seek opportunities to use and promote Web technology. Having an online account and familiarity with the Internet would be a plus.

Raid a Web Site

Look for Web sites that are creative, well-orchestrated, and convey the intended meaning with pithy text, and you may find potential Web service employees there. Just send a query note to the WebMaster's electronic mail address at the bottom of the site's Home Page or call the company.

Online Searching

A non-traditional source of Web personnel is the online arena. Use any of the larger search engines, such as NetSearch, Lycos, or Excite, with a keyword search of "WebMaster," "Web Page Designers," "Internet Consultants," or "Web Consultants."

The Mac Webmasters Consultants Directory (http://www.macweb.com/consultants) and CommerceNet's Directory of Internet Consultants (http://www.commerce.net/directories/consultants/consultants.html) are also two sources to locate Web expertise online. These pages, as

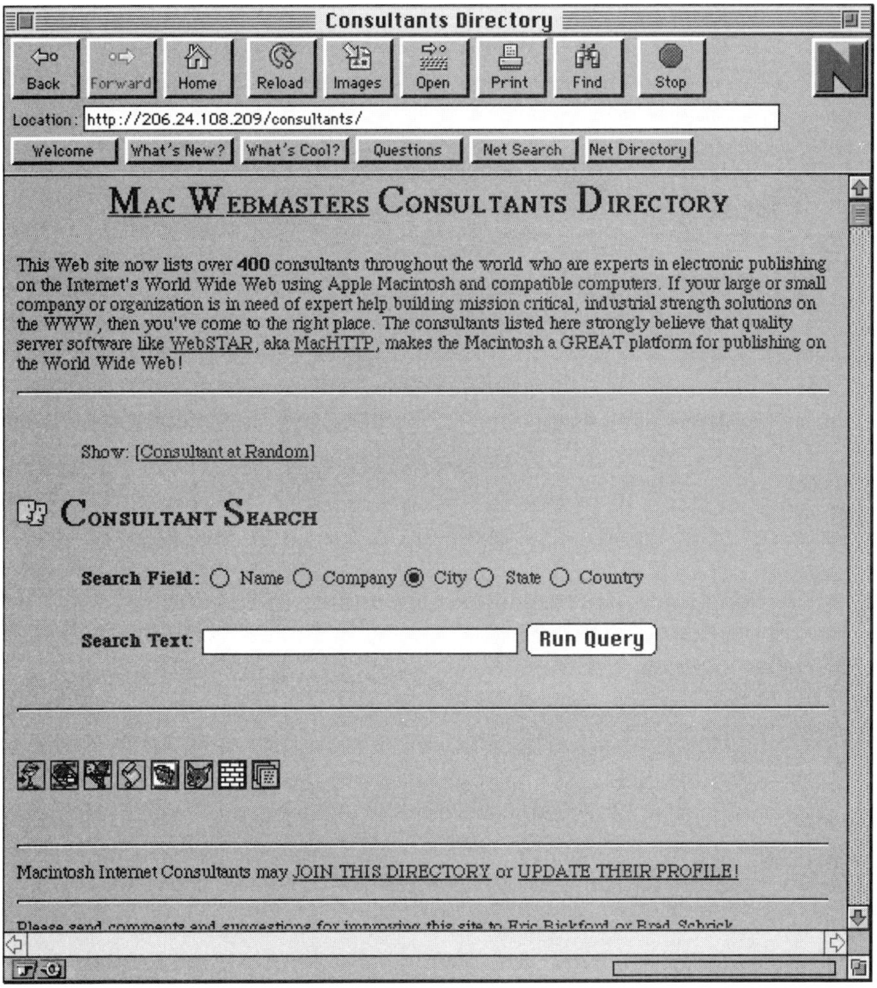

Figure 5.4   Mac Webmaster Consultants Directory Home Page

shown in Figures 5.4 and 5.5, permit the user to search alphabetically for an individual consultant by firm and by geographic area.

Online Recruiting

Another non-traditional means to locate Web personnel is to post job openings online in one of the various job or career opportunities listing services. These services charge a fee to display your listing, but it is visible to millions of potential employees with the experience and abilities you are seeking. Jobs can be posted to lists that are geographical and

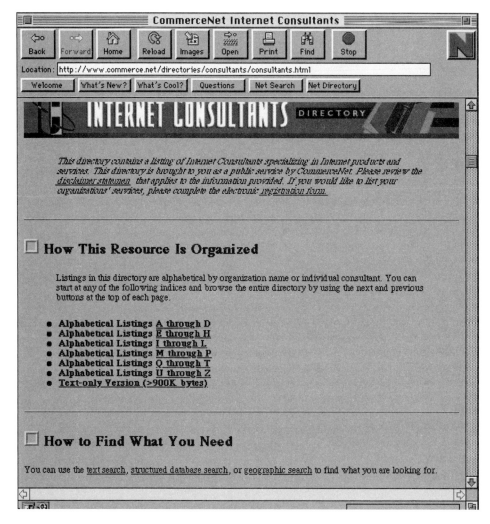

Figure 5.5 CommerceNet's Directory of Internet Consultants Home Page

specialize in a certain industry, such as real estate, healthcare, or academia, for example, or are more general in nature. To locate these services, use any of the larger search engines, like NetSearch, Lycos, or Excite, with a keyword search of "Jobs Listings" or "Job Offerings."

Recruiting Firms

Select a recruiting firm to furnish you with potential Web service employees. A high-tech firm that has generous experience in the information and marketing communications industries would provide better candidates.

Media Articles

Magazines, newspapers, and technical publications such as *Internet World, Interactive Age, WebWorld, Web Master, Communications Week, Information Week, USA Today, The Wall Street Journal, Journal of the ACM*, and others all provide articles featuring hot Web sites and technology. The Web site's URL and the name(s) of the people supporting the service are usually printed along with the articles. Many of these publications are also online, so that searching using keywords makes finding articles about Web sites easier and faster.

Newspaper and Magazine Classified Advertisements

Advertise in local and national newspapers and computer magazines for Web professionals, using the job descriptions presented in the previous section.

Additional Sources

Industry trade shows and conferences such as "WebWorld" are sources of prospective employees with Web and Internet experience. High-technology or computer-oriented job fairs held within the local region are another more traditional means of finding personnel. Also, check out trade associations such as IEEE, ACM, AMA, or IAIWC for members with the qualifications you are seeking.

Outsourcing

Outsourcing all or portions of the Web business service is a viable option today, especially if the organization is experiencing budget, personnel, or time constraints; will not risk the investment in rapidly changing technology; or has absolutely no in-house expertise. This section focuses on what to outsource, hiring consultants, and outsourcing contracts.

DECIDING WHAT TO OUTSOURCE

Outsourcing can be accomplished in varying degrees. For example, consultants may be retained as analysts for industry trends, information reports, technical briefings, and conferences. Firms such as the Gartner Group or the Meta Group offer this type of consulting service. This service is useful for keeping the organization's personnel up-to-date with the technology and what is going on within the industry.

The organization may request information or consulting services from consultants representing specific products and services. These are really vendors in the guise of consultants and may or may not charge a fee for their services. Their main interest is fitting their particular product and service suite to that of the client's needs. The advantage is a single point of contact; the disadvantage is vendor bias.

Consultants may be retained to design and create the site, train the employees, then turn the on-going operation and maintenance of the site over to the customer. This option enables an organization to more quickly establish a Web service, while bringing their own employees up-to-speed on the technology. Another advantage is that the expertise for the system remains in-house.

Consultants may be retained for the design, creation, and ongoing operation and maintenance of the site. This is the full-blown outsourcing of the Web business service to a Web Service Provider. The advantages are the speed of getting the site in production, concentrating on the core business of the organization—not Web technology— and reducing the start-up costs of the service and the on-going labor costs to maintain the service in-house. The disadvantages are the loss of control over the site itself and working with an outside vendor who may not have the same urgency as the firm's management.

HIRING CONSULTANTS

Web consultants bring to the table a variety of capabilities, including experience with Internet and Web technology, linkages, site promotion and public relations, innovation and creativity, site design and management, and ready access to other Web professionals, as needed.

Rates for consulting services vary widely, but a typical range is $600–$1,000 per day.

The International Association of Independent Web Consultants, IAIWC, (e-mail hambrook@worldtel.com) (http://www.worldtel.com/iaiwc/temp/announce.html) is a professional organization dedicated to developing site-building criteria and standards of construction, as well as ethical industry standards. IAIWC will provide a database directory of members. Other sources include those mentioned previously under Online Recruiting, plus the Internet and Web Service Providers listed in Chapter 4.

What the Consultant May Ask

Web consultants may want to have the following questions answered by the organization prior to responding to the Request for Proposal or entering into contract negotiations:

- Why is the organization considering hiring a consultant or outsourcing their Web service?
- What is the scope of the outsourcing/consulting to be provided?
- Who within the organization will actually select the consultant/outsourcer?
- What additional personnel will be available to assist with the project?
- Where and how is the work to be performed (on the customer's site or at the consultant's/outsourcer's location)?
- What are the payment arrangements?
- When is the contract considered fulfilled?

OUTSOURCING SELECTION CRITERIA

After all the responses to the Request for Proposal have been received, the organization must select an outsourcer to design, create, and/or manage the Web service. The following selection criteria can be used to determine an outsourcing contractor:

- Ability to create a unique, creative presence on the Web
- Ability to use existing images and text to design an efficient and functional relationship between this information and the Web site design
- Qualifications, portfolio, and current clients
- Qualifications of the project management, creative design, and programming team and subcontractors

---

Sample Outsourcing Request for Proposal

The sample Request for Proposal included in this section specifies the Fremont Office's requirements for a fully functional and interactive Web site. The scope of the proposal is for a Web consulting firm to design, create, and implement their Web site, train their employees, and then turn the site over to the Fremont Office to operate and maintain. The proposal is for a highly-active site with links to applications.

FREMONT OFFICE

INTERNET WEB SITE DESIGN AND IMPLEMENTATION ON THE WORLD WIDE WEB

REQUEST FOR PROPOSAL

I. INTRODUCTION

The Fremont Office is the official marketing organization for the hospitality and tourism industry of the State of Fremont. It is the intent of this request to solicit bids from Internet Web site design firms or agencies (referred throughout this Request for Proposal as "firm") capable of providing the development, design, and programming of an interactive application and implementation of the Fremont Office's Internet Web site on the World Wide Web (WWW).

II. BACKGROUND

The mission of the Fremont Office is to market Fremont worldwide as the premier leisure, convention, and business destination for the continual economic benefit of the state. The Fremont Office is a private, not-for-profit organization partially funded by its 1,200 members. Member companies span the full range of the hospitality, entertainment, and travel sectors of the tourism and convention industry, as well as local businesses. The Fremont Office is 11 years old and is comprised of eight major divisions: North American Tourism, International Tourism, Convention and Visitor Services, Convention Sales, Public Relations, Research, Member Services, and Administration. Fremont's Visitor Information Center is also operated by the Fremont Office and is located within a popular tourism area.

In addition, the Fremont Office has convention sales representatives in Chicago, Los Angeles, and Washington, D.C. Internationally, the Fremont Office currently has a full-service office in London, England; and tourism marketing representatives in Korea, Japan, Germany, and Belgium to expand our reach through the European and Asian communities. Two tourism marketing representatives, one based in Cord Gables, Florida, and a second based in Mexico

Continued

Sample Outsourcing Request for Proposal *(continued)*

City, Mexico, cover the Latin and South American marketplaces. The Fremont Office intends to enhance Fremont's marketing through interactive applications such as the Internet's World Wide Web, commercial online services, and CD-ROM. Audiences will be general consumers, travel trade, media, and convention and meeting planning markets. Efficient and enhanced communication capability with Fremont Office members is also a very important goal.

The Fremont Office has established relationships with America Online (AOL) and CompuServe to provide information and support for their travel information areas and forums. In addition, the Fremont Office has also established electronic addresses on AOL (Fremont@AOL.com) and CompuServe (224455.3366©compuserve.com). As part of the Fremont Office's Internet presence, a Web site domain "FREMONTINFO.com" has been registered. Currently, this Web site is inactive, pending the completion of the design and programming of the functional Web site.

III. BID PROCEDURES

A. Schedule

Timing of this Request for Proposal is as follows:

- Issued: July 28, 1996
- Submission deadline: August 25, 1996
- Design firm decision: September 15, 1996
- First presentation: October 9, 1996
- Second presentation: October 30, 1996
- Implementation date: November 13, 1996

B. Requirements

1   Overall, the firm should provide a full description of its qualifications, facilities, and a list of current clients.

2   Information such as Internet Web site home pages and URLs of current clients should be provided to enable the Fremont Office to view the firm's "portfolio" of Web site programming and creative designs. These Web site files should be provided on a source diskette in addition to being accessible by the Fremont Office on the firm's designated server as it would appear on the WWW.

Continued

Sample Outsourcing Request for Proposal (*continued*)

3 This section should also include identification and qualifications of the design team to be assigned to this project. The firm should have extensive knowledge and experience in HTML formatting and Web site development with knowledge of HTML3+ and SGML. Please document your expertise in this area in addition to your overall expertise regarding database software design and management. If any sub-contractors are to be used, they should be identified with their qualifications and a description of the role they will be providing.

IV. INTERNET WEB SITE AND INTERACTIVITY

A. Design

1 Specify your marketing, communications, and technical Internet and online services expertise. Describe in detail your design, programming, and end-user philosophy in utilizing the Internet and online services.

2 Explain your capability in terms of creating copy and unique graphical interfaces that are appealing to specific, targeted groups of consumers via electronic media. Indicate your firm's experience in this area.

3 Describe how your designs and programming will address "netiquette" in regard to the Fremont Office's Internet presence.

4 Explain your ability to market the Fremont Office's Web site across the WWW, in particular, establishing links with appropriate search engines on the Internet, such as WAIS, Yahoo, Web Crawlers, Gopher, Veronica, Hyperlinks, etc.

5 Describe your ability to program a Web site that is easily interfaced with the Fremont Office to facilitate efficient updating and expansion of the system without the assistance of the design firm. Please specify the programming language(s) used to create HTML forms.

6 Describe, in detail, your assessment of the essential elements which must be in any online presence and your plan to effect that with the Fremont Office's Web site. Please offer examples of features that would be included in a proposed Fremont Office presence and why they are impor-

Continued

Sample Outsourcing Request for Proposal *(continued)*

tant. Examples would be intuitive information access, data-base display based on customer profile, and so on.

7   The firm is asked to design a sample home page, incorporating the above, and load it onto the WWW for the Fremont Office's inspection.

8   As the proposed Web site evolves, the Fremont Office will add enhanced listings of member information and graphics. The firm should provide cost estimates for designing expansion modules and templates which will be used to standardize this information. Cost estimates for the storage and programming to have the information reside in the Web site server should also be provided and/or the cost to establish a hyperlink to the member's home page.

B. Functions

Submit a description of all, but not limited to, the functions below that can be provided presently or if enhancements would be made to meet requested programming:

1)   Capacity and operational efficiency of the server the Fremont Office's application would reside on, in specific, the telecommunications capacity, such as ISDN, T1, or T3 bandwidth

2)   Ability to create custom forms driven by the database and the ability to update the database, simultaneously affecting all forms generated

3)   Programming to facilitate existing information real-time database queries from existing information

4)   Incorporation of the Fremont Office's existing text and graphic images into the design process and any cost-savings therein

5)   Capability to create outbound hyperlinks via clickable icons with existing Web sites from within the Fremont Office's Web site

6)   Capacity to incorporate unique "doors" for inbound hyperlinks from other Web sites and online services with the Fremont Office's Web site

Continued

Sample Outsourcing Request for Proposal (continued)

7) Extent of programming capability to capture Web site user information, demographics, and usage duration of the site, such as indicating the number of "hits," user registrations, what the path the user followed to get to a specific page, length of time spent on each page, and the duration/time-of-day.

8) Ability to receive and forward group and individual e-mail seamlessly between the Web site server and routed directly to the Fremont Office's LAN server for member companies and other specified groups to utilize.

9) Information transfer, Web site content remote maintenance and off-site storage capabilities, including backup procedures and mirror sites during high server utilization

10) Make, model and capabilities of the Web server software and operating system the software will operate on, along with a description of any other services sharing the server and any possible capacity limitations. (As part of this description, the Fremont Office requests a cost analysis statement—see Section VI-9—between renting server space verses purchasing a server based on capacity required for current design and future enhancements.)

11) Application must support CGI (Clickable Graphic Icons) scripts and PERL embedded custom enhancements

12) Ability to program forms and e-mail templates which will efficiently interface with Fremont Office mail fulfillment procedures to download user requests for printed visitor information

13) Ability to program data and graphical display to accommodate the wide-range of modem speeds, graphic and text capabilities under all current Web browsers formats—both character-based and GUI—and operating systems available to consumers now and in the future (such as Mosaic, Archie, Gopher, Netscape, Netcruiser, AOL, etc.)

14) Ability of users to choose between graphic-text and text-only versions

15) Ability of users to choose preferred international languages at home page

Continued

Sample Outsourcing Request for Proposal (continued)

16) Ability to create discussion groups and chat forums, newsgroups, and other features suitable for the Fremont Office's marketing

C. Implementation

To ensure the proper management of this service and the highest level of utilization, all Fremont Office staff members will be available for consultation during this process. Status reports and presentations will be scheduled to facilitate this communication.

1   The firm should provide an itemized timeline of implementation from initial consultation to presentation for approvals to beta testing to consumer accessibility.

2   The firm also should indicate existing resources available to expedite the implementation of the web site and provide examples of previous timelines from consultation to launch.

3   A description of the information gathering and manipulation should also be provided in terms of how this information will be transferred into the design of the Web site. (Note the Fremont Office's Publications Department currently maintains all text and graphic images via electronic media.)

D. Maintenance

Ownership of the Web site, the data therein, its design and programming will become the property of the Fremont Office. All information maintenance of the system will be managed by the Fremont Office's information specialists. The Web site should be designed to facilitate efficient FTP and other capabilities for uploading and downloading information in addition to the creation of expanded listings using the Web site's expansion module format (as designed by the firm). Assistance from the firm for specific maintenance projects will be contracted as needed.

V. FUTURE ENHANCEMENTS

1   Enhancements such as accommodations' bookings, sale of attractions' tickets, and other products should be explained in terms of how such a system would complement existing information, or how such a system will reside in or link to the Fremont Office's Web site.

Continued

Sample Outsourcing Request for Proposal *(continued)*

2 The security of such a system should also be explained in terms of protecting submitted addresses and credit card information (and/or the ability to utilize E-cash).

3 The capabilities of sound, full-motion video, QuickTime, QuickTime VR, and SGI VR should also be taken into account when designing the site.

4 Alternative interactive media such as CD-ROM storage and distribution of information should be addressed.

VI. COST PROPOSAL

1 Define an hourly fee schedule based on programming, design, and implementation requirements, including copy, story boards, artwork and image scanning (or file transfer from existing media when possible).

2 Provide a copy of the terms of a service contract agreement, including space rental, maintenance of system, administration, and warranty against all viral infections (inherent and through downloadable files) and information backup.

3 Costs should be presented as a separate document, be sealed in a separate envelope marked "project costs," and identify the firm's name.

4 Costs should consider the Fremont Office's existing electronic graphics, images, and text available for transfer into the design of the web site and any savings this will allow.

The costs should be delineated into:

1) Staff time (charge per hour times estimated time to completion)

2) Programming and design fees

3) Information transfer and/or storage fees

4) Optional design/programming fees for enhanced applications (if applicable)

5) Cost of expansion modules and/or ability to hyperlink with member Web sites

6) Costs for any additional hardware or other materials, beyond those service-based in nature

Continued

Sample Outsourcing Request for Proposal (*continued*)

7) Implementation costs

8) Optional fees for storage and Internet access via designer's Internet service provider

9) Optional fees for purchasing a file server, whereby the Web site and information can reside on a server owned by the Fremont Office. This cost would be contingent on the size of the Fremont Office's Web site file, the capacity of the server and any expansion limitations due to shared space on the server.

10) Costs should also consider the possibility of modular development (therefore a modular cost for development)

1 Finalists may be asked to present their proposal in person at the Fremont Office in Fremont.

2 The Fremont Office should retain complete ownership of the application, source code, and all rights for future marketing efforts. Any documentation required to meet this requirement should be supplied by the firm.

- Existing and future enhancements
- Ability to interface efficiently with mail fulfillment procedures to download requests for printed information
- Understanding of the relations between the organization and its customers and ways to use interactive applications (such as e-mail and bulletin boards) to better that relationship
- Understanding of the marketing capabilities of such a Web site across all the organization's departmental lines and ways to exploit these capabilities
- Ability to meet the time schedule
- Reasonable cost and contract terms

ELEMENTS OF AN OUTSOURCING CONTRACT

A good outsourcing contract will contain a clear and concise statement of work, plus the following essential Web-oriented elements.

The contract will spell out the specific responsibilities for both parties. Outsourcing contracts will also contain the standard terms and conditions designed by the organization's legal counsel.

Introduction and Background Information

This brief statement of introduction serves to describe the organization and relate the organization's purpose and mission to the contractor. The background statement cites the organizations' requirements and objectives in designing and creating their Web site. These two statements together specify the overall scope of the project for the contractor.

Site Design

The contract specifies the functional design of the Web site as proposed by the contractor in the response to the RFP, including Web page navigation and flow. The design also specifies hypertext links, logos, graphics, multimedia, interactive forms, etc. The model of this design is the prototype developed by the contractor, which is then modified to suit the organization's needs.

Content

The content of the Web site may be owned and controlled by either party to the outsourcing contract. Just who owns what must be explicitly detailed. Any changes, updates, and upgrades need to be specified as to the method used, frequency, and penalties if the customer doesn't provide them as stipulated or the contractor doesn't implement them on time.

Implementation Process

The contract should specify the time schedule for the design, creation, and implementation of the Web site. Specific dates (and penalties if they aren't met) should be listed. The contractor will have provided a project schedule as part of the response to the RFP; this should be attached to the outsourcing contract if there were no modifications.

System Configuration

This section specifies the hardware, software, and communications facilities used for the Web site. The contract should detail exactly how much disk space is allocated for the Web site, software versions used, and the line speed.

Monitoring

This section specifies how the Web site will be monitored for traffic flow, problems, and performance, and when these statistics will be made available to the organization in the form of reports (daily, monthly, quarterly, or on-demand).

Operations and Maintenance

This section details how the contractor will perform problem detection, isolation, escalation, and resolution. The contract also specifies penalties if the system is unavailable and lists scheduled downtime.

Marketing and Public Relations

The contract specifies which online search engines will be given links to the new Web site and what additional media, such as radio spots, magazine ads, etc., will be used to promote the site.

Sales Revenue

If the Web site will be used to generate electronic orders, the contract will detail the expected sales revenue and what percentage the outsourcer will derive. This is similar to a sales percentage given to the retail leaseholder based on gross receipts.

Fees and Payment Schedule

The fees detailed in Chapter 4 for Internet and Web Service Providers will be specified in this section. The payment schedule will show progress points in the process of delivering and maintaining the Web site, along with the percentage of the overall contract price which would be drawn down after customer acceptance of each phase.

Summary

Finding qualified and creative people to design, create, and manage your Web site is no easy task, due to the newness of the technology and the blend of computer, content, and communications skills required. In this chapter we explored the ways to find Web employees, to size the Web service organization, and to outsource the Web site, if warranted. Smaller companies use outsourcing as a way to become familiar with the Web and take advantage of its potential without having to risk a heavy investment in time, personnel, and equipment. Larger companies are turning to outsourcing today in response to the high volume of traffic on their networks and security concerns.

In the next chapter we will tackle the financial considerations for launching a Web business service—budgeting and selling the service to management. Whether the Web service is operated in-house or outsourced, financial matters are of paramount concern.

Financial Considerations

BUDGETING, ACCOUNTING, AND SELLING TO MANAGEMENT

"It seems that more children accessed the Bronto Brats virtual reality page this month than ever before!" noted Chris, analyzing the Web site's statistics. "This would be a great spot for the free screen saver showing all the dinosaurs frolicking in the wet and wacky fountains and, of course, a $10.00-off park admission downloadable coupon for the parents! This new form of advertising has already given us a very healthy rate of return."

Once the Web business service has been architected, and planning for staffing or outsourcing has been completed, certain financial issues must be worked out prior to selling the service to senior management. An all-up budget must be generated to determine the cost model for the service; a cost recovery model will then be built from this information to account and bill for the service. Management will want statistics about the service gathered and analyzed, including exactly which pages are most frequently accessed and by whom. The service's return on investment must be calculated and presented within a comprehensive cost justification package to management. This chapter explores

Web service costing, income generation, statistical analysis, and accounting for billing and chargeback, as well as getting the service funded by management.

Budgeting for Web Services

What does it actually cost to establish and run an active Web business service? Costs are extremely difficult to pin down for a Web service, since a typical site may have many software products installed and running—some commercial, some shareware, and some free—but all with installation costs and some level of ongoing maintenance expense. Costs will vary, depending on the size of the organization and the activity and complexity of the Web site. The best approach in building a budget for the Web service is to develop a general cost model that can be used as a foundation for any size organization or any activity level of Web site. Then apply this model to cost scenarios for small-, medium-, and large-sized organizations.

WEB SERVICE GENERAL COST MODEL

The Web service's general cost model has two main components as shown in the summary below. Start-up costs and recurring costs, described in detail later in this section, are combined to present the financial information needed for budgeting for a Web service.

Start-up Costs
- Capital Items
  - Hardware
  - Software
- Expense Items
  - Hardware
  - Software
  - Communications
  - Miscellaneous
  - Labor

Recurring Costs

- Hardware
- Software
- Communications
- Miscellaneous
- Labor

Assumptions

This cost model assumes that all Web service hardware, software, communications, and miscellaneous items will be procured by the organization from commercial sources, not downloaded as freeware or outsourced to Internet or Web service providers. Many organizations have a policy stipulating that no software will be placed into production that is not commercially available and fully supported by the original vendor or acceptable third party. All required LAN connectivity and personal computer hardware (486s or better) for end users are already in place within the enterprise. Labor for the installation of the site as well as for ongoing support will also come from within the organization and not be outsourced. The model assumes that all content for the Web site will be developed in-house and not by consultants. Therefore, this model represents the high-end budget for a Web service. Hardware costs will dominate in the first year of the Web service's implementation, with labor costs taking the lead thereafter. Estimated costs are shown later in the Cost Model Scenarios section.

START-UP COSTS

Start-up costs—one-time, set-up, non-recurring, or installation costs—occur only once, at the beginning of the Web business service implementation. These are all costs associated with the actual launch of the new service. Start-up costs are composed of capital and expense costs.

Capital Items

Capital items are typically physical assets, such as computer hardware, machinery, vehicles, etc., and are depreciated over time. Generally, each organization has an amount established for determining which items can be capitalized and which will be expensed. The amount is usually a minimum of $1,500. Depreciation is the amount of worth that a capital asset loses over time due to use, and is expressed as a percentage. For example, computer hardware is generally depreciated over five years at a rate of 20% of the original purchase price per year. There are several accounting methods used today to depreciate assets over time. Software applications and systems purchased for amounts equal to that of capital items can be amortized. For example, firewall server software can run as high as $6,000, and would be considered a capital item to be amortized. Amortization is an accounting method similar to depreciation in which the software's value is reduced at a defined rate over time. Costs such as consulting fees, training, installation of the hardware, software, or cable infrastructure can also be capitalized if they are a lump sum associated with the initial purchase of the capital item.

Typically, an organization will treat the component parts of a computer—the CPU, monitor and keyboard/mouse—as one entire system for accounting purposes. The entire system can then be either expensed, if under the capital limit, or capitalized, if over it. Capital items for the launch of the Web business service are

Computer Hardware
- Web server system
    — CPU
    — Keyboard and mouse
    — Monitor
    — Firewall/Proxy server system
    — CPU
    — Keyboard and mouse
    — Monitor

Software
- Web server software
- Firewall server software
- Additional software products in excess of $1,500

Communications
- Router
- DSU/CSU

Installation
- Cable, hardware, software

Miscellaneous
- Training, consulting services, etc.

Expense Items

Expense items are those than can be accounted for as ordinary disbursements within the accounting system of the organization. Expense items are under the capital limit for the organization (under $1,500, for example) and can be written off as the expense occurs, rather than depreciating the item over time.

Expense items associated with the initial launch of the Web business service include

Hardware
- Scanner
- Web and firewall server's LAN cards

Software
- Web browser for each desktop
- TCP/IP stack
- Statistical reporting package
- Accounting/billing package

Communications
- Telco line installation
- Internet service provider installation

Registrations
- Domain Name
- UUCP mail
- NNTP newsfeeds

Training
- Classes, seminars, conferences for technical support staff

Documentation
- System, software, and user documentation

Labor
- Install new hardware and software
- Prototype and test
- Perform benchmarking and capacity planning
- Content development
  — Web page development—coding and scripting
  — Graphics and illustrations
  — Conversion of documents to HTML
  — Scanning images into Web pages
  — Integrating applications with the Web service
  — Advertising and promotion

RECURRING COSTS

Recurring costs are those that continue for the life of the Web business service after all installation and implementation costs have been allocated. They include such items as hardware and software maintenance, usage costs, administration, and operation of the system, as well as any planned hardware and software upgrades. Recurring costs typically fall under the expense category and will be either fixed costs or variable costs. Fixed costs are those that are the same month after month, such as a flat-rate connection to the Internet. Variable costs are those that fluctuate over time, such as fees based on the number of server hits.

Recurring costs for a Web business service typically include

Hardware
- Planned hardware upgrades
- Hardware maintenance

Software
- Planned software upgrades
- Software maintenance

Communications

- Monthly fees for telco lines, Internet access
- Monthly fees for usage
- Upgrade/downgrade service level

Miscellaneous

- Electricity to run the Web and firewall servers

Labor

- New content development
- Content maintenance
- Ongoing administration and management
- Desktop support and software upgrades

COST MODEL SCENARIOS

Cost models are shown below for three types of organizations: small-, medium- and large-sized enterprises. The cost model scenarios use the minimum suggested server configurations, activity levels, and number of employees and desktops equipped with Web browsers in Table 6.1. This information is taken from Chapters 3 (Web Server Hardware)

Table 6.1 Enterprise Classification for Cost Model Scenarios			
Classification	Small Enterprise	Medium Enterprise	Large Enterprise
Number of desktops	to 300	to 2,000	to 50,000+
Company locations	1	2	3+
Web site traffic	30,000 hits/day	150,000 hits/day	300,000 + hits/day
Server processor	75MHz	100MHz	133–166+ MHz
Server RAM	16MB	32MB	64+ MB
Web site content	1GB	2GB	4GB
Internal Web site(s)	1	2	3+
External Web site(s)	1	1	1
Employees	1	3	6+

and Chapter 5 (The Web Services Organization), where the rationale for the classification is explained.

The costs reflected in Table 6.2 are the minimum amounts to be expected in the launch of a successful Web business service if the organization uses new, commercial, off-the-shelf products and systems. The costs include the software, hardware, communications, etc., items detailed in the start-up and recurring costs sections discussed previously. The major expenses are the start-up costs of providing labor and a commercial Web browser (at $30 per seat) for each and every desktop within the enterprise. And with 300, 2,000, and 50,000 desktops in the small, medium and large organizations, this gets very expensive. Most companies therefore opt to use a free Web browser downloadable from the Internet.

Table 6.2   Cost Model Scenarios for Establishing a Web Business Service

Cost Item	Small Enterprise	Medium Enterprise	Large Enterprise
START UP COSTS			
Hardware (server and firewall)	$5,600	$17,200	$76,800
Software (server and firewall)	$13,500	$26,500	$51,500
Browser software	$9,000	$60,000	$1,500,000
Communications (CSU/DSU, router)	$5,000	$10,000	$20,000
Miscellaneous	$2,000	$4,000	$6,000
Labor and fringe	$15,750 (3 months)	$94,500 (6 months)	$304,500 (9 months)
RECURRING COSTS			
Hardware	$1,200	$2,500	$5,000
Software	$1,200	$2,500	$10,000
Communications	$12,000	$18,000	$24,000
Miscellaneous	$250	$500	$750
Labor and fringe	$47,250 (3 months)	$94,500 (6 months)	$101,500 (9 months)
TOTAL FIRST YEAR COSTS:	$100,600	$330,200	$2,100,050

Labor for all models is estimated at $45,000 for the salaries of a Web-Master, Web page designer, and graphic artist, and $65,000 for a Web business service manager's salary—plus 40% to include fringe benefits.

The first cost model shown in Table 6.2 represents a small enterprise with a low-content, low-activity-level Web site and a small number of desktops equipped with browsers. The server is a Windows-based machine with a 56Kbps link to the Internet service provider. The second scenario is for a medium-sized enterprise of 2,000 desktops with active Windows-based Web sites in two locations and a larger amount of content. For this organization, a higher-end server would be required, as well as a T1 link to the Internet service provider. The last scenario is for a very large organization of 50,000 desktops with multiple, highly-active and complex Web sites. This enterprise would typically have UNIX servers as Web sites and would also use a T1 interface.

Statistical Analysis, Billing, and Accounting of Services

The Web business service must have measurement technologies to provide the raw data (statistics) as input to the billing and accounting systems. The statistics gathered are necessary to describe, qualify, and quantify the user/customer. Statistics are used to determine site visitors and usage patterns, including who is reading the particular Web page, banner, product announcement or document, and the navigation and flow of customers through the site. Statistics are also used to provide service cost justification, user demographics, trend information, capacity planning; to compare sites; to optimize pages based on user behavior; and to create customized information and products/services for the user base.

Statistics, billing, and accounting for a Web business service are discussed in the sections below. A survey of the current offerings of Web software packages is shown in Table 6.3.

WEB SERVICE STATISTICS

With today's technology it is quite difficult to isolate a particular user of the Web business service, since the source destination address pair of the message header identifies hosts, not individual users.

Table 6.3 Survey of Web Statistics, Billing, and Accounting Software Products and Services

Product	Vendor	Platforms	Source	Cost
Access Watch	NetPresence, Inc.	UNIX, Win	http://netpressence.com/accesswatch/	Free
Analog	University of Cambridge Statistical Laboratory	DOS, Win, OS/2, UNIX	http://www.statslab.cam.ac.uk /~sret1/analog/	Free
Armor	Armor Systems, Inc.	DOS, UNIX	http://armor-net.com/	Commercial
Counter 4.0	NetForce Development, Inc.	UNIX	http://www.nforce.com/	Free
Genesis Surveys	Web Genesis	Mac	http://www.webgenesis.com	Commercial $495
I/Count	Internet Profiles Corp.	Win, Mac, UNIX	http:/ipro.com	Commercial to $5,000 (traffic usage basis)
Internet Audit Bureau	IAB	Win NT	http://www.internet-audit.com	Free
Internet Billing	Coolworld.com, Inc.	Win 3.1, Win 95, Win NT	http://www.coolworld.com/intbill/	Commercial $ (per user basis)
Internet Power Suite	Data Pro Accounting Software, Inc.	UNIX, Win	http://www.dpro.com/	Commercial $23,000—Intel $28,000—DEC Alpha or RX/6000
Lilypad	Streams Online Development Corp.	UNIX, Win, Mac	http://streams.com/lilypad/	Commercial $695/month
Market Focus	Interse	Win 95, Win NT	http://www.interse.com	Commercial $695 ($3,500 developer)
net.Analysis	net.Genesis Corp.	Win 95, Win NT, UNIX	http://www.netgen.com	Commercial $2,995

Continued

Table 6.3 Survey of Web Statistics, Billing, and Accounting Software Products and Services (*continued*)

Product	Vendor	Platforms	Source	Cost
NetCount	NetCount, Inc.	UNIX, (Win 95, NT, Mac future)	http://www.netcount.com	Free—Basic Commercial—$195+ per month
Optimal Internet Monitor	Optimal Networks Corp.	Win 95, Win NT	http://www.optimal.com	Commercial $1,000–1,500
Personal Web Site	W3.COM	UNIX	http://w3.com	Commercial $2,500–5,000
Pro Series 3.0	SBT Accounting Systems, Inc.	DOS, Win	http://www.sbtcorp.com	Commercial
ServerStat and ServerStat Lite	Kitchen Sink	Mac, Power Mac Software, Inc.	http://www.kitchen-sink.com/	Commercial $20–99.95
SiteTrack	Group Cortex	UNIX, (Netscape)	http://www.cortex.net	Commercial $3,500
Stat*X	Netforce Development, Inc.	UNIX	http://www.nforce.com/	Commercial
User Tracking and Accounting 2.0	RTD Systems and Networking, Inc.	UNIX	http://www.rtd.com/software/uta.html	Commercial $1,000–20,000 (per user basis)
WebReporter	Open Market, Inc.	UNIX	http://www.openmarket.com/products/reporter/	Commercial $495
WebScope	TLC Systems, Inc.	UNIX	http://www.tlc-systems.com/	Commercial Service
WebStat	Huntana	UNIX (Python Browser)	http://www.pegasus.esprit.ec.org/people/sijben/statistics/advertisment.html	Free

Continued

Table 6.3	Survey of Web Statistics, Billing, and Accounting Software Products and Services *(continued)*			
Product	Vendor	Platforms	Source	Cost
WebTap	Electronic Book Technologies	UNIX (HotJava applet)	http://www.ebt.com	Free
WebTrac	Logical Design Solutions	Win 3.X	http://www.lds.com	Free
WebTrack	Webster Network Strategies	UNIX	http://www.webster.com	Commercial
WebTrader	SBT Internet Systems, Inc.	Win NT	http://www.sbtcorp.com	Commercial
WebTrends	e.g. Software, Inc.	Win 3.1, Win 95, Win NT, UNIX, Mac	http://www.webtrends.com/ webtrend.htm	Commercial $299
WebWatch	Virtual Office, Inc.	UNIX	http://www.office.net	Commercial

Another drawback is that most Web-tracking packages today count hits, the number of times that a user accesses any file at the site. For example, a user may access the home page itself, four images, and an audio file, and this activity would be reported as six hits on the system. A few of the more sophisticated packages are now offering a means to count visits and sessions, not just hits. This measurement provides more detailed information on repeat visitors, how long they stay, and how they navigate within the site.

This section explores the statistics that are useful to gather and analyze and the features and functions to look for in a good statistical reporting software package.

In the very near future we will see many practical enhancements in the area of statistics gathering and analysis, including the tracking of

- secure Web servers with authorizations and authentications
- financial transactions
- attachments to corporate databases
- user interactions and queries
- Web robots

Gathering Statistics

Statistics packages today offer a wide variety of raw data and consolidated reports for the analysis of Web site usage, performance, and monitoring. The mechanism whereby statistics are gathered may be a software package located on the Web business server that provides data and reports to the management locally. Subscription services are also available that tap into the dynamics of the Web server, send the data back to the vendor for analysis, then return reports to the customer. Subscription services typically bill the customer by the number of hits on the Web site, as in the case of NetCount Plus (http://www.net-count.com) shown in Figure 6.1.

Stat*X (http://www.nforce.com/), a statistics gathering and analysis software package, is an example of the first type of software product. Stat*X collects a variety of statistics; in addition, it has each user answer one question prior to taking the next step in the navigation of the Web site. In this way, the product does a broader survey than

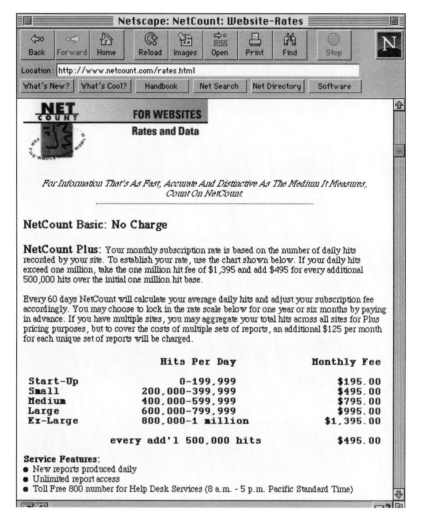

Figure 6.1 NetCount Rates for Web Subscription Services

those home pages that force the user to complete a registration form before entering the site. Stat*X then collects user demographics from a sample of the site's visitors. Lilypad, representative of the subscription service type of software product, is a response assessment service developed by Streams Online Development Corp., a Web analysis and marketing firm (http://streams.com/).

Statistics useful to gather include those on Web site usage, server performance, link statistics, Web page usage, and information about the user. The expense of procuring the tracking software and the labor to analyze the results needs to be balanced with the added value of information. The major statistical categories are more fully defined in the following sections.

Web Site Usage

- number of hits
- number of errors (file does not exist, send timed out, etc.)
- total failed requests
- total redirected requests
- number of status messages (document moved, found elsewhere, etc.)
- busy hours
- busy day of week
- activity levels by day of week and hour of day
- daily activity summary
- total bytes transferred
- average bytes transferred per day
- number of distinct files requested
- most downloaded files by type
- most submitted forms and scripts
- most active domains—com, edu, net, gov, org, and mil
- most active countries—e.g., UK and Canada
- activity by state and city
- most frequent host accesses
- number of distinct hosts served
- number of new hosts served in last 7 days
- sites accessed by proxy server
- directories accessed sorted by amount of traffic
- most active sub-directories
- corrupt log file lines
- unwanted log file entries

Server Statistics

- hourly server load

Link Statistics

- site's broken links
- links users coming from to get to the Web site
- links used within the site
- which search engines point to the site
- which queries within search engines point to the site

Web Page Usage

- usage report per page
- most requested pages
- total successful requests
  — printing all pages with at least 10 requests, sorted by number of requests
- average successful requests per day

User Statistics

- demographics
  — location
  — income
  — marital status
  — age
  — gender
  — race
- browser and operating system used
- referred by—which site the user came from
- where the users go within the site
- where users exit the site
- number of users bookmarking the site

Statistical Report Features and Functions

Several features and functions are desirable to have when selecting a good statistical reporting software package or subscription service. These features are categorized into six major areas, including user features, report display, report generation, logging, security and privacy, and additional features discussed below.

User Features

First and foremost, the package should be easy to use, install, and configure. It should feature a graphical user interface and offer online help and documentation. The system should display information consolidated into concise and easy-to-understand reports, and it also should be customizable, so that you can design and produce reports uniquely suited to your Web business environment.

Report Display

The manner in which the reports are viewed is an important discriminator when selecting a statistical package. Reports may be viewed online or within an e-mail message. Reports may also be displayed in a Web browser, as a spreadsheet, as a hard copy printout, or as text. Some packages enable reports to be displayed in real time for monitoring the site's activity. User queries of the report database should return reports for analysis formatted in 2-D or 3-D graphics or in text mode.

Report Generation

Actually generating or producing useful reports by means of the statistical package is another essential feature. The product should offer flexible data collection and query tools. It should provide a built-in scheduler for automatic reporting, as well as the ability to select report time ranges from minutes to years. The report package should offer the ability to filter in and out specific domains and pages. Report summaries should be produced as Web pages automatically. Report generation should have the capability of being distributed to any or all Web sites within the user's domain. The package or service should offer predefined (or default) as well as customizable templates for report generation. The package should enable export facilities and support HTML, Microsoft Word, and/or comma-delimited files. A user should be able to generate and save reports and graphs as standard HTML files, in plain text, or in formats for use in spreadsheet programs.

Logging

The report package should easily work with compressed or uncompressed log files, as well as multiple log file formats. The package should use common log file formats (Common Log File, Combined Log Format, EMWAC, and Microsoft Information Server) and be able to easily convert from one log file format to another. The speed to import log files into the program and to generate reports is a consideration that should be benchmarked within a vendor's test environment similar to that of the planned Web business service. Multiple servers should have the capability to log to the same machine. The package should offer a way to easily and efficiently archive the statistical logs.

Security and Privacy

The statistical package should offer a basic level of privacy for the users of the system and be password protected at the server administration level. The system should not require a user to sign on or to register prior to entering the Web site. The system should monitor for unauthorized access. The product should also have the capability of analyzing proxy server files and capturing users from behind firewalls or through proxy servers

Additional Features

The statistical package should store statistical data in a database. The package should also offer a database containing the names of companies and domains on the Internet cross-referenced to their IP addresses. This is quite useful, since Internet addresses are just a string of unintelligible IP numbers. This database will be used to provide reverse IP lookup to resolve IP addresses to domain names, which are more intelligible to the end users.

The reporting package should provide the location of the user, including domestic and international geographic areas.

The reporting package should collect statistics on other Internet services used, such as FTP, Usenet News, gopher, Telnet, listserv, etc.

BILLING

Billing for Web services rendered has not yet evolved to a high degree of sophistication within most organizations. Most enterprises are merely swallowing the start-up and recurring costs as overhead. As the service matures and more robust billing packages appear, organizations may move toward billing or charging back for their Web business services. They may decide to bill based on the actual number of internal users of the Web service, or by which specific services they use, or they may still roll up all the costs into an overhead pool and distribute them accordingly.

In creating a cost recovery or cost allocation model for the Web business service, the issue of whether to bill based on a flat rate service or on a usage-sensitive service must be taken into consideration.

Flat Rate Billing

In the flat rate billing model, all the costs predicted and associated with the Web business service are collected and divided by the number of users within the organization. This method is similar to a corporate per capita tax for Web usage. An organization may also opt to roll up all the costs and allocate them to the departments most benefiting from the Web service, such as sales and marketing, human resources, or public relations.

Either of these methods allocates costs based on the number of users or departments. The advantage of this method is that it is fairly easy to implement and maintain. The disadvantage is that, since no detailed level billing is accumulated, no capability of measuring or controlling direct costs exists.

Usage-sensitive Billing

The usage-sensitive billing method allocates costs based on what the user or department actually does while interacting with the service. This is the "user pays" or measured usage approach to cost recovery. The advantage is that costs are detailed and can be measured and controlled. Another advantage is that users can receive feedback on which services they are using most frequently and can regulate themselves in an effort to reduce usage and costs. The disadvantage is that accumulating and analyzing the statistics required to arrive at the usage-sensitive costs is itself costly to implement and maintain in terms of time and labor.

Usage-sensitive billing takes into account both the quality and the quantity of service rendered to the user. Users may be willing to pay extra for a higher level of throughput during peak traffic times or for more sophisticated services, such as credit card transactions, videoconferencing, or virtual reality.

Items to consider when building a cost recovery model for usage-sensitive billing include

- number of hits
- number of visits
- session time
- per packet or byte level of detail
- size of files downloaded
- number of forms or user queries submitted
- number of messages sent/received
- real-time applications such as desktop videoconferencing or video dialtone vs. non-real-time such as e-mail

Other Billing Issues

Several other issues revolve around billing and cost recovery for the Web business service, including

- How will the bills for the Web service actually be rendered?
- How will bills to external users for hosting, software distribution, etc., be rendered?
- Will online billing be available so that users can monitor their current charges?
- Will bills be consolidated or will users get one bill for Internet access and one for services actually used?

ACCOUNTING

Very few options today provide accounting software integrated with the Internet and the World Wide Web. These systems will enable orders placed, inventory changes, and electronic funds transactions to be automatically downloaded into the organization's accounting systems. The systems will also eventually offer accounting for fixed assets, time billing, inventory, order entry, point of sale, and job cost functions.

One of the earliest products to appear on the market with integrated Internet accounting is Pro Series 3.0 by SBT Accounting Systems, Inc. (http:// www.sbtcorp.com). This package supports Windows and DOS platforms and integrates Internet-sourced data with the accounting database. All the typical accounting functions are offered, including General Ledger, Accounts Payable and Receivable, Inventory Control, Purchase and Sales Orders, and Payroll. Pro Series offers WebSeries, a turn-key Web site creation and support solution. In addition, the product provides a graphical user interface, supporting clickable access to spreadsheets, automatic mail merge, and graphics.

Features of an Internet Accounting Package

As Internet accounting software evolves, look for products offering at least the following feature set.

- Multi-platform support—DOS, Windows, UNIX, and Mac
- Web browser support
- Full accounting functions—GL, AP, AR, etc.
- Integrate accounting functions with the Web site(s)
- Graphical user interface—ease of use
- Audit logging to master files
- Database query tools
- Customizable reports, templates, and forms
- Import/export from spreadsheet and other software applications
- System management
- Online help and clear, concise documentation

Selling to Management

Before the Web business service can become an efficient and highly-used business tool and completely change the way the organization provides and distributes information to its employees, customers, and suppliers, the system must be funded by management. This selling effort involves considerable time and energy and is definitely not for the faint of heart or the lethargic. The selling effort involves securing the backing of an executive champion, developing a prototype of the service, doing demonstrations to anyone who will listen, and keying the sales presentation to what management wants.

EXECUTIVE CHAMPION

This project will get funded faster, be more widely accepted, and be used more extensively if a well-placed and highly-respected executive champions the service from the start. The foundation that this person builds will pave the way for getting the funding for better-quality hardware and software as well as human resources with a higher level of expertise. Plus, the executive support will generate a higher level of excitement about the new service and what it will offer than trying to achieve the same results from a grassroots level.

Executive champions can be found virtually anywhere in the organization. Likely targets are the head of information systems, public relations, or marketing. Someone who has a studied propensity toward high-tech endeavors and has been recently successful in launching new programs or products within the organization would be a good executive champion for the launch of the new Web business service.

PROTOTYPING THE WEB BUSINESS SERVICE

"Let's see what you've got." You have to show management something! The quicker you can prototype the system and get it in front of management, the sooner the service will be approved and implemented—or at least the sooner you will know what else management needs to make the decision. The prototype need not be fully functional, but should be simple and straightforward. It can be the proposed home page with the organization's logo and a couple of recognizable images, a few subsequent pages with links to more information, and a customer feedback/e-mail form. Management will feed back their comments and suggestions, which will then be rolled into the next phase of the prototype to be used in the demonstrations.

DEMOS, DEMOS, DEMOS!

Demonstrations are the life blood of the new Web business service. Demonstrations should be quick, colorful, and lively, with time for questions. Always give the listeners a way to contact you for more information after the demonstration. The Web group should be showing off the prototype of the service to anyone who will listen—anywhere, anytime. Make the demonstrations very convenient. Plan them for the noon hour as Lunch and Learn or Brown Bag sessions. Cater to the executives in one-on-one sessions at their convenience. Visit the third shift support groups. Don't leave anyone or any department out. This is the way you will build your backlog of new pages and services as people think about what is possible, then come to you for help in designing something to meet their needs and business objectives. This is also where you will build support for the service.

WHAT MANAGEMENT WANTS

In funding a Web business service, management basically wants three things: a healthy return on investment (ROI), a solid competitive edge, and a hassle-free service, as shown in Figure 6.2. How do you calculate the Web business service's ROI? How will the service provide the organization with a competitive edge? And how can we assure management that the service will be easy to use, maintain, and administer?

Return on Investment

Typically, Web sites are installed within organizations without much regard or need for complex return on investment justifications. Just the

Figure 6.2 What Management Wants

simple fact that a main competitor has a Web site is often enough for management to launch their own. And after the system has been in production for a few months, just the daily hit count is enough to keep the service funded. Eventually, however, when management keeps getting the depreciation and amortization expense and the monthly bills to support the service and connect to the Internet, the piper will have to be paid. Management will demand that the system provide an acceptable return on investment. What is acceptable as an ROI and the payback period for the Web service varies from firm to firm.

Determining the Web service's ROI or tangible benefits requires three steps:

1. Identifying all the costs
2. Identifying the savings and revenue generated and costs avoided
3. Performing the ROI calculation

All costs associated with the Web service must be identified and quantified. The costs outlined in the first section of this chapter for hardware, software, registrations, and communications are typical and can be used as the cost model for the ROI calculation. An all-up cost model includes one-time implementation costs, as well as recurring costs.

Establishing a Web business service will lower the cost of doing business. All savings, cost avoidance, and revenue generated must be identified. Savings will be identified in areas such as the expense and local mileage reports being posted via electronic forms on the Web site; reduction in the printing and distribution of corporate telephone books, policies and procedure manuals, working documents, and news events; moving technical support to the Web from a voice-oriented help desk; etc. Also, placing advertising online reduces the costs of using traditional media such as print, radio/TV advertising, or direct mail.

Cost avoidance funds can be identified by looking for upgrades, new systems, new applications, etc., that were planned but now do not need to be funded. Revenue figures will be derived from estimates of orders placed from the Web site and income derived from hosting the home pages of trading partners and other associated organizations.

The data generated from the first two steps will then be rolled into the ROI calculation (use any standard calculation available on most spreadsheet or accounting software programs). The output will be then be placed before management as an integral part of an overall cost justification package that will include the cost and tangible benefits analysis, as well as a review of the intangible benefits that will accrue with the implementation of the new service. Intangible benefits would include creating a better image, building better customer relations and goodwill, building name/brand recognition, and building top-of-mind awareness or mindshare in new or existing markets.

Competitive Edge

What the competition is doing is one of management's most pressing issues. And in today's fast paced environment, just keeping up with the competition is not enough. An organization must excel, must be able to show and demonstrate added value to the customer, and must be open and accessible to the customer. Exploring the competitive edge angle with management involves several interrelated aspects:

- being completely informed about what the organization's direct competition is doing with Web services
- showing management their competitor's home pages
- showing the links on those pages to products, services, and additional information
- making suggestions on what types of things are possible with the organization's own Web services.

Hassle Free Service

Management does not want the phone to ring in the middle of the night about some problem or critical situation involving the Web business service. To alleviate the prospect of this happening, the Web service team must develop measures to enable the service to run smoothly and efficiently. Ensuring that the service is constantly monitored for security breaches, that the content is up-to-the-minute accurate, that customers have their problems and concerns addressed quickly and with a high level of expertise are the essential parts of the "service" part of the Web business service. These concerns and more will be addressed in detail in the next chapter.

Summary

Nailing down all the costs associated with the launching and subsequent support and maintenance of an active Web business service represents quite a challenge. In this chapter we have detailed a general cost model, as well as cost scenarios for small-, medium-, and large-sized organizations to use in gathering costs to feed information into a budget for the proposed service. We have developed a cost recovery model for the service to be used in allocating and charging back the costs of the service. We have cited those elements of a well-thought-out Web business service that will appeal to management so as to get the service funded. In the next chapter we will explore what it takes to efficiently run and manage a successful Web business service.

Running an Efficient Web Business Service

"Where are we going to put all this data? There must be 10 gigabytes of stuff here. Incredible!" thought Jason as he clicked through thumbnail views of colorful images and icons leading to 3-D animated sequences and video and audio clips planned for the new Bronto Brats Web site. "And how are we going to manage and support this new service?"

Running an efficient, highly-active, and content-rich Web business service is a day-in, day-out proposition, the subject of shimmering praise and hair-pulling anguish. As such, it is important to revisit the vision and goals that were initially developed in order to focus on what levels of service to provide. Goals such as 24-hour availability, current content, reliability, data integrity, and the ability to locate information quickly and easily should be uppermost in the minds of those establishing the service management foundation. After a clear focus has been re-established, the next step is to design a formal Service Plan to enable the Web business service to achieve management objectives and to be an efficient "just-in-time" information source for both internal employees and external users.

This chapter presents the development of a Service Plan detailing Web business service management and support. Topics like troubleshooting, performance measurement, content, network, storage, problem management, training, and customer service are also explored.

Web Business Service Plan

The Web business service plan is a commitment to both users and management as to what will be accomplished in the coming year, given operating constraints such as budget, time, human resources, etc. The plan supports the organization's objectives and seeks to strike a balance between the constraints and the vision.

The elements of a Web business service plan include

- Overview
- Vision, goals and objectives
- Service management and support
- Service level agreements
- Service organization
- Planned service enhancements
- Policies

The service plan should include a brief overview of the Web business service and what it intends to achieve. The plan should cite the service's vision, goals, and objectives, along with any identified needs and mission critical requirements.

The service plan specifies how the service will be managed and supported in the coming year, including the organizational structure of the service, accounting and chargebacks, training, help desk and customer support, and maintenance. Just as a reminder, the Web is a distributed environment and needs a distributed approach to service management. Not all management components will be capable of being centralized, nor should they be.

The plan details Service Level Agreements between organizational departments which commit to measurable goals in the areas of response time, reliability, availability, and accessibility. Sub-second response times, a reliability percentage of .9999 uptime, 24-hour-a-day availability and accessibility by 100% of all authorized users are typical. Statistics forming the basis for these metrics are discussed in the service management and support section below.

Providing a service plan is useful in managing user and departmental (marketing, human resources, public relations, etc.) expectations in the areas of planned enhancements and upgrades and items to be deferred to out years.

As a natural follow-on, procedures and policies for the processes to configure, maintain, and operate the Web business service must be developed. The service plan includes relevant policies such as appropriate use, security, privacy, retention, archiving, etc. Security and privacy will be discussed in the next chapter.

Web Service Management and Support

As shown in Figure 7.1 and discussed Chapter 2, Web service management and support extend throughout the entire architectural model, touching all components, such as the network infrastructure, server and client systems, the application content, and the financial system. Service management and support provide the organization with tools and utilities to facilitate the smooth operation of the entire Web business service.

Components of the Web service management system would include

- Server management
- Content management
- Client management
- Network management
- Problem and change management
- Project management

Web service support can be segmented into two categories:

- Customer service
- Training

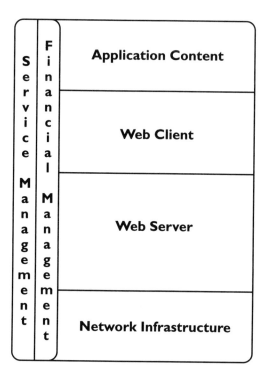

Figure 7.1   Web Service Management Permeates the Architectural Model

Web Server Management

The pulsing heart of the Web business service is the Web server. This computer system must run continuously at an acceptable performance level and be available to all authorized users requesting services. The Web server administrator functions at the core of the Web service. The role of the administrator is typically to configure, monitor, and troubleshoot the system; conduct performance analyses; backup the data; perform routine diagnostics and maintenance; install new hardware and software; and perform upgrades to the server. Luckily, new Web server and site management tools designed to ease the administrator's burden are just appearing on the market.

WEB SERVER CONFIGURATION

The Web server initially will be configured based on predictions of the number of hits, the interaction of the users, and the size of the files requested. The hardware platform, the amount of memory and hard disk space, and processor speed are the hardware configuration elements to consider. The software configuration is composed of the Web server and other application software, the TCP/IP stack, and the operating system. Both hardware and software configurations need to be updated periodically due to changes in load and content. A proactive approach of conducting performance measurement and benchmarking analyses will determine the best configuration for existing loads and for any planned enhancements. Ways to tune the system are discussed later.

The server administrator should also have procedures for managing changes in the server configuration, such as upgrading software to newer versions, installing new hardware, and reconfiguring communications services. This becomes increasingly more imperative as the Web business service grows and more hardware and software are added, along with new special function servers.

A list of vendors offering configuration management products and tools can be found at http://www.iac.honeywell.com/Pub/Tech/CM/CMTools.html.

SERVER AND SITE MANAGEMENT TOOLS

Several new and updated software tools are available for managing Web servers and sites, as shown in Table 7.1. Tools that provide a means to view all the pages, images, links, and documents within a Web site are beneficial. The package selected should accommodate growth in the amount of content, traffic, and complexity of the Web server and in the number of Web servers within the enterprise. The management tool should permit the Web administrator to look simultaneously at every one of the Web servers in the organization, creating a virtual network map on one screen. The product should have enhanced capabilities regarding the site's hyperlinks, since they are both the essence of the Web and the most dynamic element. Specifically, the product should verify that the links are still active, proactively prevent broken links, update them automatically, and log the activities and errors.

Additional features to look for in Web server and site management software tools include

- graphical user interface
- hierarchical view of Web server's contents by categories

Table 7.1		Web Server and Site Management Tools		
Product	**Vendor**	**Platforms Supported**	**Source**	**Cost**
Cyberleaf	Interleaf	UNIX	http:// www.ileaf.com/ip.html	Commercial
LiveWire	Netscape	Win 95, Win NT, UNIX	http://home.netscape.com/	Commercial $199
PureDDTS WebTracker	Pure Software	Win, Mac, UNIX	http://www.pure.com	Commercial
SiteMill	Adobe	Mac	http://www.adobe.com	Commercial $795
WebView (in WebSite)	OíReilly and Associates	Win NT, Win 95	http://website.ora.com	Commercial $495
WebWATCHER	Caravelle Networks Corp.	Win 3.X, Win 95	http://www.caravelle.com 800.363.5292	Commercial $295

- view several Web sites at once
- remote task automation and management
- directory synchronization
- access control
- scripting facility to automate routine maintenance
- error and orphaned link logging
- automatic link mapping
- automatic link verification and restoration
- search and index tools
- security
- monitoring and notification

TROUBLESHOOTING

Troubleshooting—the detection and isolation of faults, errors, and problems—is quite involved in the case of Web services. This is due to the fact that each Web site will typically have a variety of hardware platforms for the server, the firewall, and the client, as well as a variety of different software applications and processes, all running over high-bandwidth communications facilities. Each of these components have different problems and troubleshooting mechanisms to aid the system administrator.

Server and Firewall Software and Hardware

In the case of server and firewall/proxy hardware and software, the two most problematic components are the server's response and configuration. The server's response may be slow or erratic, responding to some requests and not others. The server may be configured improperly so that access to the configuration files by the applications is inhibited. The server may be using too much disk space, memory, or processor time to fulfill requests. Again, a proactive approach in conducting performance measurement and benchmarking will serve to alleviate or mitigate these common problems.

Client Software

The users of the Web client software will typically have problems in the following areas:

- Downloading files—Users will find that the file they wish to download is not found on the accessed server or that the file cannot be opened or converted at their desktop.
- Viewers—Users will find that the file they are downloading requires a viewer not available on the accessed server or not available on their own desktop. Users will also have difficulty in successfully using viewers.
- Connections—Connectivity problems will include the LAN being down, the server being down or busy, an outage along the network path, etc.
- Permissions—Users may be arbitrarily denied permission to access a particular server, files on that server, or specific functions, like e-mail.
- URLs—Users will constantly run into dead-end links or inactive links.
- Scripts—Users may input data into forms and receive inconsistent responses, may not be able to access the scripts published on the home page, or may not be able to locate the scripts referenced.

A list of the most common errors relating to Web client software and suggested remedies for these problems are at the end of this section.

Communications Facilities

The entire communications path that handles any and all requests made by users of internal or external Web services may fall prey to faults and failures.

The communications facilities pertinent to the Web business service are

- Network—the TCP/IP communications facilities, the Ethernet LAN, or other local area networks
- Gateways—access to different networks, protocols, and applications
- Routers—inaccuracies in routing tables
- Communications links
    - Local—the organization's internal communications links to the ISP
    - Internet Service Provider—the ISP's links to the Internet or access points

Common Client Error Messages

Several error messages will be seen by the users from time to time in the course of interacting with both the internal home page and external Web sites. These error messages generally fall into five categories: errors having to do with downloading files and using viewers, errors associated with URLs, errors regarding the user's access rights and permissions, errors in the connection between the user and the server, and errors relating to a Web server or client. Then, there are always the general errors, such as number 400 "Bad Request" or 404 "Not Found." The format of the error message is typically:

Error Number	Error	Error Description
404	Not Found	The requested URL was not found on this server.

Files and Viewers
- File not found
- Bad file request
- Unknown file type
- File contains no data

- No viewer configured
- Viewer not found
- Unable to launch viewer

URLs
- URL not found
- Host unknown
- Cannot add form submission result to bookmark list

Permissions
- Permission denied
- Proxy server denied access
- Unauthorized
- Forbidden
- You can't log on as an anonymous user

Connections
- Service unavailable
- Host unavailable
- Socket is not connected
- Server does not have a DNS entry
- Connection timed out
- Network connection refused by server
- Too many connections—try again later
- Too many users
- Connection refused by host
- Broken path
- LAN is down
- Can't route to destination address
- Unable to locate host
- Failed DNS lookup

Server
- Server not responding

- Server is busy
- Unable to locate the server
- Internal error

Client

- Bad version (of the browser)

Remedies for Errors

The most common remedy for an error of any type is to repeat the action. Sometimes the user has inadvertently typed in the incorrect URL address, which will prompt a "URL not found" or "unknown host" error. If a typing error is not the case, the user should be instructed to use the Web site's short URL instead of entering in slashes and the text between them. For example, the URL of *http://www.xyz.com/pub/index01/story0696/* would be shortened to *http://www.xyz.com* to see if the site itself is responding.

Errors having to do with permissions generally cannot be overcome since the user is being denied access. The only remedy here is to directly contact the WebMaster of the particular home page for access, using either e-mail, fax, or the telephone if this information is known.

In some cases, the network is busy and just reloading the URL or performing the function again will clear the error. If this doesn't remedy the situation, the user can try a few other things, such as disconnecting and reconnecting or pinging the site in the case of a connection or server error.

Pings use the Internet Control Message Protocol and are like probes. Pings send a message to the site to verify that the site is valid, up and running, and available for requests. To ping a site, key in "ping" followed by the domain name or IP numerical address—for example, *ping www.xyz.com.* If the site is alive, the return message from the site will so indicate. Otherwise, the site will be either unknown or down.

If all attempts the user makes to remedy the error fail, the user should place a call to the Help Desk, technical support, or customer support center and report the problem.

WEB SERVER PERFORMANCE MODELING

As we have discussed previously in this chapter, using performance modeling provides for more proactive management of an efficient and smoothly-running Web business service. Establishing the performance models by covering such predicted scenarios, such as an increase in the number of users, an increase in the amount of content requested by the users, a new interactive database query facility, a new server release, etc., will enable the Web service to experience orderly and trouble-free growth.

For an excellent white paper on Web server performance modeling and benchmarking, see http://www.microsoft.com/infoserv/docs/Iisperf.htm.

The benefits of performance modeling are many. Server performance analysis enables the evaluation and testing of

- Different proposed configuration scenarios
- Upgraded hardware
- New software releases, bug fixes and patches
- Increased traffic loads and file transfer requests
- Solutions to known problems

In addition, performance analysis permits the determination and isolation of bottlenecks, is useful when the Web Service must be expanded by adding new Web servers within the enterprise, and is an aid in Web server tuning.

As shown in Figure 7.2, the Web server performance measurement process consists of three steps:

1. Creating the performance model
2. Generating the workload
3. Analyzing the results

Creating the Performance Model

The first step in measuring Web server performance is the design of a particular scenario to be evaluated, such as a 50% increase in traffic or the effect of a new interactive catalog capability for the users. The model

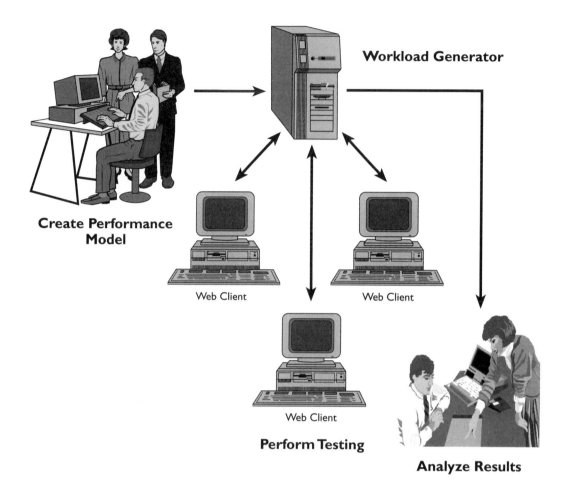

Figure 7.2 Web Server Performance Measurement

scenario would be constructed using a predicted workload for the server. The workload may be a very simple script such as:

```
read a URL
look up the URL address
connect to URL's web server
issue a request (GET)
read the data
log the activity
```

The workload may also be tailored for more active and complex Web server environments. The workloads may include CGI scripts, several servers, or clusters of files to simulate images embedded in the Web pages.

The workload is a configuration file that contains the number of pages to be accessed, the number and size of the files to be accessed, and the percentage of times each page will be hit (for example, the home page will be hit more often than subsequent pages). This file is then used during the performance testing and the results are generally displayed on a page-by-page basis and in a composite form.

There is a difference between performance and workload. Performance is how well the server is handling the requests made of it; the workload is the actual activity the server is performing. For example, a server's performance is measured in how much data is transferred to the client in megabits per second (throughput), how many connections the server handles per second (connections/second), the time the server takes to fulfill a request (response time), and the number of errors the server produces (errors). The workload would be the scripts, files, or requests the server is expected to handle during the test.

It is extremely important to standardize on the configuration of the server and client hardware and software and on the workload for the performance measurement. This is invaluable in controlling the testing, in getting uniform results, and in gathering trending information across the enterprise. The performance model should closely model the existing Web server environment in content, security, transactions, scripts, Java applets, imagemaps, database queries, e-mail messages, etc., so that any change brought about during the testing will be noticed and tracked.

Components of the performance model to standardize include

- length of the test
- how many times the test will be repeated
- arrival rate of files, so server can process requests simultaneously
- size of files
- number of files
- type of files—images, audio, video, text, etc.

- number of pages accessed
- scripts used
- number of clients
- number of processes per client

The performance model should be designed to provide metrics on the following:

- number of clients
- average connect time
- maximum connect time
- requests per second
- bytes per second (throughput)
- average response time
- maximum response time
- number of pages retrieved
- number of files retrieved
- errors

Table 7.2 shows suggested performance models for small, medium, and large organizations. The models in this table can be used to build performance measurement tests for the different enterprises, based on the amount of traffic predicted, the amount of content, and the complexity of the site. Again, the configuration on which the performance model is based should closely mimic the existing Web service at the outset so that any deviations will be quickly seen.

Generating the Workload

Once the model and the sample workload are created, the next step is to run the model on a workload generator. In this case, the workload generator would be either one or more personal computers dedicated to testing, development, and evaluations, or it would be the production Web server (not recommended). The workload generator actually runs the model scenario and manages the flow of traffic through the system. The test patterns should be varied to tune the Web server. The data formed from running the model scenario is then output to a report generator for analysis.

Table 7.2   Sample Performance Model Variables for Web Sites

Model Variable	Small, Low Activity Site	Medium Activity Site	Large, Complex, High Activity Site
Clients	2	16	24
Processes per client	2	4	4
Number of files	3	8	15
Total size of files	30KB	1.7MB	10MB
Number of pages	1	3	6
Number of scripts	0	3	5
Number of networks	1	2	4
Number of database queries	0	6	10
Number of e-mail messages	0	8	12

Analyzing the Results

The results of the performance measurement testing will be analyzed to determine which scenario and configuration provides the best levels of performance for the particular Web server(s). Results may be analyzed using historical log files to illustrate trends such as traffic flow, throughput, response times, and bandwidth utilization. Results may also point out the most efficient and reliable routing paths for the Web server, as well as the effects of hardware, software, and communication line-speed upgrades. Performance measurement can also be used to analyze log files on active servers, including real-time dynamic monitoring and the monitoring of the operational servers.

Performance Measurement Tools

WebStone is the de facto standard for measuring Web server performance. This software tool was created by SGI and is rather vendor, platform, and operating system (UNIX) specific. The product measures connect and response times, throughput, and the number of pages and files retrieved per minute by the server.

Webperf is a relatively new performance measurement tool from SPEC (Standard Performance Evaluation Corporation). SPEC is an independent, non-profit, benchmarking organization. Webperf, therefore, is platform independent and measures the response time on any HTTP Web server. The product measures the server's ability to process requests, server throughput, and average response times. Webperf is available for system vendors and software developers.

NetBench and ServerBench are two performance measurement tools developed by the Ziff-Davis Benchmark Operation. NetBench measures file servers for input/output throughput and ServerBench measures application servers for how well they handle client requests.

All of the performance measurement tools shown in Table 7.3 are free today, but we expect more sophisticated and feature-rich commercial products to become available in the near future.

SYSTEM BACKUP AND RESTORATION

System backups need to be conducted for the Web service on a routine and well-defined basis. Backups can be performed in-house using tape archival mechanisms or by a commercial service, such as WebStor by McAfee, Inc., or DataSafe by Connected Corporation may be used. Several options exist for the type of backup performed and the timing of the system backups:

- Full—Backups are taken of everything associated with the service. This is a total system restoration, usually conducted in the event of hardware or software failures or flood, fire, power outages, etc.

Table 7.3 Web Server Performance Measurement Tools

Product	Vendor	Platforms Supported	Source	Cost
NetBench, ServerBench	Ziff-Davis Benchmark Operation	Win NT, Mac (NetBench), OS/2, UNIX	http:// www.zdnet.com/zdbop/	Free
Webperf	Standard Performance Evaluation Corporation	Win NT, UNIX	http://www.specbench.org	Free
Webstone	Silicon Graphics	UNIX	http://www.sgi.com	Free

- Partial—Backups are taken of just part of the service, such as the content
- Differential—Backups are taken of any changes made to the service
- Continuous—Backups are made as soon as a transaction has been completed
- Daily—Backups are taken once every 24-hour period, usually late at night
- Weekly—Backups are taken once every 7 days
- Monthly—Backups are taken once every 30 days

The amount of time that it takes for an administrator to perform a system restoration is a consideration, because downtime incurred is costly to a highly-active, commercial Web site. Care should be given in selecting backup and restoration methods that balance the cost of the equipment required (tape backup and tape drives) with the time to complete the task.

Administrators are generally required to perform the system backups and restorations. However, the newer systems will permit users to restore their own files. Companies backup their Web sites to a remote location for security, for archival purposes, and to give them more local storage space. Backups are now frequently analyzed in lawsuits, as well.

Disaster Recovery

In order to provide for the recovery of the Web Business Service in the event of a disaster, management must develop a Disaster Plan. This plan will include the definition of a disaster, when a disaster is declared, by whom, and under what conditions. The plan also includes a detailed inventory of all hardware and software and communications facilities that are used in the service—down to serial numbers and release versions. The plan will provide a means for storing system tapes off-site as part of routine backup procedures. The plan will include details regarding the restoration of the system, such as hardware, software, system files, data, authorizations, passwords, content, and links. The plan may also include instructions on conducting a simulated disaster in order to test the planned recovery mechanisms.

WEB SERVER MONITORING

The Web servers within an enterprise can, of course, be monitored using traditional tools such as HP's OpenView. Just coming to market, however, are system-monitoring products developed specifically for Web servers. One such product is WebWatcher from Caravelle Networks Corporation (http://www.caravelle.com). WebWatcher is a Windows-based product that dynamically monitors Web and Internet applications, providing alerts by means of an electronic mail message, beeper, or console screen. WebWatcher monitors such Internet applications as WWW, FTP, SMTP, Newsgroups, WAIS, gopher, and Archie, as well as routers and gateways.

Content Management

Comprehensive and efficient content management for the Web business service encompasses several different areas of concern. Content management needs to address, at a minimum, the following questions:

- Who places content on the Web server(s)?
- Who are the content owners and consumers?
- How will we structure the content?
- What access privileges are given to various users?
- How will we keep the service current?
- How will content storage be managed?
- How can we standardize the service?

PLACING CONTENT ON THE WEB SERVER

The first step in managing what can grow to become multi-gigabytes of Web content is to decide who places content on the Web server(s). Most companies take one of three approaches, as illustrated in Figure 7.3:

1. **Anyone** can place content on the Web server—This approach is convenient, fast, and easy, but it can lead very quickly to a chaotic environment that slows down everyone's access to critical information.

2. **WebMaster only** places all content on the Web server—The advantage here is that all content will be uniform and consistent,

Web Server

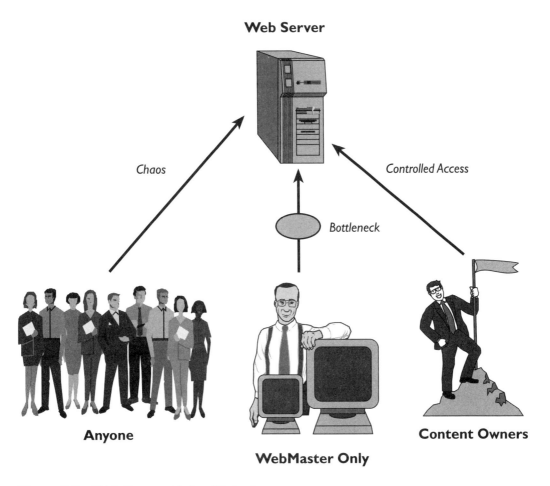

Figure 7.3   Web Content Update Methods

and the service will provide better response times. This approach is constrained by time, as the WebMaster becomes the bottleneck in the process.

3. **Content owners** as delegates of the WebMaster place content on the Web server—This approach provides more-controlled access, consistency, and uniformity. Also, it is faster than option 2. Individual users or departments are stakeholders and can own and manage directories and individual files. This approach will need to be managed to avoid chaos in the content access and structure.

DETERMINING CONTENT OWNERS AND CONSUMERS

The next step in managing the Web business service content is to define the content owners and consumers, as well as their hypertext links. A content owner is the source of the data for a specific amount of Web content. The content owner may be a person, group of people, or a department (such as the Human Resources Manager, the technical services group, or the Marketing Communications Department, respectively, for example) that creates, modifies, and updates the content. The content owner is ultimately responsible for what is displayed on the Web page. The owners must be identified and an entry made on each Web page as to who owns the content, when it was last changed, and how they may be contacted regarding it (a hypertext e-mail link). For example, an entry at the bottom of a Web page might read, "Last updated on 08/21/96 by JCC. E-mail your comments to JCC@Fremont.com".

Several questions must be answered in dealing with content ownership. Where is the source of the data? Who feeds the content of the Web service? Where is the source data located? What is the format of the data? What are the data dependencies for the source data? Is this content static or dynamic?

Next, it is imperative to rank the content/source data as to critical, essential, or normal importance to the organization's business goals or key users. This will give the Web service management a priority listing to use when dealing with system failures, posting content updates, etc. Content may be manually or automatically updated, depending on the source of the data (people or applications).

A consumer is anyone who accesses, downloads, or in any way interacts with the Web content. Internal users, other applications, external suppliers, vendors, and customers would all be content consumers.

Keeping a directory or listing of all hypertext links between content owners and consumers will enable more rapid isolation of link problems, provide more consistency in the naming of links, and provide faster link updating. Several of the Web site management tools provide the capability of hypertext link display, update, and management.

Structuring the Web Service Content

The content of the Web business service needs to be structured in order to provide faster access, search, and response times for content consumers. Imposing a structure on the Web content also will alleviate the chaos that sometimes erupts when too many owners are making changes to too many files. Helpful hints in establishing a logical document structure include creating a

- directory index file
- hierarchy of documents
- naming standard for home and subsequent pages, files, and directories
- structure of links correlated to the structure of the directories

Granting Access Privileges

Access control is used in conjunction with system file permissions to grant access privileges to users to perform various functions (see/view, copy, create, delete, execute, write, and modify) on the files and directories on the Web server. Privileges are usually granted or denied to all users (the world), the owner, or to a defined group of users. Typical access privileges in the Web service would parallel the following:

- **Read Access**—Anyone can view, see, or read the file (the file owner, a group, or any user).
- **Write Access**—The owner or group can create, delete, or modify the file.
- **Execute**—The owner or group can run the file (script files) or execute the program.

While not specifically required for small sites, formal Access Control Lists (ACLs) are beneficial to more carefully define permissions. ACLs are essential, however, in a large and complex Web service environment.

Keeping the Service Current

It is imperative that the content of the Web business service be kept as current and accurate as possible. Content consumers require the most recent information to order products and services, to perform research, and to generally be more productive in their endeavors. Nothing turns a user off more than to see a site updated last month or years ago, see the same thing they saw the last few times they accessed the site, or see inaccuracies in the content. Content owners and Web site administrators also need to keep up with new technology and services that will enhance the site and encourage users to return again and again. Keeping the service current involves, at a minimum, the following activities:

- validating the links
- validating the CGI scripts
- validating the HTML code
- updating the content
- developing new content
- evaluating new technology and services
- promoting the site
- monitoring changes made to the server(s)

Validating the Hyperlinks

Hyperlinks change frequently, and rather than frustrating the users with broken or stale links, the Web service should perform a routine analysis of all hypertext links. Links both on the organization's Web servers and downstream servers should be verified. Fortunately, there are tools available to help automate what would be an arduous and time-consuming manual task. There are various Internet-available robots, spiders, worms, wanderers, and crawlers that perform this activity, as well as commercial Web site management tools.

Products and Services

- lvrfy
  - http://www.cs.dartmouth.edu/~crow/lvrfy.html
- missinglink
  - http://www.rsol.com/ml/
- MOMspider
  - http://www.ics.uci.edu/Websoft/MOMspider/

Validating the CGI Scripts

The CGI scripts used to develop forms for user input must also be routinely verified. The scripts may not permit the proper access or may return erratic data, or the user may be unable to locate the script.

Areas to verify on CGI forms and scripts include

- hidden data
- hidden lines
- image input
- buttons not supported
- text area value
- multiple text area
- content length
- no selection

Products and Services:
- Windows CGI Testing
  - — http://128.120.58.122/cgi-win/cgitest.exe
- Digital HTML Form Testing
  - — http://www.research.digital.com/nsl/formtest/

Validating the HTML Code

Validating the HTML code involves checking each and every Web page document for errors and non-compliance to the HTML standard. The reason to validate the HTML code is to ensure portability and reusable content across the enterprise. Also, code conforming to the HTML standard will not need to be reworked as new browsers come online.

Typical validation involves the following areas:

- table, form, and document structure
- heading levels
- anchor tags
- cross-references
- mapping
- syntax
- spelling
- image analysis
- options and option values
- elements

Products and Services:

- Anchor Checker
  - http://www.ugrad.cs.ubc.ca/spider/q7f192/branch/checker.html
- Doctor HTML
  - http://imagiware.com/RxHTML/
- HTMLchek
  - http://wsk.eit.com/wsk/dist/doc/admin/webtest/verify_links.html
- HTML_Analyzer
  - ftp://ftp.ncsa.uiuc.edu
- Webtest
  - http://uts.cc.utexas.edu:80/~churchh/htmlchek.html

Updating the Content

The Web service plan should provide procedures and practices for the routine and as-required content updating. Content must be fresh, accurate, and easily understood for users to fully and completely "consume" the organization's information. Each page should carry a "Last Revised" entry at the bottom. Each page should also have the e-mail address of the content owner. The Web administration can then develop an automated means to send an e-mail message to the content owner at appropriate intervals, requesting that the page be reviewed for content update. Update intervals can be negotiated by the WebMaster with the content owner at the time the page is loaded onto the server.

Developing New Content

The Web business service must constantly search for opportunities to develop new content. This often will happen naturally as word of the potential of the Web service spreads within the enterprise. The main concern of most Web services is that requests for new content and interactive capabilities will come much faster than time, budget, and human resources can satisfy them. This situation begs for a good project management system in which the requests are prioritized based on their capability to contribute to the overall success of the organization and on their contribution to the enterprise's critical business needs.

Content also should not be developed in a vacuum. Enlisting content owner input and feedback early in the planning stages is crucial to producing a quality product in less time and at less cost.

Evaluating New Technology and Services

Most Web professionals are a forward thinking lot, spending time researching new ways to add value to the Web business service. The Web service team must constantly seek and evaluate new technologies, such as virtual reality, Java applets, and legacy system integration, in order to keep the service positioned strategically within the organization. The team should look for and evaluate new services that may enhance the product offerings, management, and notoriety of the Web service. The team should spend a fair amount of time "surfing" the Net, looking for "hot sites," "what's cool," and "what's new" on Web pages of general interest, plus those competitive with the organization. The team should also attend Web- and Internet-oriented conferences, seminars, and training to keep current on the direction of the industry.

Promoting the Web Site

The Web team must constantly place the Web site in every nook and cranny of the Internet to gain customer visibility and top-of-mind awareness. The Web site should be on at least 100 of the top directories and search engines, such as InfoSeek, Lycos, Excite, etc., and should also promote itself on sites in the enterprise's industry or vertical market. The Web team can undertake this promotion in-house or use a third-party service to actively promote the site. To locate a Web promotion service, look under keywords "Web Site Promotion," "Internet Marketing," "Web Advertising," "Interactive Marketing," or "Web Presence Providers." Also, consult A1's Directory of Free Promotion Sites at http://www.a1co.com/index.html.

The Web site may also be promoted through traditional means, such as including the URL of the Web home page on company brochures and catalogs; on invoice fliers; in radio, newspaper, magazine, and television advertising; and on employee business cards.

Monitoring Changes on the Server

The Web service administrator must keep a watchful eye on changes on the server. This task can be automated, with any changes sent as e-mail messages to the server administrator. If administrators keep up with changes made by approved content owners, problems can be detected, isolated, and resolved more quickly. Changes on one server have a tendency to ripple throughout the organization's Web servers; so having a good change control practice in place will enable updates to be made more effectively.

Informing users of changes in your site is beneficial, as this encourages them to return to your site. Changes may be placed on the "What's New" icon on the organization's home page. Another way is to have an entry at the bottom of the page that will automatically inform an interested user of any changes. For example, "If you would like to keep up-to-date on progress at XYZ Company, then **register for our update notification**, which will advise you directly of updates and revisions by e-mail."

MANAGING WEB CONTENT STORAGE

Managing the storage of Web content is just beginning to be of concern to the larger, more content-rich and active Web business services. Content storage management seeks to strike a balance between the cost of storage and the time it takes a user to access the information. Users demand quick response times for critical and current information. At the same time, management is concerned with constantly providing more and more expensive local storage options. Content storage management uses a hierarchical scheme based on keeping the most frequently-used, dynamic, and critical content on local server disks. Content that is static or infrequently-used is stored on different storage media, such as CD-ROMs. Content storage management has several benefits:

- reduces backup time
- improves network performance
- reduces the cost of data ownership
- reduces the cost of distributed hard drive storage space among the Web servers

The first step in creating a Web content storage management system is to survey the Web server files and obtain their access history. Determining how often files are accessed or changed will determine where they will be stored. Some storage management systems will use the last accessed date to automatically migrate infrequently-used files to other storage media. Typically, the larger multimedia files will be migrated, including images, audio, video, animation, movies, etc. Similar types of files or frequently-used files may be located on the same storage device.

HSM, or Hierarchical Storage Management systems, have been around for quite some time and are now beginning to use Web-based graphical user interfaces and tools to perform the migration and management activities. HSM uses both network and user data management to handle the massive volumes of files generated by an organization.

HSM uses various devices connected to the network to migrate and store data. Devices include mainframe and mini-computers, jukeboxes to hold CD-ROMs, tape storage devices, hard disks on network servers, and the user's local storage drives. Jukeboxes should offer the capability to rewrite CD-ROMs. Data may also be stored off-site in climate-controlled vaults. The type of device or location for the data is dependent on how often the file is accessed. A typical migration path for a file would be

user hard drive → server hard drive → tape → jukebox → mainframe → off-site storage

Primary storage locates frequently-used data on devices closest to the user of that data and includes computer RAM storage, the user's local drive, and the server hard drive. Secondary or nearline storage would include optical jukeboxes or tape libraries. Tape—especially digital linear tape (DLT)—is becoming the primary storage medium due to the increase in the speed in which data on those tapes may be accessed by the user. Off-line storage is locating data on devices that are not network connected. Off-site storage is locating data in places that are distant from the organization and are also not network connected. Remote storage is transferring data by means of a public or private network connection to a storage location. This option is becoming extremely viable for backup services as more storage services are now coming onto the market.

To integrate HSM systems into Web content management, the data would be backed up to the mainframe or other host computer using a Web browser front end. The system creates a URL for the host, which directs any requests from the user to that location. The system will place an indicator or icon on the user's hard drive as to when the file was migrated and where it is now located.

The reliability of the various storage devices has traditionally been measured as the mean time between failures (MTBF). However, with Web storage, how long the device is merely on and running is not as accurate an indicator of the reliability as the average time it takes to exchange one CD-ROM or tape for another. Mean cycles between failure or MCBF is the average time between swaps and is a more accurate gauge of the actual usage of the storage device.

Features of a Web Content Storage Management System

Typical user interface, system management, and file-handling capability features to look for in a good Web content storage management system include

User Interface
- use of Web browsers as front ends
- notify a user that a file has been migrated
- notify a user when the file has been retrieved

System Management
- ease of set up and configuration
- use of browser to monitor system components
- preventive maintenance schedule
- self-diagnosing and self-correcting actions for worn components
- adequate provision for growth—headroom
- interoperability across multiple devices
- security—passwords, encryption, etc.
- mirroring of disks, fault tolerance features
- redundancy

Handling Content Files

- automatically migrate files overnight
- migrate content from several different servers
- customizable data migration
- keep track of off-line storage of files on CD-ROMs, tapes, etc.
- control where and when the file is archived—administrator or user
- speed of initial and subsequent migrations
- transparent file access by users

Web Content Storage Management Systems and Tools

A variety of tools and management systems are available for the migration, storage, and retrieval of Web content, as shown in Table 7.4. These systems were either developed specifically for Web storage or they are existing systems upgraded to include Web tools and interfaces.

STANDARDIZING THE WEB SERVICE

There are several opportunities to begin to standardize the various components of the Web service. The benefits of standardization include reduction of support costs, reduction of product procurement costs, quicker and easier access and retrieval of information, interoperability among the components, and portability of applications across various hardware platforms and networks. The downside, of course, is that the organization may become effectively locked into a particular vendor, thereby limiting support options and raising the procurement price.

Web service components and content on which to standardize include:

- full pathname for all URLs
- document styles
- presentation of information
- representation in internal and external meta indexes or search engines
- server hardware and software
- browsers and other client tools

Table 7.4 Web Content Storage Management Systems and Tools

Product	Vendor	Platforms Supported	Source	Cost
Adstar Distributed Storage Manager	IBM	Win NT, OS/2	http://www.storage.ibm.com	Commercial
DataSafe	Connected Corp.	Win 3.1, Win 95, Mac	http://www.connected.com	Commercial Service
ArcServe	Cheyenne Software, Inc.	Win 95, Win NT, Mac, OS/2, UNIX	http://www.chey.com	Commercial $1,995
Cheyenne HSM	Cheyenne Software, Inc.	Win 95, Win NT, Mac, OS/2, UNIX	http://www.chey.com	Commercial
NearNet	StorageTek	UNIX, NetWare	http://www.stortek.com	Commercial
Networker	Legato Systems	DOS, Win, Win NT, OS/2, Mac, UNIX	http://www.legato.com	Commercial
NetSpace	Avail Systems	DOS	http://avail_web.avail.com 303.444.4018	Commercial $3,995
Open Storage Manager	Cray Research	UNIX	http://www.cray.com	Commercial
OpenV*NetBackup	OpenVision Technology, Inc.	UNIX	510.425.6417	Commercial
Storage Manager	Palindrome	NetWare, DOS, OS/2, UNIX, Mac, Win NT, Win 95	http://www.palindrome.com	Commercial $995–3,500
WebStor	McAfee, Inc.	Win 95	http://www.mcafee.com	Commercial Service
Web Storage Manager	Andataco	Win 95, UNIX	http://www.andataco.com	Commercial
Solstice Backup and HSM	SunSoft	UNIX	http://www.sun.com/solstice/	Commercial

Web Client Management

Running an efficient Web business service is not a matter of simply installing the latest version of a browser on every user's workstation and then sitting back complacently while the system chugs merrily along, a fully-functioning and independent life form. Web service administrators must manage the system, hardware, and software upgrades at both the server and the client levels. In most larger, more complex environments, administrators experience incompatible HTML versions and browsers among various Web servers within the same organization. Staying on top of what the users have on their desktops and enabling the timely and smooth update of their software are two key elements in Web client management.

DETERMINING CLIENT DESKTOP CONFIGURATIONS

Any Web business service would do well to know exactly how each desktop is configured. The information collected would include the hardware platform, disk storage, memory, operating system and version, and software applications and utilities and their versions for each desktop within the organization. Also very relevant to know is the client's means of network connectivity (remote, mobile, WAN, LAN, etc.) and line speed, the IP address and which IP addresses are active, and which users need software upgrades. This information will enable the Web business management to plan ahead for system upgrades and enhancements, and it will also be useful for disaster recovery purposes.

Several products on the market today have the capabilities just described. Norton Utilities and NetManage have the largest market share.

PERFORMING CLIENT UPDATES

Performing client updates must strike a careful balance between the needs of the users to stay current with the technology and the needs of management to reduce costs for labor, hardware, and software acquisition and maintenance. The distribution of software may take several methods, some fully electronic and automatic, some manual, and some using a hybrid approach. The various approaches used to perform Web client updates are discussed next and are illustrated in Figure 7.4.

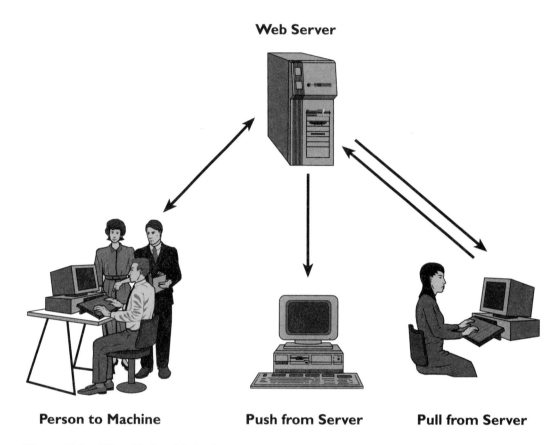

Web Server

Person to Machine   **Push from Server**   **Pull from Server**

Figure 7.4   Client Update Methods

Method 1: Person to Machine

This method of client update is the purely manual approach, requiring a personal visit to each desktop by a member of the Web service support staff. This method is labor intensive and should only be used in very small organizations with limited desktops or for the personal, attentive, one-on-one service provided as a routine at the executive level. The support person interacts with the Web service and manually downloads the newest client software version to the desktop, testing and verifying a successful upgrade.

Method 2: Push from Server

The push from server method is entirely automated. This approach requires agent software on the client machine to interact with the server to perform the upgrade. The user may be informed automatically that the upgrade will take place or, in some cases, will be informed subsequently to the upgrade. This method is costly on the front end to configure every desktop in the organization with the required hardware and software, but over time the labor costs will be significantly reduced.

Method 3: Pull from Server

In the pull-from-server method, the user initiates the update. The user would be notified electronically by means of a system or electronic mail message that the new version is available, as well as being provided with online installation instructions. This approach is a hybrid, using the manual efforts of the user along with the automatic update notifications. In some cases, this method may require upfront user training to acclimate them to performing this function on their own.

Client Upgrade Products

Many vendors have developed products for the electronic distribution of software. Most either offer or plan to offer Web-based interfaces for their products. Products for client upgrades include NetManage's NEWT-watch ($495 for Windows and UNIX—http://www.netmanage.com), Remotely Possible/Sockets from Avalan Technology, HP's netdist, Sun's swntool (Solaris), and products from Accugraph Corporation and Quadritek Systems.

Megasoft Online's Web Transporter (Win 95, Win NT, and Win 3.1, $20,000) is a fairly new Netscape plug-in module. Web Transporter enables users to perform their own software upgrades, notifying the Web server that the download has taken place. The product provides the Web service with information on the user's system configuration and also offers such features as access control and encryption using SSL.

Web Network Management

The purpose of network management is to gain information about how the Web servers and clients function on the network; to determine, isolate, and resolve problems; and to allocate network resources better, based on both dynamic and trending data. A Web network management system is used to display and configure network device settings, track packets, monitor traffic, and track application activity. This activity concerns application data flow, conversations across network, and application response times.

Currently, data communications networks are managed using a variety of tools for hardware components, applications, network operating systems, etc. What is relevant to the management of the Web business service, including the servers and clients within the network environment, is the topic for discussion within this section. If the organization already has a network management system, it is highly advisable that the Web business service hardware and software components be managed there as well.

Traditional network management systems such as HP's OpenView would place the Web server and selected client workstations on the network map display, showing graphically if any components were not performing to previously-defined criteria. Other products, using SNMP or Simple Network Management Protocol, would also lend themselves quite well to the management of the Web business service network components. SNMP is an international Internet protocol that has been incorporated into many of the network management products on the market today. The platform independent protocol is used to monitor all manner of network devices within a local and global arena.

A new network management development platform called HNMP or Hypertext Network Management Platform from Tribe Computer Works (http://www.tribe.com) will be used to create network management systems using Web technology. The platform uses a common and simple interface—the Web browser.

Network management systems that have incorporated Web-based technology are shown in Table 7.5. Features relevant to the management of a Web business service as a network component would include

- remote management
  — remotely access, configure, and manage Web servers
  — access—dial up or LAN connection
- device setup
- port configuration and network settings

Table 7.5   Web Network Management Tools

Product	Vendor	Platforms Supported	Source	Cost
CoroNet Management System	Compuware Corporation	PC, Mac, UNIX	http://www.compuware.com	Commercial $5,000–7,000
WebCheck	Thomas-Conrad Corp.	PC, Mac, UNIX	http://www.tci.com	Commercial $950
WebManage	Tribe Computer Works	PC, Mac, UNIX	http://www.tribe.com	Commercial $1,295

- multiple protocol support
- hot links between management functions/pages
- troubleshooting and diagnostic tools
- system users
    - different views and access privileges
    - user login and password
    - encoded password protection such as SSL
- network statistics, traffic analysis, and trending utilities

Web Project Management

Project management entails the development of phases, activities, and tasks related to the completion of an endeavor. Project plans generally detail the activities, who is responsible for them, the amount of time required to complete the activity, start and end dates, and status information. The Web business service requires someone skilled in the art of project management for three major activities:

1. Launching the Web business service—Project planning must be conducted initially during the vision formation stage and precede all major activities required for the launch of the service.

2. Scheduling applications development—Requests for new services, new applications, new scripts, image maps, video, etc., will be coming at the service furiously as more and more users become aware of

the potential of the Web. Management needs to develop a procedure to receive, prioritize, fulfill, and review requests for new service.

3. Developing and managing the service plan—The ongoing activities of the Web business service will be reflected in the service plan.

Features to look for in a project planning and management tool include the following:

- Graphical user interface
- Web browser interface
- Automatic project outliner
- Multilevel resource scheduling—people, workgroups, projects, activities
- Cost accounting—budget and actual costs
- Customizable reports and charts such as histograms, Gantt, Pert, Critical Path Management, work breakdown structure, cost variance, etc.
- Timelines
- User-defined dates and renumbering schemes
- Project status
- Action item lists
- Activity dependencies

Table 7.6 details a sampling of the project management software tools that are commercially available today. For more general information, resources, and services, consult the WWW Project Management Forum's home page at http://www.synapse.net/~loday/PMForum/. The PM Forum seeks to develop and support a professional and world wide project management discipline.

Web Problem and Change Management

Basically, problem and change management for the Web business service encompasses three functions: call tracking, problem tracking, and change management.

Table 7.6 Project Management Tools

Product	Vendor	Platforms Supported	Source	Cost
Artemis Prestige	Artemis International Limited	Win, Mac, UNIX	http://www.wji.com/artemis/	Commercial $1,995
CA-SuperProject	Computer Associates	Win	http://www.cai.com	Commercial $650
FastTrack Schedule	AEC Software	Win, Mac	http://www.aecsoft.com/	Commercial $495
MacProject	Claris Corp.	Mac	http://www.claris.com	Commercial $599
Microsoft Project	Microsoft	Win, Mac	http://www.microsoft.com	Commercial $695
Open Plan Professional	Welcom Software Technology	Win	http://www.wst.com	Commercial $17,000
Project Scheduler	Scitor Corp.	Win, Mac, OS/2	http://www.scitor.com	Commercial $695

Call tracking occurs when a user places a telephone call to the Customer Service or Help Desk. The call is statistically analyzed to determine how many rings the user heard before the call was answered, how long the user remained on hold, how long the completed call lasted, and how many callers hung up and when during the process. These statistics are used to determine how many representatives need to be on hand to answer calls during each hour of the day, and to determine if the facility is functioning at the level required in the Service Level Agreement. Web-based Customer Service and Help Desk facilities are now beginning to significantly reduce the number of incoming telephone calls for service.

Change management tracks changes to Web business service—consisting of software, hardware, firmware, and/or documents—from its origination, through maintenance, delivery, and support. Change management also includes software version control tracking.

Web problem and change management and tools will be more thoroughly discussed as a critical component of providing Web-based Help Desk and Customer Service facilities in Chapters 9 and 10.

Web Service Support

Support for the Web business service is of on-going critical importance. Internal users of the service, as well as external suppliers, vendors, and customers, must be able to communicate their problems with the system, have them isolated, resolved, with the resulting improvement implemented for the service to continue to be used and to grow. Support can be categorized into two basic functions: Customer Service and Training.

CUSTOMER SERVICE

External customers, suppliers, and employees need to know where to go for help on every facet of the Web business service with which they interact. Suffice it to say that a well-oiled Customer Service facility will enable the organization to retain existing customers, acquire new ones, shorten delivery times of raw materials from suppliers, and increase the productivity of employees. It is critical to provide a high level of customer service through internal Help Desks and Customer Support mechanisms. There are a number of tools coming on the market that interface Web services with those of traditional customer service. The planning, design, implementation, tools, and on-going maintenance of a Web-based Customer Service department will be more thoroughly discussed in Chapter 10.

Typical services that a Help Desk or Customer Service facility provides would include the following:

- "hot-line" toll-free telephone support
- comprehensive support
- support account management
- on-site services
- single point of contact
- named account representative
- call and problem management
- diagnostic and knowledge databases
- escalation procedures
- flexible hours of coverage

TRAINING

The amount of training given to users of the Web business service depends on the size of the enterprise, the number of users, and time and budget constraints. The various approaches for a training program discussed below are for larger, more complex sites with adequate training funds and the human resources and time to implement training for all users. Smaller sites may use the approaches to select training options more suitable for their own needs.

Ideally, an organization should conduct a training needs analysis in order to design a customized training program for the Web business service. An education program management support team would then be identified to deliver the training services required. The curriculum would be planned with the organization's input, and the mix of courses and services would be formalized. Several approaches to training, plus venues for the coursework, are available.

Training Approaches
- instructor-led training
- train-the-trainer program
- self-paced/self-study courses
- modular courses
- certification programs
- computer-based training
- hands-on training in a lab environment
- course licensing

Course Venues
- on-site training
- vendor's location
- other location
- satellite based training
- student's residence

The training program should provide all relevant student materials, such as documentation, online tutorials, course workbooks, etc. Each course developed should have the course description, course objectives, topics covered, and any prerequisites required listed for the students' information. The training program should include an appropriate mix of novice to power user training options. If the training is contracted to a third party, the vendor should license the organization to re-use the training materials for internal use after the initial training courses have been completed.

Summary

As Web sites continue to expand, to include more content, and to offer more interactive services to their users, the management and support of the service becomes a critical concern. In this chapter we have explored several approaches to service management, including the development of a Service Plan which functions as an umbrella for Web server, client, content, network, problem, and project management.

In the next chapter we will discuss current issues concerning security, legalities, and privacy as they relate to running a Web business service.

Web Service Security, Legal, and Privacy Concerns

"Chris, take a look at this awesome video clip for the Bronto Brats new home page that a friend of mine found in the Film Institute's archives," suggested Jason as he launched a captivating scene of a woman and four children running in a flower-laden meadow with a thundering herd of playful blue dinosaurs.

"Yes, it's a great fit for the new page, but there are lots of concerns about using it. How did your friend get access to those archives? And, do you realize what we'll go through if we actually use this? We'll have to get permission from the copyright holders and most likely pay royalties to everyone in or associated with the film including the musicians, songwriters—even the stunt doubles! We could check out a clearinghouse, though, to see if we can pay one fee for everything. And what about the female star? With all her troubles lately about her line of blue leather shoes being made in Korean sweat shops, will we have a privacy or defamation issue here?" groaned Chris, wondering if producing their own video sequence would actually be less costly and time consuming in the long run.

As more and more people gain experience in searching, locating, and retrieving information from the Internet, activities and issues such as those addressed in the scenario above will become commonplace and of paramount concern to the providers of Web business services. The security of Web servers, their processes, content and network connections; the legalities of copyrights, trademarks, and patents; and the privacy of the individuals who use the services must all be considered in planning and running a Web business service. This chapter discusses these thorny management issues and offers practical solutions.

Web Service Security

The promise of millions of people visiting the Web site, finding needed information, or purchasing products and services is a tremendous lure. However, it is inevitable that the Web service will draw just as many unsavory snoops and scoundrels as a typical store or business. Nothing can bring the Web business service to its knees faster than a security breach. The grand show of the Web service will summarily STOP until the breach is identified, halted, and corrective measures are put in place to ensure that it will never happen again. The Web service is every bit as susceptible to security risks, threats, and vulnerabilities as are the traditional forms of data communications and information distribution. The Web service management must be committed to the protection and safeguarding of the service's electronically-processed information. The organization should undertake measures against unauthorized or accidental access, disclosure, modification, denial, or destruction of the Web service's systems. Grappling with Web service security generally falls into two overall categories: physical security and logical security.

PHYSICAL SECURITY

Physical security seeks to protect the environment in which the Web service lives and works. The building, and the specific area within the building in which the Web service is located, must be safeguarded. It isn't enough to merely provide an air-conditioned, office-like environment for all the Web service hardware. Physical access to the server must be tightly controlled, and access granted only to trusted and authorized parties. Some organizations place the Web server in the same location as other application and network servers, thus affording it a greater degree of physical security. The area in the building for the telecommunications entry point, the Internet interface—typically a communications closet or room—must also be secured.

LOGICAL SECURITY

Logical security has to do with protecting any and all software that is a part of the Web business service. The software—Web service computer programs, processes, content, etc.—should be protected from unauthorized access and use by security mechanisms, both simple and sophisticated. Web services and Internet resources that require security measures include electronic commerce, e-mail, remote login (Telnet), file transfer (FTP), and discussion and news groups, such as listservers and Usenet.

This section will not instruct the reader on how to "tickle the keys"— to set up system configuration files for directory trees and access control lists, disabling server side includes, and the like. There are many excellent books with very detailed instructions on Web service security configuration. Rather, this section provides a management focus and will explore the design of a security model, the many and varied mechanisms employed to secure a Web service, the security risks, threats, and vulnerabilities, security policies, and employee security training.

Designing the Web Service Security Model

There are as many approaches to the configuration of a secure information system as there are varieties of systems. Options range from a completely-open Web service to that of an internal-only Web service, as illustrated in Figure 8.1.

With completely open access, anyone in the organization is permitted to exchange messages and files with anyone outside, to retrieve files, to access and post to newsgroups, to participate in chat services, etc. This model is the easiest to install, but also bears the most risk. Having your front door wide open in the global electronic neighborhood is, quite frankly, dangerous.

At the other end of the spectrum is the completely closed or isolated access model. In this configuration, the users from within the organi-

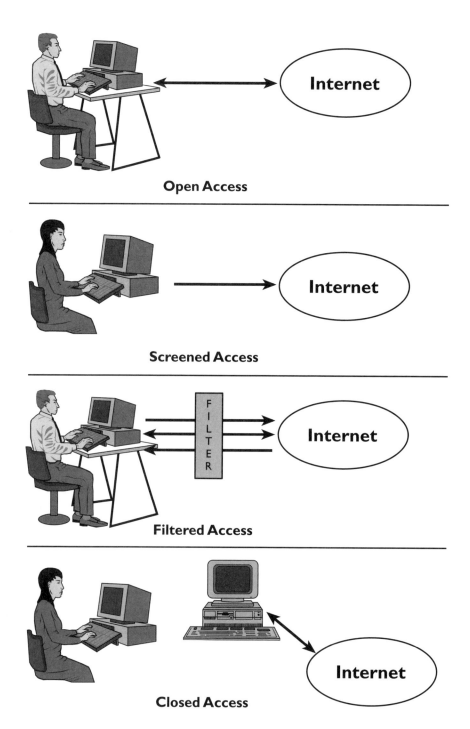

Figure 8.1 Web Service Security Models

zation cannot directly interact with the Internet. The user must physically go to the one workstation with Internet access. This is colloquially referred to as "sneaker net," in which any information gleaned from the Internet is downloaded to a floppy and hand-carried back to the user's workstation for storage or distribution. This model bears no risk of attack from outside parties, but is the most restrictive in terms of granting easy, transparent, and flexible access to the Web service for internal users. In this scenario, the user's style will be far too cramped, and use of the Web service will certainly suffer.

The middle-of-the-road approaches are the screened and filtered access models. These approaches provide a high level of security, along with easy and transparent use for the Web service clients. In screened access, the internal users have only limited access to the Internet services, as specified by management. In the filtered access model, both the internal and external users must pass through a gate or filter in order to interact with each other or the various Internet resources.

Proxy and Firewall Servers

How firewalls and proxy servers work, as well as the security, user, and administrative features and functions required, are discussed in Chapter 3. Firewall and proxy server tools, products, and services can be found in Table 3.2.

The best policy with firewalls is to force all traffic to log onto the firewall, eliminate trusted hosts, provide file transfer services only through the firewall, and prohibit all services unless they are expressly needed. For example, outbound connections are permitted from the internal Web service, but Telnet connections to the internal Web service from anywhere are denied. In addition, it is advisable to remove any superfluous network services and any compilers and programming tools. Web service firewalls must be configured to be "paranoid." A hacker's machine will impersonate the legitimate machine. Proxy machines must have simple, minimal code and be a "crystal box," not a "black box." They must have "smoke alarms" that give notification when a user is going from port to port trying to gain access. They must also provide spoofing resistance.

Firewalls may either be external or internal to the organization. External firewalls keep the unsavory types out and the organization's information in. Internal firewalls permit the organization to specify what and how service information will be exchanged between the various operating units. Encryption between internal firewalls should be implemented so that the organization can use protocols that may not be otherwise secure on the inside.

Firewalls are moving from rather code-light boxes to offering more sophisticated features and functions—from being merely intelligent routers to becoming application-based systems offering a programmable interface, auditing, alarms, service proxies, and packet filtering. In the future, the firewall will still perform the function of granting or denying access to users, but it will accomplish this task with far more robust mechanisms. Firewalls will function as gateways for each of the Internet services used. The firewall may also eventually contain the public key cryptography system which will authorize user entry and also authenticate the user, as shown in Figure 8.2. Public key cryptography is discussed later in the section on Access Control.

Filters

Filters allow the Web service to define the amount of protection applied to messages, files, and data flowing within and without the organization. Filters may be applied to a variety of the applications and services provided by the Web service, such as electronic mail envelopes, messages, attachments, file transfers, newsgroups, Telnet, electronic commerce, etc. Filters generally are located between the internal user and the firewall.

Authorizing Users of the Web Service

Permission must be granted to users or processes prior to their accessing secure components of the Web service and systems. This is a two-part process that includes the granting of access rights and the administration of access controls. Access rights are the specific privileges extended to different types of users of the Web service. Some users will have access only to certain applications and services, while others will be able to access everything. Access control are the mechanisms by which entry of networks, computing systems, application systems, and data is granted to those with the proper privileges. Access control lists are created to enforce these rights. To view, use, interact with, configure, or change a system generally requires two components. The user or

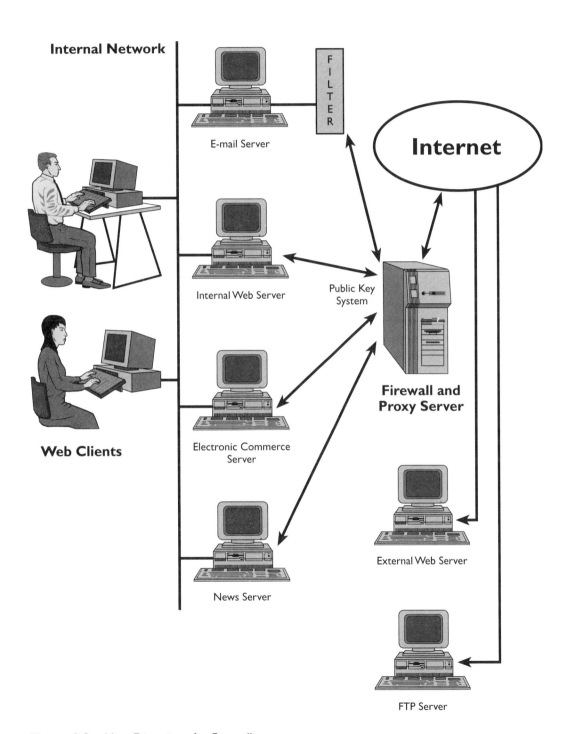

Figure 8.2   New Directions for Firewalls

application process must be *authorized* to use the system and must be correctly identified or *authenticated* to the system ("Are you allowed to use this system?" and "Is that really you?").

Authenticating Users of the Web Service

There are two accepted and commonly-used ways to authenticate users to the Web service. *Simple authentication* is the most basic, and requires the least amount of labor and cost to implement and administer. It is also the most risky, as far as security is concerned. The scheme uses passwords and user IDs to authenticate users to the system. Passwords can easily be compromised. A bit more sophistication—such as using time stamps and random numbers in addition to the password and user ID—has been added to reduce the vulnerability of this authentication scheme.

The second way to authenticate a user to the Web service or application such as electronic bill paying is to employ *strong authentication*. This method uses cryptography to establish and verify the user's identity prior to access being granted. One of the most serious stumbling blocks for the world-wide use of the electronic commerce potential of the Web is the lack of global, standardized, low-cost, and easy-to-implement encryption utilities. Encryption provides confidentiality, data integrity, and authentication for all Web service transactions.

Currently, there are two methods of using cryptography for digital information. Asymmetric or private key cryptosystems, as depicted in Figure 8.3, use a single key shared by and known only to the parties of the transaction. In our scenario, Chris uses her private key to encrypt a transaction sent to Jason. He then decrypts the transaction using the same, identical key. A *key* is a complex mathematical algorithm that coverts plain text into that which is indecipherable by humans. Both Chris and Jason are assured that their identities are known and that the contents of the transaction have not been compromised by virtue of the fact that no one else has their private keys. Parties using this scheme are constantly required to change their keys to reduce the risk of a security breach.

The second encryption method used widely today is that of public key or asymmetric cryptography. As shown in Figure 8.3, Chris uses

Jason's public key to encrypt a message or transaction to be sent to him. On receipt, Jason uses his private key to decrypt the message or transaction. Public keys are either sent along with the item or can be found in a public directory such as one based on the X.500 international standard for distributed electronic directory systems

The Web service may wish to implement end-to-end encryption, connection/packet protection, or link encryption in addition to client-based public key cryptography.

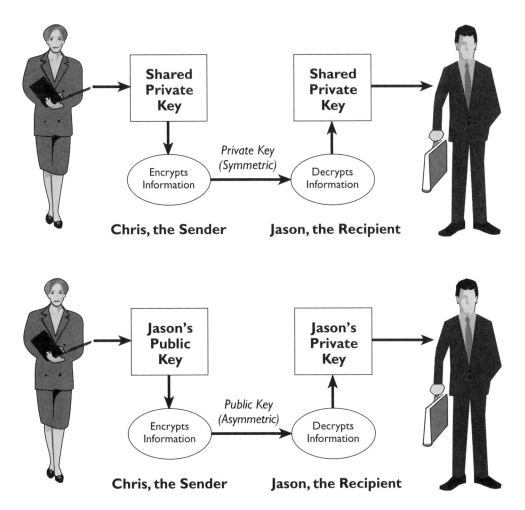

Figure 8.3 Private and Public Key Cryptosystems

Due to the crucial nature of security on the Internet, much work is underway to reduce the tight import/export controls and government-imposed cryptography that are hindering the growth of global electronic commerce. The Web service management must stay well informed on these issues in order to make judicious decisions regarding security.

Digital Signatures

Digital signatures, also known as certification tokens or seals, are becoming prevalent as a means of providing authentication, integrity, and non-repudiation for secure Web service applications such as electronic purchasing or the transmission of proprietary information. Digital signatures provide a mechanism for verifying the identity of the signer or for determining whether the content of a transaction has been altered.

The way the process works, as shown in Figure 8.4, is that plain text information is sent by a user (in this case Chris) and is received by another user (Jason). Prior to sending the information, Chris uses her private key to encrypt the information, then applies a hashing utility to create a summary of the information. This summary is the digital signature. The summary is then sent to the recipient, who applies the identical hash utility and decrypts the information using Chris's public key, which has either been sent along with the information or is available to the recipient in a public directory. Jason then compares the plain text information with the results of the decrypted hashed summary and—if the two are the same—can verify that the user was indeed Chris and that the content has not been altered.

Non-repudiation

Non-repudiation means that neither a user nor an application process can deny that a specific action was taken. If a user places an order for 500 dozen red roses, then tries to deny that the order was actually placed or that the user was not a party to the transaction, this is termed repudiation. Secure information systems seek to establish mechanisms by which a user or application cannot deny the actions taken. Non-repudiation may also act as a safeguard against one user or process masquerading as another.

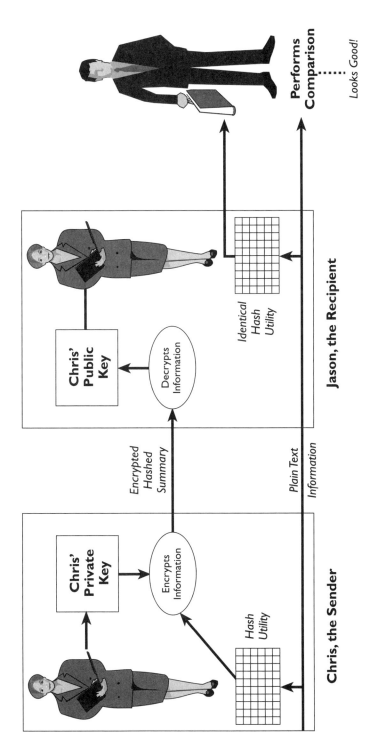

Figure 8.4 How Digital Signatures Work

Virus Checking

Malicious software, such as viruses, worms, time bombs, logic bombs, Trojan horses, executables, postscript files, etc., may result in inappropriate disclosure, use, modification, destruction or denial of electronic information systems. Mechanisms must be put in place to detect and thwart malicious software at the firewall, application, and/or client level before it has a chance to perform its intended destructive purpose.

Web Security Risk Assessment

A risk assessment is a working estimate of the risk of a security breach based on the relationship between vulnerability and the value of the Web service. The risks associated with operating a Web service must be balanced against the ability to provide, fund, and administer security protection. Some companies set a cost per user in order to allocate funds for implementing security measures. Serious risks, such as the network or operating system configuration, default settings, user authentication, passwords, and accounts, and directory and file protections, must be assessed. All security risks cannot be identified or eliminated, but organizations that take the time and effort to perform a risk assessment are better prepared, quicker to act, and faster to recover in the event of security breaches. There are four levels of security risk ranging from no security to a hardware- and software-based solution:

- Level 0—no security—very high risk
- Level 1—software based security—high risk
- Level 2—hardware-based server security—some risk
- Level 3—hardware-based client and server security—least risk

Level 3 offers the least risk as it reduces the exposure if the firewall is compromised Performance is always better in hardware-based security. Success factors for security solutions include lower cost, seamless and transparent implementation, worldwide standards, and high performance.

Web Service Threat and Vulnerability Analysis

A comprehensive analysis to measure the Web service's security threats and vulnerabilities must be performed at least annually. Information gathered to provide a foundation for the analysis includes the size and complexity of the Web service and associated network, the various types of Internet connections, the service ports, existing security features, monitoring levels, and audit logging, and the operating system security. This analysis identifies various mechanisms that can be used to invade the system and provides a basis for planning defenses and protections against them. The objective here is to reduce the inherent security risks associated with operating the Web service.

Web Service Security Threats

Common security threats the Web service may experience include

- Probes
- Password attacks and interceptions
- Trusted hosts
- Session hijacking
- File transfers
- Sendmail forgery
- Data integrity, compromise, destruction
- Denial of service
- Invasion of privacy
- Message interception
- Illegal software
- Malicious software
- Sniffing

Web Service Security Vulnerabilities

Common areas of vulnerability for the Web service include

- Theft
- Damage
- Tampering
- Reprogramming
- Monitoring
- Recording
- Rerouting
- Intrusion

- Unauthorized access
- Tapping
- Viewing

Web Service Security Policies

The formulation of a comprehensive Web service security policy is a key element in the design and management of a reliable and efficient service. The Web service security policy would pertain to all organizational elements that plan to use, develop, maintain, modify, or acquire information from the Web service. The policy would apply to all Web service systems, databases, content, computing platforms, software, and networks that process, interact with, or provide access to the service.

The Web service security policy should specifically detail the implementation procedures to establish and maintain proper security controls and mechanisms. The Web service should perform the following key elements:

1. Designate a security coordinator with overall responsibility for coordinating and monitoring the implementation of the security requirements.
2. Conduct an annual Web service protection awareness and education program.
3. Perform an annual threat and vulnerability analysis.
4. Identify Web service systems that require access controls; implement access controls for these systems and annually review the suitability of these controls.
5. Provide backup and recovery processes to protect the Web service commensurate with its risk assessment and it prescribed requirements.
6. Document and test plans for disaster recovery based on risk assessment.
7. Implement procedures to prevent, detect, and respond to malicious software attacks.
8. Adhere to software license agreements and copyright laws.
9. Preserve any classification, restricted notice, or other security marking associated with the paper form when written information is converted to electronic form.

The Web service security policy should also clearly specify the responsibilities for the implementation of the policy. These responsibilities would require

1. groups, companies, and other operating elements to develop guidelines and operating instructions to ensure compliance with this Web service security policy
2. each employee and other users of the Web service to be individually responsible in complying with the Web service security policy

Employee Security Awareness and Training

Training and orientation of employees and users is the most important element of Web service security. Not only must they be aware of the procedures and guidelines, they must be motivated to adhere to them. Some organizations will require that a user sign a security oath or agreement prior to being given authorization to use the Web service. The Web service security coordinator must take the initiative to provide meaningful training in this area. The coordinator will provide assistance for security briefings. When appropriate, briefings may cover technical security subjects such as:

1. Computer password security
2. Computer hardware and storage media security
3. Electronic eavesdropping
4. Industrial espionage tactics and techniques
5. Malicious software

Legalities of a Web Service

As if there weren't already a blue million things to consider when planning and running a Web service, the legalities of using information created by others is also of primary concern. It is so easy to download information gleaned from the Internet. Often, users and developers find just the perfect graphic or musical score and simply click it into their own Web content without regard for the rights of the originator of the work. The information used in Web content typically will be video and audio clips, movies, animated sequences, text, tables, charts, 2-D and 3-D graphics, still images, and very soon, virtual reality and holographic imagery. Once these information types have been digitized, they can quickly and easily become part of the Web service's content. The information can be reused, altered in both audacious and subtle ways, and stored—often without the knowledge of the originator.

One of the most glaring concerns in this area is the global nature of the information and the inevitable clash with local, state, federal, and international laws. Protections afforded in this country as a matter of legal and historical precedent have no basis for safeguard in other countries. For example, an animated sequence produced by a film studio in the United States may have no copyright protection when used in a product created and distributed in Singapore. A consortium known as the Internet Law Task Force is currently working on these and other legal issues of concern to the Internet community as global information sharing and electronic commerce emerge.

Several legal protections are available for Web content, including copyrights, trademarks, patents, and trade secrets. Legal protections work both ways in safeguarding the originators. Works originated by those outside the organization are protected from misappropriation, and works that are created by the organization are also protected from being misappropriated by others.

WEB CONTENT TYPES AND THE LAW

Most Web content types have a long history of specific protections under the law. These content types include text, music, film, and still images. New Web content types such as virtual reality and holographic imagery are just now beginning to have specific protections afforded to them.

Text Web Content

Text is the most basic and traditional form of Web content. Text is protected by copyright laws and permission must be obtained for its use. The copyright owner for the text will generally be either the author or the company that published the work in which the text selection is found. Traditional forms of text may be found in newspapers, magazines, pamphlets, and books. Newer electronic media, such as online services, also will contain text that may be used in Web content. Work is underway in the National Writers Union to protect the electronic rights of authors as well.

Music Web Content

Musicians in this country have national organizations that represent them for permission to use their works. Broadcast Music, Inc. (BMI— http://www.bmi.com) and the American Society of Composers, Authors, and Publishers (ASCAP—http://www.visualradio.com/ascap) together represent over 200,000 musicians, songwriters, composers, and publishers. BMI and ASCAP grant permissions for use and collect royalties for their members. Rights for use include public performance, specific performance, and synchronization licenses.

A public performance is one in which the music will be heard in a public place, such as in an elevator or when on hold during a telephone call. This would apply to users "tuning in" to music played on your public Web page as well. If you want to use a bit of music that was played at a certain place and time, a "live" performance, then you must obtain specific performance permission. If you want to play this music with a video sequence, then you must obtain a synchronization license.

Both BMI and ASCAP are working on agreements that protect their members when music is downloaded or played over the Internet.

Still Images Web Content

The copyright for still images or photographs has traditionally belonged to the photographer. Permission to use a still image as part of Web content would be obtained from the photographer, publisher of the work in which the photograph appeared, or from the executor of the photographer's estate.

Many images have now passed into the realm of public domain and are available for use without permission. The copyright on images of famous works of art may be owned by private individuals, corporations, or museums.

Film Web Content

The foregoing content types of text, music, and still images are all fairly straightforward when it comes to obtaining permission for use. Film is quite different and far more complex. Films include such works as feature films, news broadcasts, animated sequences, and videos. The film is copyrighted by the film studio, but individual permissions must also be obtained from just about everyone who worked in or on the film. These people include the actors, stunt performers, directors, and screenwriters. Permission may also have to granted by companies whose products (a can of soda or name brand of tool) appear in the film.

The Screen Actor's Guild and the Harry Fox Agency are the big names to contact when first exploring the use of film in the Web business service content.

Virtual Reality and Holographic Imagery Web Content

Virtual reality and holographic imagery technologies represent the new ground in determining copyrights and in the granting of permission. VR is being used in the more advanced Web sites for applications such as tours through museums, displaying catalog merchandise, and real estate showings. For now, they are covered under traditional copyright law. There will be other forms of digital expression in the near future over which the legal system will wrestle for the right of use, distribution, and just compensation.

LEGAL SAFEGUARDS FOR WEB CONTENT

As more and different content becomes widely available, ways to protect the interests of the originators of that content will proliferate. Traditional legal protections are applicable to Web content only in the strictest sense. To produce a book to be sold in a bookstore is not the same at all as producing a snazzy Web page to be viewed, copied, modified, or redistributed electronically by millions of people worldwide. The legal system is already in the throes of updating various laws to reflect the complexities of electronic distribution, download rights, and online real-time access to protected information.

Traditional legal protections most applicable to Web content include copyrights, trade and service marks, trade secrets, and patents.

Copyrights

From its moment of creation, any original work is protected under the modern Copyright Law of 1976. The originator has exclusive rights to the work for life plus 50 years. Copyrightable works include images, text, film, animations, plays, music, software, databases, anthologies, etc.—in short, just about anything that a Web service would desire to use as content. Due to the nature of the new Web medium, it is almost impossible to determine if a work has been copied, reused, or modified in any way.

A copyright holder may divide the copyright among different media, as in the case of an author producing a book, a movie, and an audio tape of the work. The three versions of the work may then have three different copyright holders. So, the quest to obtain permission to use a work in this case may be more complex and time consuming.

Content may also be produced as a "work for hire." An originator may be employed by an organization to produce a certain work. The originator then assigns the copyright to the employer. Works for hire include those that are created by an employee while employed by the organization and those that are specifically ordered or commissioned, such as work done by contractors or freelancers. The copyright for Web content produced by providers of such services must be negotiated and resolved up front.

When a work is copyrighted, the holder has several benefits, including the right to

- reproduce the work
- create derivative works based on the original work
- sell and distribute copies of the work
- perform or display the work in public places

Copyrighted works display the copyright symbol (©), generally followed by the name of the owner and the date of copyright. For example, © *Van Nostrand Reinhold, 1996.* The symbol also means that the owner has made application to the Register of Copyrights and has paid a $20 fee. Copyright owners today have expanded their admonitions against unauthorized reproductions of their works to include electronic distribution and copies stored on servers.

Providing links to copyrighted documents is another area of current legal concern. This action changes the whole notion of derivative works. If an author can point to images and other documents within his or her work, what copyright protections are afforded for all of the originators? Also, most Web servers use extensive caching of accessed Web URLs to reduce network traffic. Copies are made in the store and forward mechanisms of electronic messaging systems, as well as in the buffers of switches, routers, and gateways for the same reason. Are the copies made in this manner protected under copyright law? What effect will pending legislation—The National Information Infrastructure Copyright Protection Act of 1995—have on the global electronic communications industry? As can be seen from this discussion, the status of digital copyright law is still fuzzy. It behooves the Web service management to stay informed on the issues and progress being made in this area.

Trademarks

Trademarks protect product names, unique symbols, and recognizable labels from misappropriation and use. It is very simple for a developer or content owner to copy a digital image of another company's logo, alter it somewhat, and place it into the Web service content. Or, an image of a brand name product may be used in the Web content without the permission of the trademark holder. Trademarks must be registered with the U.S. Patent and Trademark Office to be valid and protected by law. Care must be taken to review any proposed content to determine if trademarked brand names, symbols, logos, labels, and the like have been used. Trademarked items such as those mentioned above will display the symbols ® or ™ prominently next to the name, logo, etc. Should the Web service misappropriate a trademarked item for use within its content, a trademark owner has the right to file an injunction to stop the service from displaying or distributing the item. Fines and damages may also be levied. So, it's good business practice to carefully review any proposed Web content for such potential trademark violations.

Trade Secrets

Trade secrets are those processes, designs, ideas, etc., that an organization knows are necessary to its competitive survival and those for which great care is taken to protect against disclosure. Web service content featuring a unique computer process would fall under this category, as would the visitor and customer list of an active Web service. Trade secrets are protected by the states under the Uniform Trade Secrets Act. Securing trade secrets against unwarranted access and disclosure is essential to protect the organization's ability to compete.

Patents

Patents on computer processes, unique ornamental digital designs, or other computer utilities have specific applicability to Web service content and processes. Developers and content owners, in their quest to provide the most current and useful content, may unknowingly draw down patented products or scan in design images that have patents. Original processes and designs created by the organization may also be protected by means of a patent award. Patents—or the right to exclusively produce, sell and use and invention—are awarded to inventors for a period of up to 17 years. Patents are granted through the United States Patent and Trademark Office. Patented inventions will display the "U.S. Patent No.12346" or "U.S. Patent Pending" notification prominently. Consulting an attorney experienced in patent law early on in the Web content design process would be beneficial to avoid any potential conflicts.

Sources for Web Content

In addition to obtaining content from traditional print media, the Internet, and other electronic or online services, information for use on the Web site may be obtained from clearinghouses, stock houses, purchased images, and the public domain. The organization may also decide to create its own content as a standard procedure.

Clearinghouses

Since it is extremely tedious and costly in both time and money to locate the copyright owners of a particular work, clearinghouses have stepped in to fill the need. These organizations locate and negotiate with the copyright holders and individuals who participated in the work's creation. The clearinghouse then markets the work to those who seek permission to use it and collects the royalties and fees on behalf of the owners. The clearinghouse secures from the user an agreement on the intended use of the work, including where and how the work will appear.

Stock Houses

Stock houses have traditionally handled still images, collected from photographers and then resold. Today, these same houses are also beginning to carry digital still images, as well as other content types. We will see the nature of the services provided by traditional stock houses begin to change as they incorporate more sophisticated electronic capture and storage technology.

Purchased Images

Various software companies market collections of images, such as clip art and photographs. The company then sells the rights to use these works to the purchaser. As long as the purchaser adheres to the intended use licensing provisions on the purchase agreement, the user may use and reuse the images at will in the Web content.

Public Domain

Due to their age, many works of art or literature are now in the public domain. If created prior to 1906 or produced by a government agency, the work is in the public domain and no permission to use it needs to be obtained. Never guess on whether a particular work is actually in the public domain. Always verify prior to use.

Developing Original Web Content

Some organizations routinely use Web content from their own repositories. Creating an internal clearinghouse of images, film, music, and text has proven to be more cost effective in the long run if the organization requires the use of original content for their Web service and has the expertise, personnel, technology, time and funding to create the works. Searching for copyright holders, working with attorneys, paying royalties and fees, etc., may override the start-up costs of originating the content.

Original works should bear the copyright symbol of the organization or individual who created the work in a visible place. If the organization will make the original content available to the public by means of the public Web site, then the copyright notice should appear prominently at the bottom of every page. If the symbol would detract from the aesthetics of the work, then a unique digital image or mark, like a watermark, should appear within the image.

WEB SERVICE LIABILITIES

The notion of liability for Web content, stored data, electronic messages, and information posted to bulletin boards and newsgroups is now becoming of major concern to providers of Web services. And—with the ability to store, post, and send information around the globe—holding providers liable on the international scene is also emerging. Liability is defined as being held legally obligated and responsible. To what extent are providers liable for Web content and services? Discussed below are a few of the more obvious areas of concern and questions that should be addressed. For accurate and timely advice on this subject, seek qualified legal counsel.

Retention of Information

How long should Web content not in active use on the server be stored? How many back versions are appropriate and legally correct to keep? What content types should be stored? Where should the content be kept? Should an organization keep any back content at all, to protect itself against litigation?

Most administrators of electronic messaging systems routinely delete subscriber's messages still in the inbox after a specified time period, typically 60–90 days. The users are informed of this retention policy and have the option to store or archive their mail on their local disks, on floppies, or on other storage media. This approach of automatic deletion by date is one option for Web content retention. Another would be to only retain content that pertains to critical applications, such as order entry or electronic commerce interactions, and delete the rest.

Messages

What is the extent of liability of an organization regarding the use by its employees of the electronic messaging system? What if an employee sends company-sensitive or proprietary information to competitors? What if an employee sends or receives insider trading information, trade secrets, pornographic material, etc.? The e-mail address of the employee generally gives the organization's name. Even if the employee acted alone without management's knowledge or approval, the organization may still be implicated.

Bulletin Boards and Newsgroup Postings

Typically, anyone who is authorized can post a message to a bulletin board or a newsgroup. These electronic media are usually organized by topic and are open to comments. The message will reflect the user's e-mail address, thus again tying the user back to the organization. What if the employee posts defamatory comments about another person or vilifies a competitor's product? Is the organization liable for the content placed by their employees? Is the owner of the bulletin board or newsgroup liable for the content therein?

WEB SERVICE APPROPRIATE USE POLICIES

The issue of liability is critical since we live in an extremely litigious society. Appropriate use policies can go a long way in informing employees of acceptable behavior regarding the Web service and other forms of electronic communication. Employees may also be removed based on failure to adhere to published and enforceable company policies regarding the use of the Internet and the Web service.

Any Web service should create and distribute guidelines for the appropriate use of the new medium. The guidelines may be in the form of a policy statement prominently displayed on the home page of the Web site or may be a written statement that every employee is required to sign prior to gaining access to the service. The organization should have a policy and it should be openly communicated to every employee authorized to use the system. This policy protects the Web service in the event that an employee communicates something illegal or indecent while using the service. For example, an employee may discriminate against or harass someone in an electronic mail message or an employee may download illicit material from an external Web site and distribute or store it.

The appropriate use policy should seek to balance the rights of employees to individual expression of ideas with the prevailing laws of decency, both within the United States and internationally. The policy should also address censorship. With the global nature of the Internet technology, it is difficult at best to determine what constitutes offensive, indecent, or pornographic material. Also, no one can accurately predict the path that information will take between sender and receiver. What is extremely objectionable in Boston or Riyadh may be viewed quite differently in San Francisco.

Sample text for an appropriate use policy statement should include the following key points:

- The Web service must not be used to send, post, or download messages or information that contains obscene language or images.
- Use of the Web service must not be in support of a personal business, the business of any other corporation or firm, consulting effort, or similar profit venture; nor should it be used for any illegal purpose or purpose which would cause embarrassment to the organization or otherwise be adverse to its interests.
- Use of the service may not be in support of political interests.
- Use of the Web service must not compromise the security of the organization.
- The Web service must not be used to send an electronic message containing company-sensitive or company-proprietary information to a recipient external to the organization.
- The Web service reserves the right to monitor or access information or messages within the system.
- Personal use of the Web service must take place during non-work time, be of reasonable duration and frequency, and must not interfere with or adversely affect the employee's performance or other organization requirements.

SEEKING LEGAL COUNSEL FOR THE WEB SERVICE

Web content and services are a new field in the legal arena. Experienced legal counsel with a specialty in this area is difficult to locate. The best approach is to retain an individual or firm that has a great deal of experience in working with copyrights and permissions within traditional media like print, music and film. A group that has done recent research or litigation concerning the Internet, cyberspace issues, and electronic distribution of media would also be a good choice. If your organization conducts business globally, counsel experienced in international law and the import/export of information would be a requirement.

Web Service Privacy Concerns

Workplace privacy as a whole has become a concern of both management and employees as electronic technology continues to advance and provide people with more ways to access, store, and transmit digital information. Employers must strike a reasonable balance between their need to protect company resources and the need of the employees for individual privacy.

Employers generally feel that any company asset or resource used within the scope of an employee's duties is owned by the company and is, therefore, subject to search, monitoring, and disclosure. Employees, on the other hand—without any written and disseminated guidelines to the contrary—believe that their desks, files, computers, and the application programs they use, such as e-mail, are private. To clear up this obvious rift, a workplace privacy policy must be formulated and clearly communicated to every employee. Privacy pertaining to the Web service and systems should be included in the overall policy. In fact, the Web service internal home page is an ideal place to locate both the appropriate use and privacy policies, as well as other company policies.

Privacy also extends to the external users of the Web business service. Some Web sites routinely request demographic information and preferences of their visitors. As more sites develop the security mechanisms required for electronic commerce, people will purchase goods and services by means of the Internet, providing their credit card numbers and other financial information in order to consummate the sale. To what extent should the customer or visitor's personal purchasing habits, demographics, medical information, and preferences be made available to third parties? Mail order companies have been selling their mailing lists for years. Now that so much more information can be easily captured electronically, how will organizations resist the lure of disclosing it? Purchasers must be made to feel secure that information about themselves will be held in trust and not be shared or sold. Current thought in this area is that the American people have more to fear about disclosure of personal information by corporations than they do by the U.S. government!

Web service management should know exactly what type of information is being gathered and stored about which particular users. Users should also be informed that certain information is being gathered and exactly how that information will be used. The users must also be given the ability to prevent the information from being gathered in the first place or used in the manner specified by the Web service management (http://www.cdt.org/privacy).

The privacy policy should be developed using a team approach. Team representatives should at least include legal, human resources, communications, and technical people. Once established, the policy should be reviewed annually by this same team to adjust for advancements in technology, new federal and states laws, and precedent-setting court cases. An excellent tool kit for the development and distribution of a privacy policy is available from the Electronic Messaging Association (http://www.ema.org).

CURRENT LITIGATION

The only piece of legislation even marginally relevant to the notion of workplace privacy is that of the Federal Electronic Communications Privacy Act of 1986. This act states that telephone calls and electronic information transmitted over public transmission utilities are private and cannot be intruded upon by the companies carrying the information, such as MCI or AT&T. The act specifies no privacy guarantees for private business or for the employees therein. To date, there is only meager federal constitutional protection for government employees.

Court cases that have actually been carried to a final decision have overwhelming come down on the side of the employer in privacy-related litigation. The burden of proof of privacy invasion rests on the employee and the employee must prove that they had an "expectation of privacy." While most employees feel that their personal passwords used to gain access to the company computer systems guarantee them privacy, this is simply not the case when managers with authority or systems administrators with technical expertise can access an employee's records, files, and message stores.

Employers may or may not have had "just cause" to breach their employee's desks, files, computer disks, or e-mail files. Employees who filed suit typically disclosed something in their electronic mail messages or paper mail that was defamatory, company proprietary, or embarrassing. The employees were dismissed and then filed suit against their former employers for wrongful discharge and/or invasion of privacy. These cases generally involved firms without any formal and/or widely-communicated privacy policy.

COMPONENTS OF A WEB SERVICE PRIVACY POLICY

The Web service privacy policy should clearly specify the privacy limits of the organization and the employee. The policy should be straightforward, concise, brief and easy for both management and the employees to understand. The organization should foster an atmosphere of sensible restrictions and the full and complete disclosure of them to the employees. Topics to include in a privacy policy are a clear definition of the resources and assets covered, who will have access rights, under what circumstances access will be made, how the employee will be notified, management's responsibilities, and procedures for handling employee complaints.

Company Assets and Personal Resources

The company may declare that all hardware, software, communications facilities, and other corporate assets such as desks and filing cabinets are company resources, and therefore open to access by management and other authorized individuals as warranted by business reasons. Some companies even have policies stating that an employee's car parked in the company parking lot, purses, and briefcases may be searched. Whatever the company's policy on the use of its assets and resources, the Web service should fall under these same guidelines.

Circumstances for Intrusion

The Web service privacy policy should clearly state the circumstances or conditions under which management and system administrators will monitor, access, and view an employee's related files and messages. Examples of reasonable conditions include the following:

- as a result of a Web service system failure or recovery
- while under court order, search warrant, or discovery process

- when obscene, libelous, threatening, harassing, abusive, illegal, or criminal activity is suspected
- when downloading of harmful computer programs or viruses is suspected
- when the employee is out of the office and unreachable or unable to perform his or her duties
- in an emergency situation (as specified by management)
- to ensure the quality of the products and services produced by the organization
- to locate lost data information, files, or messages

Persons Authorized Access

Management should specify exactly who is permitted access to employee's desks, files, and computer systems and applications. Managers in the normal course of performing work-related business will generally be permitted access to their employee's work areas under the circumstances outlined above. Systems administrators and programmers may also be authorized to enter the private domain of the employee for the same reasons.

Employee Notification

How and when employees will be notified if an employer has accessed any of their business tools or resources is a key issue. Several approaches are available, depending on how much deference to the employees management wishes to show. Management may specify that an employee will be notified, for example, in writing, by personal visit, or by electronic mail. Management may notify the employee as soon as access is made, only in the event that misappropriate activity was found, or only under the advice of legal authorities.

Management Responsibilities

The Web service management, system administrators, and the organization's senior management have a responsibility to their fellow employees to not arbitrarily and capriciously invade their privacy. No one with the authority or the technical capability should peruse the files or electronic messages of another for personal reasons or amusement.

Handling Employee Complaints

Employees must be allowed to review the results of the access and monitoring so as to have the opportunity to dispute them. Users of the Web service who have complaints about intrusion and invasion of privacy must have recourse. The notion of due process is fundamental, and users must have a procedure in place whereby their complaints may be heard and resolved. The Web service may choose to adopt existing organizational complaint, grievance, dispute, or ethical violations procedures. Or the service may refer the user to the legal or human resources department in the event of a complaint. It is not advisable or practical to handle privacy complaints within the confines of the service; seek the advice and guidance of the internal experts on the subject.

SAMPLE PRIVACY POLICIES

The following are examples of the typical scope, key elements, and wording found in privacy policies of large corporations.

> "The Web service and systems are the property of (organization name). Unauthorized access and improper use are prohibited. Activity on the service is subject to monitoring by the organization. Anyone using the service consents to monitoring and agrees the organization may use the results without limitation."

> "The Web service is a company asset and is provided as a business tool. Management and systems administrators may have a legitimate need to monitor, access, and view your interactions with the Web service. The Web service is not considered private. Users of the system are encouraged to use good judgment and common sense when interacting with the Web service. Please contact the Legal Department with any problems or concerns."

Summary

Unaddressed concerns of security, legalities, and privacy could well prove to be show stoppers when implementing a Web business service.

Web management must not only implement a secure service, but must also stay informed on current developments in the areas of workplace privacy, disclosure, and use of information gathered about Web visitors and customers, as well as the legalities of copyrights, trademarks, and patents developed or used in Web content. In this chapter, these issues have been discussed, along with recommendations and suggestions for resolving them.

The next two chapters will show how to pull it all together to provide Web-based internal and external services, such as electronic mail, help desks, electronic commerce, database integration, and catalogs.

CHAPTER 9

Providing Internal Web Business Services

"Uh, oh, my desktop videoconferencing system is on the fritz again,"
grumbled Leslie, thumping the digital camera once more while clicking on
the Help Desk icon. Scanning through the supported products list, she
linked to the database holding the product's current troubleshooting guide
and began the recommended diagnostics. "Hmmm, still isn't working. I'll
fire off an urgent e-mail message to tech support and search the Web for
the vendor's advice." Within seconds the Fremont Help Desk returned her
query with additional diagnostics and the vendor's page provided
model-specific assistance. Performing the steps recommended, her crisp
image appeared once more on screen.

Not one telephone call was made in the above scenario. The Help
Desk was accessed by means of the user's Web browser, the e-mail
message was sent from the same screen, a corporate database was
checked for more information, and a search of the World Wide Web
turned up product-specific information. This is the most compelling
reason to implement Web-based business services for employees—
instant access to relevant, accurate, and useful information anytime,
anywhere, anyplace.

According to a recent study by the Business Research Group, the most common Web-based internal services are document publishing, e-mail, database access, discussion databases, workflow, and transaction processing.

In this chapter, specific examples of internal Web business services, such as e-mail, Help Desk, database integration, employee benefits, and research services, will be explored. For each service, the business drivers and stakeholders will be addressed, citing the benefits of moving to Web-based services. Each service will be reviewed in terms of the essential system requirements, system design, features, and functions to look for; available software and tools; and service output. Examples of these internal services will be also be shown to give the reader a view of what is possible and what has been done by other organizations in providing these internal Web-based services.

Providing E-mail Services

Electronic messaging, or e-mail, is one of the most powerful utilities that the Web business service can offer to its users. E-mail benefits both internal users and external users, such as suppliers, vendors, customers, and other affiliated parties, connecting them in minutes with a rich information-sharing capability.

This section will address providing e-mail as a service integrated with the user's Web browser. This is a very new way to deliver messaging services. Few products exist, and they are not as robust in user features and functionality as traditional standalone messaging systems. They are also lacking in management and administration tools, as well as an integrated directory system.

Existing electronic messaging systems are now quickly moving to integrate Web technology with their own products, in some cases using the Web browser as the front end for the messaging system. We can expect the major messaging players, such as Lotus Notes, Microsoft Exchange, HP Open DeskManager, and Novell GroupWise, to have fully-functional and robust Web-based technology integrated seamlessly with their products in short order.

Traditional messaging systems are typically built as applications that ride on top of the user's hardware platform and/or operating system—for example, cc:Mail for Mac or Microsoft Mail for Windows. Web-based messaging systems use Simple Mail Transfer Protocol (SMTP) on top of the Internet's TCP/IP transport. Most Web browsers will support any messaging system that uses a POP (Post Office Protocol) interface.

BUSINESS DRIVERS AND STAKEHOLDERS

Offering electronic messaging as an integrated part of the Web business service is beneficial in several ways. First, and most importantly, offering e-mail in this manner eliminates the thorny problem of cross-platform compatibility which plagues providers of traditional messaging systems. The second reason is that the learning curve for Web-based applications is significantly shorter than for traditional products. These two benefits mean a sharp reduction in the cost in time, software, hardware, and labor to provide support and training for the product on multiple platforms. A third benefit is that, in most cases, the messaging component is bundled in with the Web browser and is either free or available at a very small cost for the client software.

Another major benefit is the hypertext-linking capability that is inherent with Web-based messaging. The level of sophistication with hyperlinks varies greatly among today's products. The optimal functionality is for any text within the message or attached document that begins with http:, ftp:, mailto:, telnet:, file:, or is an Internet e-mail address (jsmith@xyz.com) to automatically be treated by the messaging system as a hyperlink. Users simply click on the highlighted link and the messaging system will either work through the Web browser to establish a connection with the Web site or Internet service, or it will automatically open a new message with the Internet address inserted in the "To:" field.

Stakeholders in an integrated messaging system would be the users who benefit from the productivity gains experienced in using the system; management, who now has a quick and easy means to notify users of events and to distribute information; and support personnel, who only have to learn and work on one product. Messaging is a great leveler. Anyone can send mail to anyone else who is on the system. This means that a file clerk can send a message to the president of the company. The movement toward the flattening of the organization is enabled by technologies such as electronic messaging.

SERVICE ESSENTIALS

To provide an electronic messaging system as part of the Web business service, the user must have access to a TCP/IP-based local area network running SMTP. The organization will need to establish a messaging server or post office which, if internal messaging alone is desired, would be located inside the firewall. To do this, though, is short-sighted; the users would clamor almost immediately to exchange e-mail with recipients outside the organization. So, it is advisable to establish the messaging server inside the firewall, but provide secure access to the outside world. The service would also require a directory system to hold and manage the addresses and routing information for all users on the system.

SYSTEM DESIGN

Web-based electronic messaging for the Web business clients uses a simple system design. Web browser users are connected by means of their internal network to an e-mail server that is dedicated to the messaging function. This server is the post office from which the user will access the inbox; send, receive and store messages; and perform the other features inherent in the messaging software, such as sorting and filing messages. The messaging system is also connected over the internal network to the internal Web server, enabling the user to click on a hypertext link in the body of the message or document and be automatically connected to the requested Web site or Internet service. Some organizations may want to insert a filter for their messaging between the e-mail server and the firewall to specifically prevent messages from being exchanged with competing firms or other prohibited parties.

A basic system design for a Web-based electronic messaging system is illustrated in Figure 9.1.

FEATURES AND FUNCTIONS

The features and functions included in this section are far more than typically found in any one Web-based electronic messaging product or

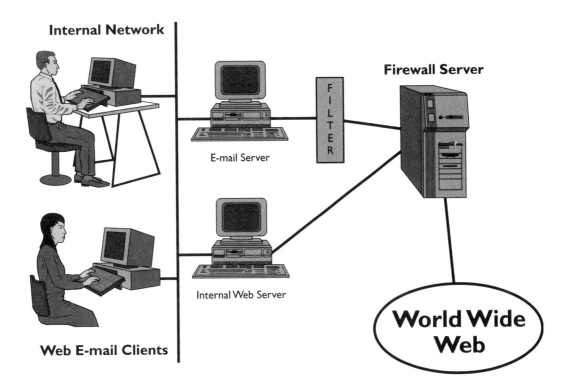

Figure 9.1 System Design for Providing Web-based Electronic Messaging

service. The organization may either elect to use the minimal feature set now contained in the Web-based e-mail products, or they may opt to use a product compatible with their Web browser.

User Interface

- Send mail while using Web browser
- Preview area for scanning inbox messages
- Folders to organize sent, deleted, saved, draft, etc., messages
- Remote capability for modem and network attached users
- Pull-down menus, icons, and toolbars

Message Composition

- Hyperlinks
- Spell-checking

- HTML 2.0 and CGI
- MIME compliant (quoted printable)
- Fonts, text styles and sizes
- Plain text, Rich Text Formatting
- Multiple language support
- Automatic signatures
- Permit attachments—documents, files, and URLs

Mail Addressing

- Simple address structure (jsmith@xyz.com)
- Compose address in "To:" field

Directory

- Integrated directory service
- Directory synchronization with other messaging platforms
- Personal address books
- Distribution lists

Message Management

- Threaded mail messages
- Copy outgoing messages to a folder
- Rules-based messaging management
- Remote diagnostics and troubleshooting
- Standards-based protocols, SMTP, POP3, and SNMP
- Search function
- Sort messages by date, message number, subject, sender, etc.
- Ability to copy messages to a local disk for archiving

Delivery Options

- Check for mail at user defined intervals
- Deferred delivery
- Priorities of urgent, normal, or low

Reply and Forward

- Retain reply address path
- Carbon copy and blind carbon copy
- Reply to all recipients
- Retain forwarding history
- Retain original message in forwarded message

Security

- Password protection
- Access control
- Encryption capability
- Privacy of messages

TOOLS

Basically, all the Web browsers on the market today offer a built-in messaging component (for a list of Web browsers, refer to Chapter 3). Additional products that are plug-compatible with Web browsers (and in most cases with Netscape Navigator, specifically) are included in Table 9.1. New Web-based messaging products are being developed and brought to market literally every day. And traditional vendors are

Table 9.1 Web-based E-mail Application Software		
Product	**Vendor**	**Source**
AlisaMail	Alisa Systems	http://www.alisa.com
cc:Mail for the WWW	Lotus Development Corp.	http://www.lotus.com/ccweb/
Chameleon	Netmanage	http://www.netmanage.com
Eudora Pro	Qualcomm	http://www.qualcomm.com
Microsoft Internet Mail	Microsoft Corp.	http://www.microsoft.com
Netscape Navigator	Netscape	http://www.netscape.com
Simeon	Esys Corporation	http://www.esys.ca/
Solstice Internet Mail	Sunsoft	http://www.sun.com
Z-Mail	Netmanage	http://www.netmanage.com

scurrying to include a Web component in their messaging products. A case in point is Lotus Development Corporation's upcoming release of Lotus Notes V4.5 with messaging, groupware, and Web access—all rolled into the same client. The Web business service management will need to stay up-to-date with this market segment to provide the most advanced messaging services available.

SERVICE OUTPUT

The output for the Web-based messaging service would be an online user guide or tutorial, the messaging traffic, and the repository of user messages, addresses, and routing information.

EXAMPLES

Examples of integrated Web-based electronic messaging are the user interface for Microsoft Internet Mail and Netscape Navigator's e-mail component, shown in Figures 9.2 and 9.3 respectively. Both systems offer a graphical user interface, replete with icons and pull-down menus to speed access to features and functions. Of the two systems, Microsoft offers far more end-user features.

Providing Database Integration Services

Linking the employees to the information locked in the organization's databases and applications is an essential element in leveraging the power of Web technology to provide internal business services. This one service alone establishes interactivity between the user and the organization's repositories. Simply providing static or even dynamic content is not going to be enough over the long term. Users, suppliers, vendors, and customers will all clamor for access to special purpose databases and indices to get information and conduct electronic commerce. They will demand a platform-independent, quick, easy-to-use interface linking to them to distributed information and workgroups. The Web, with its capability of providing simple scripts on HTML pages, will enable this next demand for increased functionality.

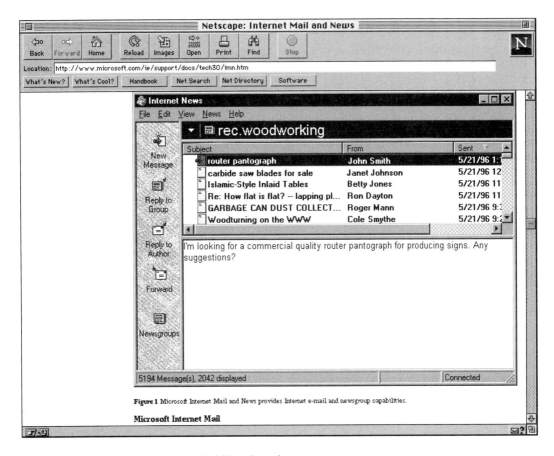

Figure 9.2   Microsoft Internet Mail User Interface

BUSINESS DRIVERS AND STAKEHOLDERS

The most crucial business drivers for providing Web-based database integration services are to give employees access to more than static content, to truly leverage the interactive nature of the Web, and to empower users to search, locate, and retrieve relevant information in the most efficient and cost-effective manner possible. The organization will provide a personal computer platform and operating-system-independent front end to access information stored in multi-vendor databases on multiple computer hardware platforms. All these disparate systems, technologies, and vendors hold separate repositories of data that employees must continually access and mine in order to perform their duties and become more proactive.

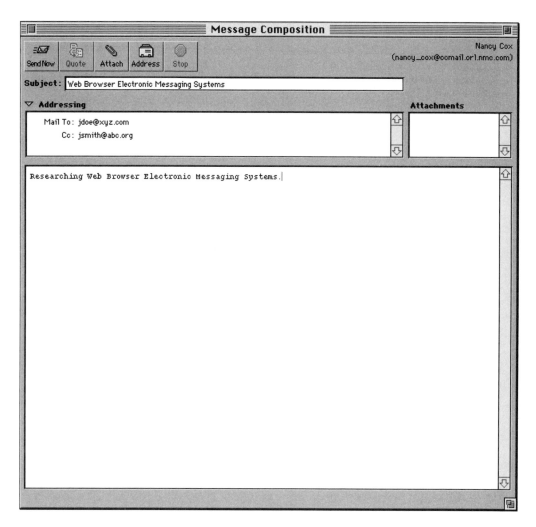

Figure 9.3   Netscape Navigator's E-mail User Interface

The stakeholders in the database integration service are the management chartered with reducing costs and increasing profits by streamlining functions, the information services organization that provides on-going support and maintenance, and the employees who can now quickly and easily use a platform-independent front end to access any legacy data.

SERVICE ESSENTIALS

The basic elements required for a simple database integration service are the Web browser, the internal Web server, a database access server, and the databases themselves, functioning either on servers or mainframes. Since the language of the Web, HTML, does not support the access language of databases, Structured Query Language (SQL), developers will have to use either the Common Gateway Interface (CGI) capability of the Web, or turn to industry-standard Application Programming Interfaces (APIs). Also required is a template or mechanism to format the raw data received from the database into HTML recognizable by the user's Web browser. In some recent products, the Internet Server Application Programming Interface (ISAPI) is supported, which offers faster performance than a CGI script

A much more powerful Web database access server is required to implement integration with existing databases and applications. Heavy traffic will flow through this server constantly as users issue queries and receive the formatted results.

The organization will require personnel with extensive distributed database application development expertise in the company's installed products. Oracle, Sybase, Informix, Ingres, Microsoft Access, FoxPro, Clipper, and PowerBuilder are typical corporate LAN-based database products. Mainframe-based products, such as IMS or DB2, may also exist as legacy systems within the organization and may necessitate additional knowledge in SNA gateways. Expertise in data communications, personal computers, the Internet (HTML, CGI, and HTTP), Structure Query Language (SQL), and Application Program Interfaces (APIs) will also be valuable in providing database integration services.

SYSTEM DESIGN

The system design depicts the user of a Web browser interacting with an area dedicated to database queries. The user interface for this service should be intuitive, offer several easy to use and understand search criteria, and should display the results in a useful and uniform manner. The user issues the query in the Web's native language of HTML. The request is processed by the Web database access server and converted into SQL, the standard database access language. The database server processes the SQL request and responds with the desired raw data. The Web database access server then uses an HTML template to format and return the results in HTML to the user's Web browser.

Security is a fundamental requirement in linking organizational databases and processes to the internal Web business service. Prior to being granted access to the entire process, the user must undergo rigorous security gates, such as access control, authorization, and authentication. Internal Web-based database integration services are located behind the firewall so that no one from the global Internet community may access the organization's guarded and proprietary information.

A basic system design for providing a Web-based database integration service is shown in Figure 9.4.

FEATURES AND FUNCTIONS

Typical features offered in commercially-available Web database integration products and tools include

- HTML, HTTP
- CGI
- ISAPI
- Automatic generation of CGI code
- Convert HTML templates into HTML documents
- Application Programming Interfaces
- Data population and manipulation
- Integrated visual HTML editor
- HTML output functions
- Ad hoc query facility
- Tables
- Cross reference checking between functions and objects
- Visual display of object tree
- User security—authentication, authorization, and access control
- System security—SSL, S-HTTP, S-MIME
- Encryption
- Native SQL drivers for common database systems
- SQL gateways
- SQL, C/C++, or Perl language support
- Software Development Tool Kits

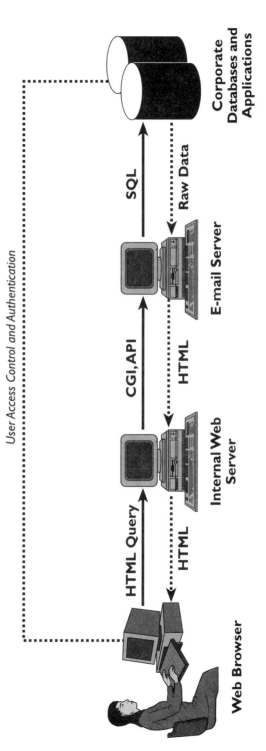

Figure 9.4 System Design of a Web-based Database Integration Service

- Visual development environment
- Add, change, delete hypertext links
- Online tutorials and documentation

TOOLS

Every day major database vendors are announcing the release of new Web components in their traditional products. Start-up companies with both Web and distributed database expertise are launching similar, more streamlined products as well.

A sampling of Web-base database integration software and tools is located in Table 9.2.

Table 9.2 Web-based Database Integration Software and Tools		
Product	Vendor	Source
DB2 WWW Server	IBM	http://www.ibm.com
Electronic Workforce	Edify Corp.	http://www.edify.com
Internet Connection Server	IBM	http://www.ibm.com
Internotes Web Publisher	Lotus	http://www.lotus.com
Java	Sun Microsystems	http://www.sun.com
Netscape LiveWire Pro	Netscape	http://www.netscape.com
OnLine Workgroup	Informix	http://www.informix.com
OneServer	Connect One	http://www.connectinc.com
Sapphire/Web	Bluestone, Inc.	http://www.bluestone.com
Spider	Spider Technologies	http://www.w3spider.com
SQLweb	SQLweb Technologies	http://www.SQLweb.com
WebBase	ExperTelligence	http://www.expertellligence.com
WebConstructor	NeXT	http://www.next.com
Web DataBlade	Illustra Information Technologies	http://www. Illustra.com
WebServer 2.0	Oracle	http://www.oracle com
web.sql	Sybase	http://www.sybase.com

EXAMPLES

Examples of internal Web-based database integration services are located behind the firewall and permit only authorized access. General examples of linking Web technology with the organization's databases include

- Retirement and financial planning
- Changing 401K allocation percentages
- Performing "what if" analyses
- Ordering hardware, software, and supplies
- Checking inventory levels
- Time reporting
- Travel authorizations
- Tuition reimbursement

SERVICE OUTPUT

The output of a Web-based database integration service would be the formatted results of the user's queries against the legacy databases and statistical reports used for traffic analysis, billing, chargeback, and trending analyses.

Providing Help Desk Services

A Help Desk (also called an Information Center or Resource Center) provides end user support and services. Help Desks provide a single point of contact to assist users in resolving problems and in providing information on events and products. Help Desks may also regularly survey their users in an effort to continually improve service quality.

The traditional Help Desk function can be radically optimized by the use of Web-based technology. The Help Desk services discussed in this section are those provided to the internal users of the Web business service. A distinction here is made between Help Desk and Customer Support services, in that the former are geared toward internal employees and the latter are primarily intended for external clients and users of the organization's information, products, and/or services. Web-based Customer Support services will be explored in Chapter 10.

In the not so distant past, problems were resolved by a user calling the Help Desk during business hours, waiting for the call to be answered, talking with a service representative, and then either having the problem resolved while still on the telephone, or being referred to the next line of more experienced help. Users generally spent a very long time on hold, waiting for assistance, even though sophisticated call-processing equipment was invariably installed to reduce wait times.

This process differs drastically today with the advent of Web-based Help Desk technology. The Help Desk is now available for user query 24 hours a day, 7 days a week. User involvement in the problem reporting and resolution process is now vastly streamlined. The Web assists the support staff by off-loading the simpler, more commonly-reported problems to the Help Desk's home page. The user may now browse the Help Desk's Frequently Asked Questions (FAQ) information, product data sheets, technical brochures, reference library, etc.; be advised of system outages or maintenance and downtime schedules by a blinking area on the screen; or consult the product or service's online product manual or user guide. The user may electronically log the problem, get a bug fix, patch, or the newest software version by simply clicking on the download icon on the Help Desk's page. The user may also send an electronic mail message to those technicians with the desired product expertise listed on the home page. In most cases, the user will resolve the problem, either alone or by means of e-mail, without ever making the first phone call.

BUSINESS DRIVERS AND STAKEHOLDERS

The new Web-based Help Desk services have several benefits. Telephone support personnel, equipment, and time is greatly reduced. Faster response times can now be provided for commonly-asked questions. The Web technology provides transparent and secure access to a database of a company's technical problem and resolution information. Product and service information can quickly be kept up-to-date and accurate. In addition, users may also add helpful information to the Help Desk FAQ and lessons learned repository. The Help Desk can now offer remote users the ability to instantly be in touch with the support services of the organization from any location where Internet access is possible. The organization can now also offer multi-platform support due to the nature of the Web browser software. The Web-based Help Desk is an excellent place to gather feedback information or to conduct user surveys. The output of these surveys, along with the Web site statistics gathered, enable an organization to analyze trends and become more proactive in assisting end users with their products and services.

Stakeholders in a Web-based Help Desk would be primarily the user support and internal marketing organizations. Their budgets to provide support could be reduced by implementing the new technology, and the users would receive faster and more accurate assistance in resolving their problems.

SERVICE ESSENTIALS

To provide a Web-based Help Desk, the organization will need to implement a Web page or site for the service and publicize its URL by traditional internal means of communication such as company newsletters, bulletin board notifications, or electronic mail.

The service must have an access flow chart that cites the various ways a user will interact with the Web Help Desk and flow through the site. Procedures must be established to handle users who are unable to have their problems resolved at the Web Help Desk. A logical flow must be defined—from initial contact at the Web Help Desk, to calling a service representative, to having the problem logged and referred to the next level of technical help.

The service must place FAQ on the site and keep them up to date. The service must also provide a way for the user to submit their own information for the FAQ. This may be done by means of an e-mail message sent to the content owner or by filling out a keyword form on the Web page that directs the information to the FAQ database to be automatically placed in the proper location. The service must also place and keep current product, service, event, and technical information on the site.

The service should also provide online tutorials, an area for new users, a "What's New" section, a list of supported hardware and software, a search facility, and contact information for users who want to talk with someone in person about their problem.

The Help Desk will also need the expertise of the Web business service to design, implement, and maintain the system if the operation has no one on their staff with its ability.

More sophisticated Help Desk operations may also wish to implement a software program that uses Web technology to provide the services. These tools are shown in Table 9.3.

Table 9.3   Web-based Help Desk and Customer Support Tools

Product	Vendor	Platforms Supported	Source	Cost
Apriori Hands-Free	Answer Systems Lab	DOS, Win 3.1, Win NT, Mac, OS/2, UNIX	http://www.answer.com	Commercial $10,000 per server
CA-Netman	Computer Associates	Various	http://www.cai.com	Commercial
CalTraker	2020 Solutions	DOS, Win	http://www.scsn.net	Commercial
ClearWeb	Clarify, Inc.	Sybase, Oracle	http://www.clarify.com	Commercial $7,500+
HelpSTAR for Windows	Help Desk Technology	Win	http://www.helpstar.com	Commercial
PowerHelp	Astea International	DOS, Win	http://www.astea.com	Commercial
Action Request System	Remedy Corp.	Various	http://www.remedy.com	Commercial
Scopus	Scopus Technology, Inc.	UNIX	http://scopus.com	Commercial
Silknet Support Expert	Silknet Software, Inc.	Win 3.1, Win NT	http://www.silknet.com	Commercial $2,000
VanWeb	Vantive Corp.	UNIX	http://www.vantive.com	Commercial $25,000 per server
WebAdvisor	ServiceSoft	Various	http://www.servicesoft.com	Commercial
WebQ, HelpQ, CustomerQ	Quintas Corp.	UNIX	http://www.quintas.com	Commercial $15,000 ?

SYSTEM DESIGN

Basically, the internal users of the Web-based Help Desk will access the site through their internal network. There they will peruse the site's home page, moving by means of icons and hyperlinks to areas of interest. Access may be given to relevant corporate databases which may contain up-to-the-minute information, such as technical product specifications, lists of supported hardware and software along with current prices, etc. In reality, the Help Desk site could reside on the same server as the internal Web site, if the activity is expected to be light. Typical reasons for maintaining a separate Web site for the Help Desk include heavy traffic, gathering separate usage statistics, having one content owner administer and maintain the site, and heavily-used links to service representatives.

A rather simple design for a Web-based Help Desk service is shown in Figure 9.5.

FEATURES AND FUNCTIONS

Typical features and functions offered with a Web-based Help Desk service include

- call tracking
- problem routing
- suggesting solutions
- reporting
- trouble ticketing
- intelligent query and search engines
- key word, subject, or synonym searches
- database integration
- converting documents to HTML on the fly
- inventory management
- diagnostic techniques
- training
- source code
- security

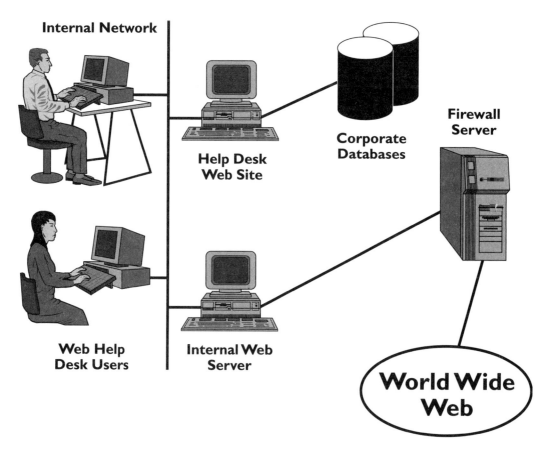

Figure 9.5   System Design for a Web-based Help Desk Service

TOOLS

Several new Help Desk and Customer Support software products are now on the market. These examples contain software for call tracking and call management, as well as for Web-based Help Desk functions. A sample of those available appears in Table 9.3.

EXAMPLES

Most Help Desks are internal services and, as such, are located behind the organization's firewall. Therefore, finding examples will be difficult. However, an example of a Web-based Help Desk service may be found at the University of Alberta's Computing and Network Services home page at http://www.ualberta.ca/HELP/, as shown in Figure 9.6. This page has buttons for all the major Help Desk-oriented services provided, including online tutorials, an area for new users, FAQs, a search utility, and a suggestion box. The page also, and rightly so, refers the user to a live service representative and gives the contact information up front.

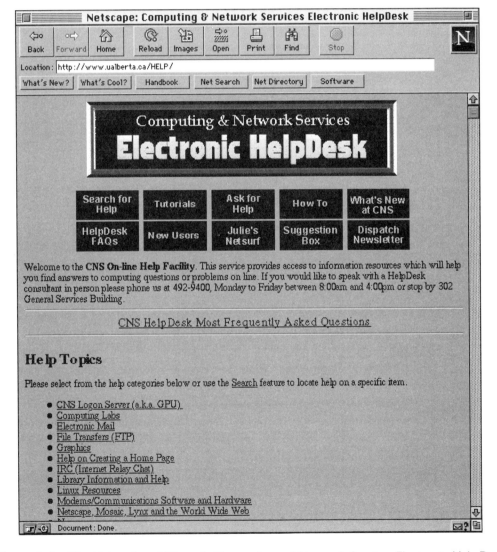

Figure 9.6   The University of Alberta's Computing and Network Services Electronic Help Desk

SERVICE OUTPUT

The output for the Help Desk service would be the database of problems logged and their resolutions. The service would also provide as output the Frequently Asked Questions information and a lessons learned area, both accepting user contributions. The service would also output information to management, such as the amount of traffic the Help Desk experienced, the busy hours, who the users were, what hardware platform and browser they were using, and when they accessed the system. Management would also be able to determine how much time and money was saved by using the new Web-based technology by analyzing usage statistics and comparing them with their traditional telephone support service.

Providing Employee Benefits Services

Web-based employee benefits services enable the organization to unleash the power of Web technology for a three-way gain: for management, for the employees, and for Plan Administrators, Fund Managers, and other third parties. A comprehensive Web-based employee benefits service empowers the employee to quickly access vital information and make decisions, the providers and administrators to access current and accurate information about the employees to more effectively and efficiently administer their plans, and the management to lower the costs of providing and administering benefits. Employees will know—in most cases for the first time—exactly what benefits they have and how much the company is paying for them. Providing this level of information to the employees may lead to more appreciation of the contribution borne by the company, may improve their morale, and may lead to less turnover in the organization.

Web-based employee benefits services lower costs by reducing the number of personnel required to answer telephone calls and respond in writing to employee and plan requests.

The time it normally takes to complete a benefit transaction will be greatly reduced with the use of Web technology. From the initial filing of the claim to the flowdown of the funds to the plan participant or sponsor, cycle times will be shortened considerably—in some cases up to 30 days sooner.

The number of human errors in rekeying plan information is greatly reduced, since information is submitted electronically and remains that way for the entire benefit process. Faulty record-keeping and inaccurate compliance results are reduced or eliminated with the Web-based service.

Authorized users of the service may view contributions and fund dollars and may explore "what if" scenarios to make better decisions regarding their benefits, loan repayments, and fund allocation percentage changes.

BUSINESS DRIVERS AND STAKEHOLDERS

The business drivers for offering a Web-based employee benefits service absolutely is the reduction in the cost to provide accurate current information, the increased responsiveness of the benefits organization, and the enhanced quality of service offered to the employees. Employees have instant, 24-hour-a-day access to current information on their benefits, rates, and schedules.

Another important driver for the benefits industry as a whole is that, with Web technology, the input received by the plan administrators and other third parties will arrive in a consistent manner and be uniform in format. Since the inception of the 401K plans, corporations have been submitting their data to the plan sponsors in a variety of ways, such as paper, electronic spreadsheets, tapes, etc. Web services will not only reduce the amount of paper handled by everyone involved, but will provide consistency of input and media of exchange.

Stakeholders in the service include management, the employees, the external benefits providers, and plan administrators.

SERVICE ESSENTIALS

To provide a simple employee benefits service—one that enables an employee to view a summary of their current benefit selection—

requires software running on the Web-server and an API or mechanism to access the corporate databases for up-to-the-minute, accurate information. Integration with the corporation's personnel and benefits databases is essential to providing the enhanced level of a benefits service to employees.

The service also requires a high level of security for the employees implemented by means of access control, authentication, and authorization mechanisms.

Typical employee benefit services that lend themselves to Web-based technology include

- Benefits statements customized for each employee
- Retirement and pension plans
- 401K plans
- Medical, vision, and dental plans
- Life insurance plans
- Disability plans
- Elder and child care benefit plans
- Health care reimbursement accounts
- Dependent care reimbursement accounts
- Education assistance and tuition reimbursement
- Employee assistance programs
- Family resource services
- Adoption assistance
- Projected Social Security
- Electronic Funds Transfer of benefit payouts
- Participant contributions and fund dollars
- Contribution allocation percentages
- "What if" scenarios and analyses—percentage changes and future value analysis to assist employees in meeting their personal financial goals
- Prescription drug ordering, payment, and delivery tracking
- Non-contribution employee data, such as hire date, birth date, salary, etc.

The benefits service home page should contain telephone and mail contact information or a hyperlink to a benefits specialist for each of the benefit plans and services offered. This enables the user who cannot resolve a benefits-oriented problem or desires more information to contact a human for assistance. The page should provide a secure hyperlink to the employee's own current benefits selections. The page should also provide hot button access to all the employee benefits provided by the organization. Summary information should include the carriers and costs of the plans, as well as co-payment or 80/20 contribution information and when coverage or contributions begin and end. Additional human resources-type information will also find a home here, such as the following:

- Sick leave
- Personal, family, bereavement, and sabbatical leave
- Jury duty
- Overtime pay policies
- Labor grades and salary ranges
- Vacation
- Holiday schedules
- Bonus and incentive plans
- Stock purchase and option plans
- Automatic paycheck deposit
- Savings bonds and charitable donations information and applications
- Credit union, check cashing, and ATM services

The benefits home page should also state the percentage of pay that is associated with the provision of benefits; for example, "XYZ Company spends another 40% on top of your compensation on your benefits."

To provide employee benefits services on the higher and more complex end of the scale requires more sophisticated software on the Web server and more database integration. The organization may want to enable their insurance providers, pension plan administrators, 401K administrators, prescription drug providers, etc., to have access to employee information. In this case, access would be given through the public Web server located outside the firewall. The provider or other third party would be issued the proper authorization and authentication mechanisms to access the organization's databases. Security for transactions and queries is of the utmost importance for this service. Security for most systems uses Secure Sockets Layer (SSL), Secure Hypertext Transport Protocol (S-HTTP), Secure Multipurpose Internet Mail Extensions (S-MIME), or a combination of all three to achieve the proper level of security for these types of transactions.

SYSTEM DESIGN

A basic system design for providing a Web-based employee benefits service is shown in Figure 9.7. The employee would access the internal Web server by means of his or her internal network. There, the employee would locate the icon or hyperlink for the benefits home page. This home page could be on the same server—if the organization is small and traffic is light—or it could be located on a separate server managed by the Human Resources or Benefits department. Extensive integration with the organization's personnel and benefits databases is essential to offering a high level of value for the employees. Also, granting the benefits providers access to authorized employee information extends the usefulness of the service for both employee and provider.

FEATURES AND FUNCTIONS

The organization will determine the level of Web-based benefit services that can be provided with the available funding, expertise, and time. The list below includes more features than the typical mid-sized organization may be able to offer. The enterprise should use this list as a guide, selecting those features and functions that can be provided within the firm's constraints. The features and functions most useful to incorporate into a comprehensive Web-based employee benefits service include

- Interactive query engine
- E-mail integration—SMTP
- Electronic Funds Transfer capability
- Payroll interface (ASCII file data or from third party such as ADP, CDC, etc.)
- Automatic computation of FICA taxes, Worker's Compensation, Federal and State Unemployment, and State disability premiums
- Handling of simple and complex calculations

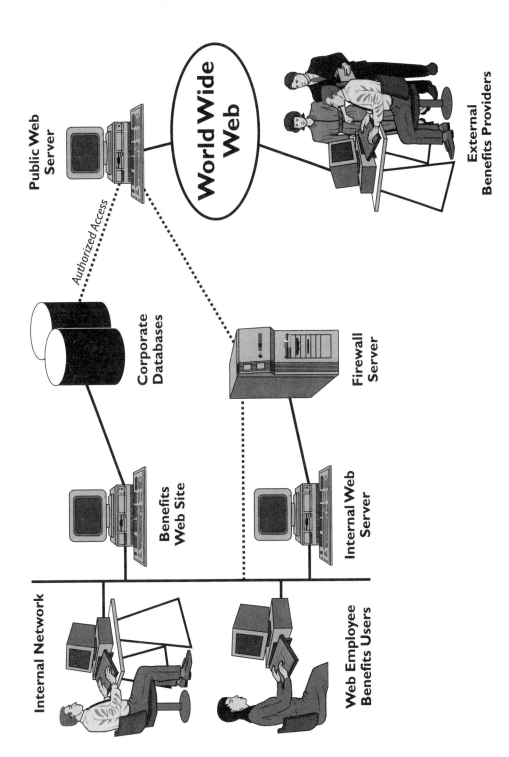

Figure 9.7 System Design for Web-based Employee Benefits Services

- Statement default templates
- Ability to customize benefits summaries or statements
- Text editing, spell check, and graphic support
- Multiple language support
- FTP transfer capability
- Bulletin board system
- Security—SSL, S-HTTP, S-MIME, encryption, data integrity, etc.
- Online Help and tutorial
- Vendor support services
- Backup and recovery
- Archiving

TOOLS

The Web-based employee benefit arena is so new that few commercial software and tools are currently on the market. Look for this area to expand as more corporate intranets are implemented, and benefit providers, management, and employees recognize the potential for Web-based services. The Web business service management will need to keep well informed on this subject, since providing even a small amount of benefits information to employees is a quick and easy service to offer and one that gives a healthy return to the organization.

A selection of benefits software and tools is shown in Table 9.4.

Two other sources on providing a Web-based employee benefit service can be found at Benefits Link (http://www.benefitslink.com/) and Employee Benefits Infosource (http://www.ifebp.org/icebinfo.html).

Table 9.4	Web-based Employee Benefit Software and Tools	
Product	**Vendor**	**Source**
FringeFacts	Benefit Software, Inc.	http://www.bsiweb.com/bsi-ff.htm
SmartForms	Smart Forms, Inc.	http://www.smartforms.com
SrsNetLink	Through the Looking Glass Software, Inc.	http://www.wolfenet.com/~hlgs

EXAMPLES

As with Web-based internal Help Desks, employee benefits systems using Web technology are also located behind the organization's firewall, making them difficult to access and view. A few examples of very robust employee benefit Web sites may be found at Smart Forms (http://www.emi.net/~smart/benenet.html and in Figure 9.8), Verity,

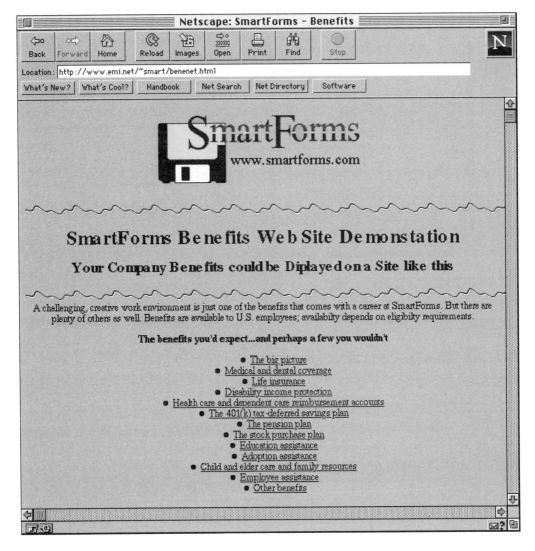

Figure 9.8   SmartForms Benefits Web Site Demonstration

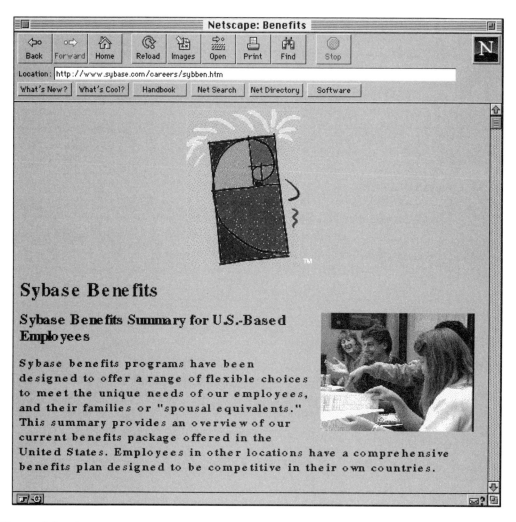

Figure 9.9   Sybase Employee Benefits Home Page

Inc. (http://www.verity.com/JOBS/benefits.html), and Sybase, Inc. (http://www.sybase.com/careers/sybben.htm and in Figure 9.9)

SERVICE OUTPUT

Output from this service may be quite voluminous. Employees will be able to see in an instant their current benefits selection, the status of their 401K plan, their pension summary, claim status, and deductible status on various plans such as medical, vision, dental, etc.

Providing Research Services

Instant access to information is a fundamental attribute of the Web business service. As such, the organization will want to provide research services to its employees. These services may be either mining the organization's own databases and processes for critical information or using a mix of free and commercial external Internet search services.

The Web business service should implement a Web-based search capability that offers a consistent user interface to a variety of internal and external information sources, flexible and intuitive search syntax, and filtering of search results. All these features are productivity-enhancing, time-saving, and profit-increasing mechanisms for the users of the research service.

BUSINESS DRIVERS AND STAKEHOLDERS

The primary business driver for providing a Web-based research service is to enable employees to quickly and efficiently locate information anywhere, anytime, anyplace. Only by obtaining relevant information in time can employees make better and more cost-effective decisions.

The stakeholders in the research service would be the management who, by offering the service, will reduce the costs of information access by providing users with a consistent interface, of consolidating search tools and engines, and of distributing information by offering the electronic return of results. The users are stakeholders in that they will benefit from reducing the learning curve to master a new interface and from getting faster, more relevant, and workable results from their queries.

SERVICE ESSENTIALS

A Web-based research service will typically offer basic storage, retrieval, caching, filtering, indexing, and Web crawling capabilities. These search services will be brought to bear on a variety of organizational and special-purpose databases, processes, indices, and search services. A consistent user interface to all search engines, databases, processes, and network connectivity is also essential.

The organization will require the technical expertise of personnel skilled in databases, APIs, Internet search technology, data communications, client software, and user interfaces.

SYSTEM DESIGN

Two key elements of a system for the research service include the consistent user search interface and access to search services, databases, and indices—both internal and external to the organization. The end user will access the uniform user interface through their Web browser and will perform searches using their internal network and the Internet as transports. The search engine, meta-service, Web crawling, and indexing software may need to reside on a separate server, depending on the amount of traffic expected, the level of cache supported, and the size of the index. As intranets continue to be implemented and flourish within organizations, more divisions will be establishing their own pages, which will also be listed in the search indexes.

A basic system design for a Web-based research service is depicted in Figure 9.10.

FEATURES AND FUNCTIONS

Typical features and functions to buy or build into a Web-based research service include

- Graphical and consistent user interface
- Interactive query engine
- Enhanced caching capabilities
- Customizable queries
- Query entry box
- Expert search options
- Rules, agents, and filters
- Intuitive and flexible query syntax
- Fuzzy searches
- Multiple keyword parameters
- Keyword, date, phrase, subject, image, object, etc., search parameters
- Required and non-desired keywords

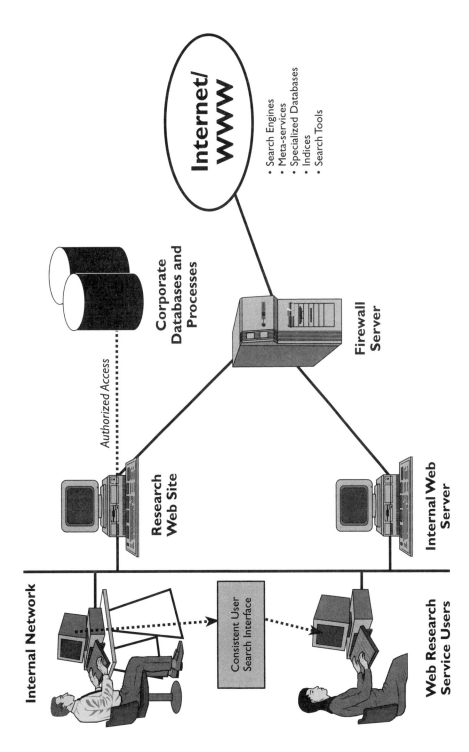

Figure 9.10 System Design for a Web-based Research Service

- Indexing
- Reference and results filtering
- Interactivity with specialized databases and indices, such as The Internet Movie Database and Usenet news
- Collating, analysis, post-processing, and sorting of results
- Confidence scores
- References to related or similar pages
- Scheduled queries for "What's New" on specified sites
- Link pre-display verification
- Least cost routing to external search engines
- Statistics gathering for accounting, billing, and trending analysis
- Performance measurement
- Logging
- Privacy

TOOLS

The enterprise providing internal research services with access to their own corporate databases and processes may use any one of a number of commercial and freeware Web crawling, indexing, searching, storage, and retrieval software products and tools to build the service. The organization may also provide internal employees access through their Web browser to external search services and tools (such as those listed in Table 9.5) plus access to free, traditional Internet search resources like gopher, Archie, Veronica, Jughead, WHOIS, and WAIS.

The downside to providing access to multiple external search services is that all of them have a different user interface—with various search rules and parameters—and have knowledge of only a portion of the Web. This forces the user to conduct searches on different services and receive search results that often are irrelevant, outdated, or have broken hyperlinks. A new brand of search engine called a meta-service is now being developed and either brought to market or provided free of charge. The MetaCrawler is a free search service and resolves most of these issues by providing a consistent interface with access to all the major Web search engines, sending queries to multiple search engines simultaneously, collating and filtering results, and verifying links. Other similar meta-services are shown in Table 9.6.

Table 9.5 External Search Services and Tools	
External Search Service	**Source**
All in One Internet Search Page	http://www.albany.net/~wcross/alllsrch.html
Alta Vista	http://www.altavista.digital.com
Configurable Universal Search Interface	http://pubweb.nexor.co.uk/public/cusi/cusi.html
Excite!	http://www.excite.com
Galaxy	http://galaxy.einet.net/www/www.html
InfoSeek	http://infoseek.com
Inktomi	http://inktomi.berkley.edu
LEXIS-NEXIS	http://www.lexis-nexis.com
Lycos	http://www.lycos.com
Magellan	http://www.mckinley.com
Open Text Web Index	http://www.opentext.com:8080/omw.html
Personal Library Software	http://www.pls.com
Verity	http://www.verity.com
W3 Search Engines	http://cuiwww.unige.ch/meta-index.html
WebCrawler	http://www.webcrawler.com
Web Search	http://www.web-search.com
Yahoo!	http://yahoo.com

EXAMPLES

Accessing any of the search services in Table 9.6 will give the reader an excellent sampling of the creativity, pizzaz, search criteria, and search results formatting found in a typical external search service. An example of a commercial search service, InfoSeek, is illustrated in Figure 9.11.

SERVICE OUTPUT

The primary output of the research service is the result of the user's query. These results may be sorted, rated, filtered, and otherwise massaged to reduce the typically voluminous response to something relevant and useful by the user. The user will receive a listing of results,

Table 9.6 Meta-services

Product	Vendor	Source
Harvest	Harvest Brokers	http://town.hall.org/Harvest/brokers/www-home-pages/
infoMarket	IBM	http://www.infomkt.ibm.com
Internet Softbot	Oren Etzioni	http://www.cs.washington.edu/research/softbots
JavaCrawler	Brian Pinkerton	http://webcrawler.com
MetaCrawler	Brian Pinkerton	http://webcrawler.com
Multithreaded Query Page	Sun Microsystems	http://www.sun.com/cgi-bin/show?search/mtquery/index.body
SavvySearch	Daniel Dreilinger	http://www.cs.colostate.edu/~dreilling/smartform.html
WebCompass	Quarterdeck	http://www.qdeck.com

along with their URLs. Service output also includes statistics gathered for trending purposes and for accounting and billing.

Summary

Providing efficient, feature-rich and reliable internal Web-based services fuels the massive growth in corporate intranets. All the services discussed in this chapter—e-mail, database integration, Help Desk, benefits, and research—bring tremendous returns on investment, plus the intangible benefits of productivity increases, improved response times, and better dissemination and use of information. All of these services—while not entirely simple to implement and maintain—are, after all, much less complicated, labor intensive, and costly than providing separate services by traditional means.

In the next chapter, we will explore leveraging the power of Web-based technology to implement external services aimed at breaking down the traditional barriers between an organization and its suppliers and customers. External Web services, such as marketing communications and electronic commerce, will enable the organization to become much more visible and, therefore, more of a known and recognizable entity to customers worldwide.

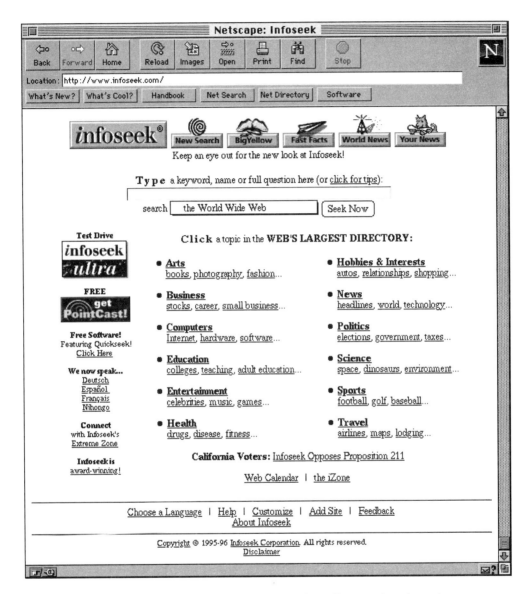

Figure 9.11   Home Page for InfoSeek Search Service (http://www.infoseek.com)

Providing External Web Business Services

"Our new online commerce system for the travel agencies has really paid off!" reported Sidney at Fremont's weekly staff meeting. "They can make reservations at any of the theme park hotels and receive discount park admission tickets for their clients—all in a matter of seconds. Plus, this new promotion we've got going with AnyWhere Airlines means that an agent can book a flight and automatically get the third night's stay free. This combination has jumped our revenue forecast for the month of September to 20% more than the same time last year."

Commerce in cyberspace is the new paradigm for the cashless society. People and businesses will come to live in the online market economy by searching for, locating, purchasing, and paying for goods and services electronically, without any paper or hard currency exchanged. Electronic commerce for business to business transactions has been around for several years, especially in the transportation, pharmaceutical, and retail industries. Only since the opening of the Internet to the commercial consumer—an individual using a Web browser—has the notion of universal electronic commerce coalesced.

In this chapter we will explore providing services to the external Web community, electronic commerce for business-to-business transactions, catalog services for individuals, customer service for users of the organization's products and services, and marketing communications services for online public relations and brand recognition. Offering external services to the global Internet community interactively bridges the gap between the organization and the individual.

Providing Catalog Services

Small and large businesses, as well as non-profit organizations and the government, are rapidly deploying Web-based catalog services to quickly and easily place information about their products and services in the hands of their target consumers. Organizations are realizing much shorter order fulfillment cycles, improving cash flow, increasing the number of inventory turns, and reducing the costs of carrying inventory and supporting the entire order process.

Many catalogs are now available on the Web. In fact, catalogs of catalogs—"meta-catalogs"—are now springing up, in which the content of a number of different catalogs are reviewed and listed for online ordering. Catalogs are using the most enhanced software available for the Web, including Java and VRML (Virtual Reality Markup Language). Catalog service providers are also becoming widely available.

In this section we will discuss catalog services that appeal to the individual consumer. In the next section, "Providing Electronic Commerce Services," we will explore business-to-business transactions and services.

BUSINESS DRIVERS AND STAKEHOLDERS

Web-based catalogs offer many drivers for the business. In addition to the ability to immediately reduce the cost of printing, storing, and distributing print catalogs, the target market for the catalog swells to the entire Internet community—over 30 million subscribers. Plus, the catalog service is available 24 hours per day, seven days per week across all the times zones, from anywhere in the world. Several other stunning benefits accrue to the organization in providing Web-based product catalog services.

- **Low service start-up costs**—The actual expense for setting up a Web-based catalog service is far less than launching a traditional print catalog service.

- **Fast, cost-effective changes**—The organization will be able to make modifications to any detail of the catalog—price, description, availability, etc.—quickly, easily, and at a much-reduced cost than modifying traditional print media. The electronic catalog can be maintained and dynamically updated from source data.

- **Searchable content**—Users have the ability to perform rapid searches on the catalog content. They may use an intuitive search engine to locate items or information by category, keywords, phrases, price, etc. Searches can be extended across all of the organization's catalogs for a specific item by automatically taking the customer to the other catalog or displaying a hypertext link.

- **Multimedia content**—Online catalogs provide a more robust assortment of multimedia content than traditional print media. Audio, video, animation, 3-D graphics, and virtual reality provide a much richer experience for the customer.

- **Customer information**—The organization can collect a wealth of information about the customer, including buying habits, preferences, sizes, etc.

- **Increased accuracy**—Support staff will no longer have to re-key order information from paper forms, reducing the number of input errors.

- **Changes in customer information**—The organization can be immediately informed of changes in their customer base, such as a move, new phone number, etc., by integrating the catalog service with electronic mail.

- **Immediate order and credit card processing**—The online catalog provides the ability for a customer to quickly place and order and have their credit card authorized for the sale.

The stakeholders in the Web-based catalog service include management, customer service, inventory control, accounting, shipping, and the customers themselves. Management will reap the benefits of a reduced cycle time and improved cash flow; customer service will have more time to process non-electronic orders and answer questions; and inventory control, accounting, and shipping will turn over product faster with the direct links into the Web-based ordering system, have more timely and accurate information, and reduce the amount of time to deliver the product to the customer.

Catalog Service Providers

Catalog Service Providers (CSPs) will develop your catalog for a fee and either deliver the finished product to your Web server or run your catalog on their Web server. If the CSP hosts your catalog service, they will typically charge you a fixed amount per day per catalog item. Each item would have its own home page, making changes faster and easier, improving the statistics gathering of hits on the page and orders placed, etc. The CSP will also charge you to make changes to your catalog and may offer a volume discount if changes are expected to be heavy. Some services will enable you, for a monthly fee, to connect to the CSP's server and make the changes yourself. This capability requires you to have secure Web access to the CSP's server and an easy-to-use change process. Some CSPs will also give you the ability to run your catalog off-line for security reasons. Catalogs may also be downloaded to the user, or the users may request that a diskette or CD-ROM version of the catalog be sent to them.

Service Essentials

Security is perhaps the most essential ingredient for a successful Web-based catalog service. The catalog server should be placed in front of the firewall to protect the organization's network from security breaches. Placing the catalog service with a service provider is also an option for improved security. The customer must be informed on the order page that the transaction they are about to perform is secure. A notation that "this site is protected by SSL" or "secure keyboard capability is available" ensure that the customer will be comfortable and willing to use a credit card online for the transaction. Much work is underway among the major credit card companies to create a standard for the use of credit cards on the Internet. The Web business service management needs to keep informed on this subject to provide the most secure environment possible for the catalog service.

The Web server for the online catalog service needs to be sized appropriately for the amount of traffic and file downloads anticipated.

In addition to the static item description pages, the service must offer an intuitive and very effective search capability; indexing, sorting, storing and retrieval of information; and different order options, such as by mail, fax, phone, or e-mail with associated links or telephone numbers.

Components of a Good Online Catalog

A useful and snappy online catalog has only a few components, but they are essential in providing the customer with an easy-to-use interface. A catalog should open with a simple home page, using either an image map or icons for the links. The page should include a What's New area, an area describing the company with perhaps a message from the president, and links to the broad, overall categories covered by the catalog, such as "apparel, electronics, appliances" or "products, support, services." The page should include a "search" button to enable the customer to quickly find an item in the entire catalog. The home page should be fairly uncluttered, the objective being to get the customer immediately deeper into the Web site.

It is preferable if each item has it's own page, but if that is impractical or too costly, then grouping similar items on one page is acceptable. The item page should contain an image and any information that the customer will need to purchase the product, such as a concise description, sizes, colors, styles, price, etc. Each item page should have a "go back" to the previous page link, a "go Home" link, a "go to Index" link, a "search" link, a "review order" button, a "delete item from order" button, and an "add to order" button. This last button automatically adds the selected item on the page to the "shopping basket" or list of items purchased, the order form that the customer selects at the end of the session. A catalog could also feature a running total for all the items selected, "your order now totals $67.83."

Components of a Good Online Order Form

As with the catalog in general, there are just a few elements in a good online order form, but they are critical to the ability of the customer to place an order. The form may be organized into three areas: the basics, the pizzazz, and the links.

The Basics

Each order form must collect the same basic type of information about the customer and the order. Customer information such as first name, last name, address, city, state, country, zip, telephone number, fax number, and e-mail address is essential. This information is there for the person who is placing the order, and it may differ from the "ship to" or "bill to" information. Also essential to collect from business people is the company name, type of business, title, mail stop, business telephone number, fax number and e-mail address when they order information on products, technical specifications, training CD-ROMs, and the like.

Essential order information to collect include the item number, brief description, quantity, price, extended price, sub-total, shipping charges, local sales tax information, and total order amount, as shown in Table 10.1. The form elements of "sales tax" and "shipping" would be taken from a small table located near the form.

The billing information should contain the method of payment, either by credit card or by electronic funds transaction like "E-Cash." The input screen should list the credit cards that the company takes, plus fields for the name as it appears on the card and the expiration

Table 10.1 Sample Basic Online Order Form				
Item Number	Description	Quantity	Price	Extended Price
A-1245	Sun glasses	1	$87.00	$87.00
G-4567	Beach umbrella	1	$39.95	$39.95
H-7891	Beach towels	2	$19.95	$39.90
			Sub Total:	$166.85
			FL St. Sales Tax (6%)	$10.01
			Shipping	$2.85
			Order Total	$179.71

date. Alternate payment options may be specified on the order form, such as by mail or by telephone.

Other essential elements on this page are "change order," "clear," and "submit" buttons. A notation as to the amount of time to allow for product delivery such as "Allow 6 weeks for order to be processed," will reduce the number of customers calling to verify that an order has been shipped.

The Pizzazz

Now for a little sizzle. In designing online forms, the more you can do for your customer, the quicker the order will be placed. This means automatically entering a selected item on the order form, keeping a running total of the order, providing the ability to review the order from any page, and performing all the necessary calculations to complete the "order total" field. For example, the "sales tax" and "shipping" fields would automatically be completed based on the customer's entry in the "State" field and on the total order amount.

The customer's credit card should automatically be authorized, either by the organization in the case of in-house accounts, or by direct link with a verification service.

Other services to offer include the ability to provide additional comments or instructions, to send the item as a gift to a third party with a personalized gift card, to request gift wrapping, or to send to an alternate shipping address.

Many companies are also collecting more information from the customer at this point, such as what browser they are using, what connection speed, if they have a CD-ROM drive, what interest areas they have, or how often they use the product or service. This information, along with buying habits, will be used to tailor future marketing efforts to that customer.

The Links

To expedite the order process, the order form should contain the telephone number of the organization's Customer Service department and at least the following links:

- Search
- E-mail to WebMaster
- Price list

- Other catalogs
- Organization's home page

Online Order Flow

A customer must be able to move through the online catalog just as effortlessly as if flipping the pages in a print edition. The way that a catalog site is structured is crucial to the ability of the customer to navigate successfully and quickly. The organization should map out the anticipated path a customer will take through the site to pinpoint any additional links or information a customer would require to complete the order. In other words, many dry runs of the entire order process—from the initial entry into the catalog's home page to clicking on the submit button—are essential to build an efficient and sales-producing catalog. Each page must give the customer the ability to search, move forward and backward, review the order, select an item, go to the index, and go to the home page. The order, when completed and submitted, should be confirmed to the customer, preferably by e-mail.

After the catalog is placed into service, the statistics gathered on how many times a particular page was accessed by a customer will be used in establishing trending information and in determining where another link or search option needs to be placed. It is advisable to periodically review the flow of the catalog to ensure that all the customer's needs are being addressed and to look for enhancement opportunities.

SYSTEM DESIGN

The system design, as shown in Figure 10.1, is fairly straightforward for a catalog service. The organization may want to offer very basic services or to enhance the online order process by performing calculations for the customer, automatic fill-in of certain fields, etc. The organization may also want to have the information updated dynamically from source data found in corporate databases. Links to inventory control are another enhancement that will enable the customer to know immediately if the item is in stock. Accounting interfaces to the general ledger or accounts receivable systems reduce the number of manual input errors. Customer buying habits, preferences, and other information can be stored in the organization's databases to provide statistical information for the sales and marketing department's use in

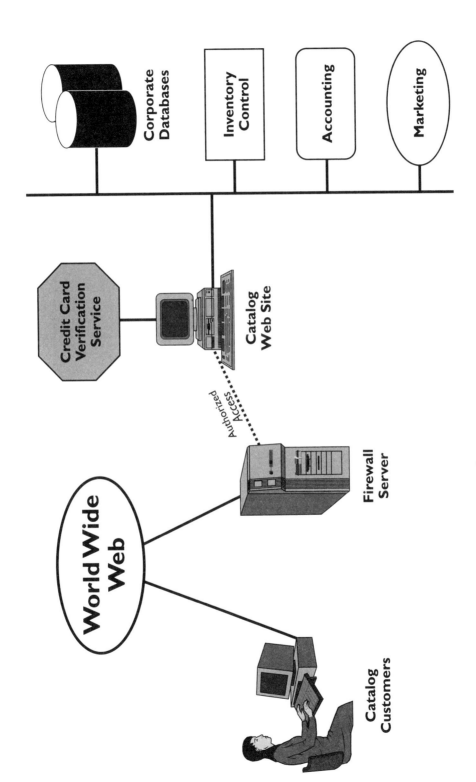

Figure 10.1 System Design for a Web-based Catalog Service

planning and delivering sales promotions. The credit card used by the customer will be verified either by means of the corporate database or by an authorization service.

FEATURES AND FUNCTIONS

A useful Web-based catalog software development package should offer the following minimal features and functions:

- Customizable forms and templates
- HTML and CGI
- MIME and S-MIME
- SSL and S-HTTP
- Search engine
- Link verification
- Ability to perform mathematical calculations
- Multiple file formats, such as TIFF, GIF, MPEG, JPEG, etc.
- Java and VRML
- Online help and documentation

TOOLS

Although many catalogs and catalog service providers are currently available on the Web, not much in the way of software development tools are yet on the market (as seen in Table 10.2).

Table 10.2 Web-based Catalog Services, Software, and Tools

Product	Vendor	Source
Catalog Development	Automated Research Systems, Ltd.	http://WWW.arslimited.com
Electronic Catalog Publishing	Ronin Paperless Publishing	http://www.register.com/number10/
Internet Catalog Software	Computer Software Systems	http://bend-or.com/css/
Yellow Pages Catalog Service	XYNet	http://www.xynet.com
Step Search	Saqqara	http://www.danish.com

EXAMPLES

Examples of good online catalog services can be found at the locations illustrated by Figures 10.2, 10.3, and 10.4. The presentation is colorful, the site navigation is efficient, and the online order forms are superb.

SERVICE OUTPUT

The output for the Web-based catalog service includes the order, customer information, buying habits, preferences, requests for catalogs, and statistical information used for trends and sales forecasts.

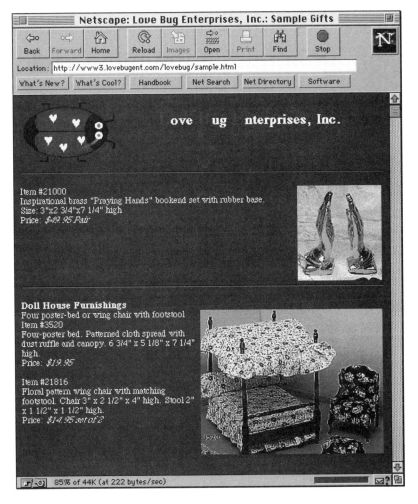

Figure 10.2   Love Bug Enterprises (http://www3.lovebugent.com)

Figure 10.3   Big Yank Sports (http://www.BigYank.com)

Providing Electronic Commerce Services

Electronic commerce (EC) is the paperless exchange of documents and funds between businesses. Traditionally, this activity was termed EDI or Electronic Data Interchange and consisted of highly-structured, formatted transactions between two cooperating companies. With the

Figure 10.4 Attitudes On Line Catalog (http://www.attitudes.com)

advent of the Web, new terminology is rapidly replacing the EDI moniker. Today's Internet-based commerce is called the "I-Market," "Commerce on the Web," or "Ecommerce." The distributed nature of the Web supports establishing more relationships in an ad hoc manner for the exchange of less structured information. Web-based EC will enable an interactive dialog between buyers and sellers, and will make mass customization possible to drive the cyberspace economy.

Businesses typically go through five stages in acquiring new products: search, validate, order, pay, delivery, and maintenance. Web-based EC will play an increasingly more important role in each of these stages. The Web may be used to perform searches of the electronic market-place for competitive products, information, and white papers to gather an initial list of products and vendors. The vendors may be validated by means of such services as Dun & Bradstreet online. The company may place an order for the selected product and pay for it electronically. If the product is electronic itself, such as music, video, or literature, then the product can be electronically delivered or down-loaded to the purchaser. Web-based customer support services will enable the company to maintain the product after implementation.

Most of the major Value Added Networks, such as Advantis, GEIS, and Sterling Commerce, are planning to provide Internet-based electronic commerce services in addition to their existing services. The browser companies and cable companies are also forming alliances to bring the Web technology closer to the consumer. And smaller companies, without legacy systems to encumber them, are coming out with EC products and services built on Internet technology.

Web-based electronic commerce is a great equalizer of companies. The "Mom and Pop" shops are able to compete head-to-head with the mega-corporations for electronically-placed orders. Much progress has been made in providing small businesses with the software and tools required to compete in this arena.

BUSINESS DRIVERS AND STAKEHOLDERS

With Web-based electronic commerce, the cost of implementing and running the system is reduced, cash flow is improved, delivery cycles are shortened, and errors are reduced. More consumers, manufacturers, and suppliers may be reached worldwide than ever before. In addition, electronic commerce enables an organization to ferret out new markets for existing goods and services as well as create new markets.

Stakeholders in the electronic commerce service include trading partners, management, customer service, accounting, and the order processing department. The partners to electronic commerce have quite a large stake in the efficient and trusted running of the service. The firm's management and customer service have a stake in the service to provide worry-free business transactions. The accounting department benefits from reduced errors and more timely information. The order processing department benefits from reduced paperwork, more accurate information, shorter delivery cycles, and quicker receipt of payments.

SERVICE ESSENTIALS

Electronic commerce relies on security as the main ingredient for success. Web-based security then becomes vital to establishing trusted relationships between buyers and sellers. Orders must be non-repudiated and buyers must be both authorized to conduct the trade and authenticated to each other. A new market has opened for trusted third parties to provide secure transactions using digital signatures, encryption, and certificates between trading partners.

On the server side, EDI translation and mapping software is required, as well as integration with the organization's databases, accounting, shipping, and inventory control processes. Trading partners must also have EDI software running on their Web servers, and each company must support the same standard, either X12 or EDIFACT.

Legally, the partners to the trade must have established a working relationship with one another in the form of trading partner agreements. These contracts specify the terms of the trade, payment, delinquencies, overages and shortages, etc.

SYSTEM DESIGN

As shown in Figure 10.5, quite a bit activity transpires between buyers and sellers in a typical electronic commerce or EDI transaction. If Company A were a small enterprise, a person using a Web browser would interact with the electronic commerce server to initiate the transactions. In the case of a larger organization, the company's internal processes would trigger an event which would automatically initiate the electronic commerce transaction.

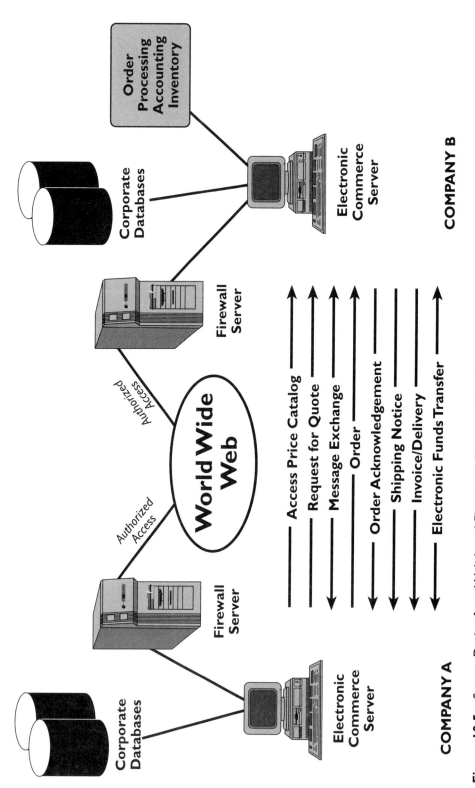

Figure 10.5 System Design for a Web-based Electronic Commerce Service

Company A initiates the EDI transaction by accessing Company B's online price catalog. Company A reviews the price for the particular item(s) sought, then sends a format Request for Quote transaction to Company B. B responds with the quote, and a flurry of messages are exchanged as technical specifications, delivery dates, terms, etc., are finalized. Then Company A electronically places the order. B sends an order acknowledgment and follows up with a shipping notice to inform A of the expected delivery date. When the order is delivered to A, B sends an invoice. A then follows up by electronically transferring the funds to B based on the amount on the invoice.

Company B has integrated its databases, accounting, order processing, and inventory systems with the electronic commerce system, and updates all the pertinent records within them as required.

FEATURES AND FUNCTIONS

A useful Web-based electronic commerce system should support, at a minimum, the following features and functions:

- A full complement of EDI transaction sets
- HTML and CGI
- TCP/IP
- Search engine
- Database integration tools
- SSL and S-HTTP
- Digital signatures, certificates, and authentication schemes
- Electronic Funds Transfer integration
- Non-repudiability
- Disaster recovery mechanisms
- Online help and documentation

TOOLS

As can be seen in Table 10.3, there are many software packages, tools, payment options, and commerce servers from which to select when implementing a Web-based EC service.

Table 10.3	Web-based Electronic Commerce Service Software and Tools	
Product	**Vendor**	**Source**
BSDI Internet Server	Berkely Software Design,	http://www.bsdi.com
Cold Fusion	Allaire	http://www.allaire.com
Commerce Builder	Internet Factory	http://www.aristosoft.com
Connect One Server	Connect	http://www.connectinc.com
Cybercash	Cybercash	http://www.cybercash.com
Digicash	Digicash	http://www.digicash.com
E-Cheque	BankNet	http://mkn.co.uk/bank
First Virtual	First Virtual Holdings	http://www.fv.com
Merchant Server and Secure Web Server	OpenMarket	http://www.openmarket.com
NetChex	NetChex	http://www.netchex.com/
Netscape Commerce Server	Netscape	http://www.netscape.com
One-to-One	BroadVision	http://www.broadvision.com
Retail Catalog	Electronic Commerce Systems	http://www.ecweb.com/catalog/
SiteTrack	Coretex	http://www.cortex.net/sitetrack
Templar	Premenos	http://www.premenos.com/premenos/
WebStar SSL Security Toolkit	StarNine	http://www.starnine.com
Zipper Translation System	Dakin	http://www.pcug.org.au/~daktec/
Online Distributor	TRADEíex	http://www.tradeex.com

EXAMPLES

Since many electronic commerce applications occur between trading partners, access to their Web pages is unavailable. Two interesting and accessible EC applications are AMP, Inc. (http://connect.ampincorporated.com), a parts distributor that has placed a 50,000-item parts catalog on the Web for online search and ordering, and CommerceNet (http://www.commerce.net), an industry consortium of over 200 members who are building a trusted Internet-based market for their goods and services. In addition, most of the major computer equipment manufacturers, such as IBM, HP, Sun, and Apple, have placed their product catalogs online.

SERVICE OUTPUT

The output of the Web-based electronic commerce service would be the transaction sets that are transmitted to the trading partners, the messages regarding the transactions, and the statistics gathered for trending and sales forecasting.

Proving Customer Support Services

Web-based customer support services, if implemented properly, will be the leading cause of the vaporization of the boundary between the customer and the organization. This service will give the customer a window into the workings of the enterprise. This service will give the customer a voice. The interactive use of this new Web service will empower customers to resolve their own problems, track their own orders, schedule their own appointments, and follow their own claims from inception to payment.

In this section we will explore the provision of Customer Support services to external customers. In Chapter 9 we discussed providing Help Desk services to internal employees, contractors, etc.

BUSINESS DRIVERS AND STAKEHOLDERS

All businesses are constantly searching for ways to provide better service to their customers, while reducing the costs of providing that service. Web-based customer support services reduce the labor costs associated with handling customer inquiries and performing problem resolution. Customers will have immediate access to a reliable and accurate source of help 24 hours a day, seven days a week, from anywhere in the world, using any type of computer system. Customers will access Frequently Asked Questions about the particular product or service, consult the Lessons Learned repository, or perform sophisticated searches to obtain the information required to resolve their problem. This reduces the number of telephone calls to the support hot line and the number of support staff required to deal with those calls. The organization will begin to render "service by exception," in which only those equipped solely with telephone access will use the traditional support system. The statistics gathered from problem reporting and trouble ticketing will enable the enterprise to become more proactive in dealing with customer problems.

Every access a customer makes of the customer support service home page represents a sales opportunity. Links to the organization's catalogs and recent product announcements are a must, as is publication of support telephone and fax numbers.

The stakeholders in the service are management, customer support personnel, sales and marketing departments, and the customers themselves.

SERVICE ESSENTIALS

The Web-based customer support service requires an external Web site located outside the firewall. Customers must identify themselves in some manner to the system—a customer ID, serial number, etc.—prior to gaining entry. Some organizations may want customer support to be an icon on their home page so that anyone who wants to browse the contents may do so. The service must establish links to corporate databases to obtain accurate customer information, parts inventory, and product technical specifications. The service must establish and maintain a FAQ area that is interactive with the customers. Telephone and fax numbers must be placed on every page so a customer can dial for help if unable to resolve the problem.

The service should also provide online tutorials, an area for new users, a "What's New" section, a list of supported hardware and software, a search facility, and contact information for users who want to talk with someone in person about their problem.

SYSTEM DESIGN

External customers would use any Web browser to access the organization's Customer Support Web site. The site would be located in front of the firewall. Customers would input a qualifier, such as their account number, serial number, PIN (personal identification number), or an order number, and be granted trusted access to the support service. Links to databases are essential to providing the customer with up-to-date information and assistance on products and services (see Figure 10.6).

FEATURES AND FUNCTIONS

Features and functions of good Web-based customer support service software and tools include at least the following:

- Call tracking
- Problem routing and trouble ticketing
- HTML and CGI
- SSL and S-HTTP
- Search engine
- Knowledge base
- Inventory integration tools
- Customer information database
- Database integration tools
- FAQ area
- Lessons learned repository
- Statistics gathering
- Report generation
- Source code
- Training
- Online help and documentation

TOOLS

The tools cited in Chapter 9 for Help Desk services are also viable for providing Web-based customer support services. In addition, you may want to review Backstage by IBAND (http://www.iband.com) and Visual Help Desk for Notes and Intranets by Brainstorm Technologies (http://www.braintech.com). We can expect to see more products that integrate groupware and the customer service function with Internet technology, as does Visual Help Desk.

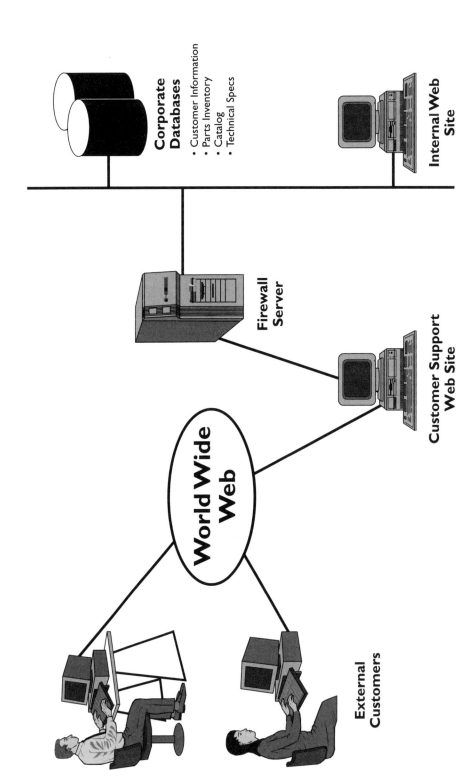

Figure 10.6 System Design for a Web-based Customer Support Service

EXAMPLES

Federal Express (http://www.fedex.com) is perhaps the most well-known example of a Web-based Customer Support service. As illustrated in Figure 10.7, the company permits a customer to input the package tracking number to determine where in the shipping process the package is at the moment. Another excellent example is the Postal Service's Zip Code Directory (http://www.usps.gov) which enables a user to determine a specified location's zip code.

Figure 10.7   Federal Express Customer Support Parcel Tracking System

SERVICE OUTPUT

The output of this service would be a database of customer information and preferences, problem resolution information, trends and forecasts, the ability to take a more proactive stance on problem resolution, and the opportunity to turn the service call into a sales opportunity through a link to the company's catalog.

Providing Marketing Communications Services

Organizations use marketing communications to establish a "top-of-mind" awareness, brand preference, or goodwill in their customers. Having an online presence on the World Wide Web is a new and dynamic advertising and public relations medium. Consultants state that an organization should spend 5–10% of its advertising budget online. This percentage will grow over time as the Web becomes more immersed in the everyday lives of consumers.

Information to make available to the public, to customers, trading partners, the government, and other interested parties would include

- "who we are"
- "what we do"
- electronic brochures
- product announcements
- product data sheets and technical specifications
- news and press releases
- white papers
- the history of the organization
- the officers of the corporation
- messages from the president
- living organizational chart
- "what's new" on the page, in the latest product version or release
- annual report
- stock quote ticker

- event ticker
- trade shows, conferences, and seminars where the firm will be represented
- charities, foundations, etc., supported
- recruiting, jobs, and benefits

BUSINESS DRIVERS AND STAKEHOLDERS

A major benefit of the Web-based marketing communications service is that all the information required for public relations is available in one place. The costs to modify, distribute, and store this information are greatly reduced while name recognition is increased. The organization's name, products, and services are now available to a much wider audience than would be found using traditional forms of advertising, public relations, and promotion.

Public relations, promotions, and advertising delivered by traditional means like print, radio, TV, billboards, etc., generally has few mechanisms to determine if the material is actually being consumed by the target audience. With Web-based marketing communications, each time someone accesses the server, much information about the customer is automatically obtained. And with a short survey, more demographic information can be gleaned. Providing links to the catalog or to the page of an account representative gives the customer an immediate opportunity to begin the buying process. Organizations with Web-based services will finally be able to determine if their advertising dollars are paying off.

The stakeholders in the Web-based marketing communications service are the stockholders, the management, and the customers. The public image of the organization is vital to its long-term success. Companies are now eager to let the public know about what they do, and about foundations, charities, and other community service activities they support. This so called "greening" and "giving back" of American corporations will foster more goodwill and hence increase the organization's opportunity to remain competitive. By means of Web-based marketing communications, this type of information can be made readily available to the public, investors, and consumers of the products or services.

SERVICE ESSENTIALS

A Web-based marketing communications service is very straightforward and quite simple, compared to providing any of the other external services discussed previously in this chapter. Basically, all that is needed is the Web server and software, an Internet connection, and links to corporate databases and catalogs. The site will contain both static and dynamic information as well as provide the visitor with the capability of feedback, either by means of electronic mail or a CGI form to complete and submit.

Another essential ingredient are content owners in the public relations, advertising, or marketing communications department that will create and have ongoing responsibility for the site's exceptional, current, and accurate content. These owners must constantly mine competitive and other hot sites for new information and new ways to present it. The site must continually change, and it's an excellent idea to provide notification to interested parties when changes do occur. The site should also offer something free to the visitor, such as a screen saver, coupon, or small promotional item that will be either downloaded or mailed to them.

SYSTEM DESIGN

A basic system design for a Web-based marketing communications service is illustrated in Figure 10.8. The external public, with access to the Web from any browser, connects to the site's marketing communications server. This server is placed outside the firewall to prevent network intrusion and other security breaches. The site may also be hosted by a Web Presence Provider to handle high traffic volumes or provide greater security for the organization. The service contains static information, such as the annual report and white papers. Dynamic information is made available by means of links to the corporate databases to obtain current product data sheets, the online catalog, promotions, etc.

FEATURES AND FUNCTIONS

The most useful features and functions to have in a Web-based marketing communications service include

• HTML and CGI

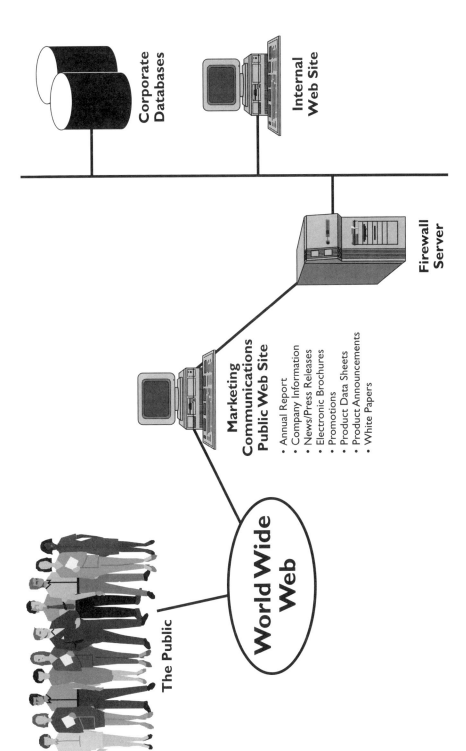

Corporate Databases

Internal Web Site

Firewall Server

Marketing Communications Public Web Site

- Annual Report
- Company Information
- News/Press Releases
- Electronic Brochures
- Promotions
- Product Data Sheets
- Product Announcements
- White Papers

World Wide Web

The Public

Figure 10.8   System Design for a Web-based Marketing Communications Service

- Electronic mail
- Search engine
- Database integration
- Statistics gathering
- Logging and tracking
- Report generation
- Link verification
- Java and VRML
- Online help and documentation

TOOLS

Tools essential to the development of a solid Web-based marketing communications service include Web server software and hardware, HTML authoring tools, database integration applications, electronic mail, and so on. Table 10.4 contains an amalgamation of these tools since the Web site will be custom constructed for the organization's own promotional requirements. Also, the products and services for Web servers and development discussed in Chapter 3 are viable options here as well.

EXAMPLES

Two interesting examples—both in the top 5% of all Web sites—are the home pages of Lockheed Martin Corporation, the nation's largest defense contractor (http://www.lmco.com), and Coca Cola Company, the world's largest beverage maker (http://cocacola.com).

As shown in Figure 10.9, Lockheed Martin's marketing communications page has all the essential elements recommended in this section. The page is colorful, has an image map as well as hypertext links for browsers that do not support graphics, and a contact link. The site showcases a "What's New" location, a Library, financial information, a corporate overview, and a link to products and services.

Coca Cola's home page, shown in Figure 10.10, is quite off-beat and playful in contrast. The entire screen is one image map that takes you to the next page, where vending machine icons are available to take

Table 10.4	Web-based Marketing Communications Service Software and Tools		
Product	Function	Vendor	Source
BSDI Internet Server	EC Server	Berkely Software Design	http://www.bsdi.com
Cold Fusion	EC Development/ Database Integration	Allaire	http://www.allaire.com
Commerce Builder	EC Server	Internet Factory	http://www.aristosoft.com
Connect One Server	EC Server	Connect	http://www.connectinc.com
Java	Application Development	Sun Microsystems	http://www.sun.com
Lotus Notes	Application Development/E-mail	Lotus Development Corp.	http://www.lotus.com
Microsoft Exchange Server	Application Development/E-mail	Microsoft	http://www.microsoft.com
Sapphire/Web	DB Integration	Bluestone, Inc.	http://www.bluestone.com
Solstice Internet Mail	E-mail	Sunsoft	http://www.sun.com
Spider	DB Integration	Spider Technologies	http://www.w3spider.com
SQLweb	DB Integration	SQLweb Technologies	http://www.SQLweb.com
Step Search	Catalog Development	Saqqara	http://www.danish.com
WebBase	DB Integration	ExperTelligence	http://www. expertellligence.com
Z-Mail	E-mail	Netmanage	http://www.netmanage.com

the visitor to investor information, mission, product, and related locations. The same type of information is made available, but the
approach of each company is vastly different.

SERVICE OUTPUT

Output for the Web-based marketing communications service would
be electronic messages received from interested parties, donations for

Figure 10.9 Lockheed Martin's Home Page

the organization's charities, requests for visits by the sales representatives, online orders, statistical information for trends and forecasts, and customer information, preferences, and buying habits.

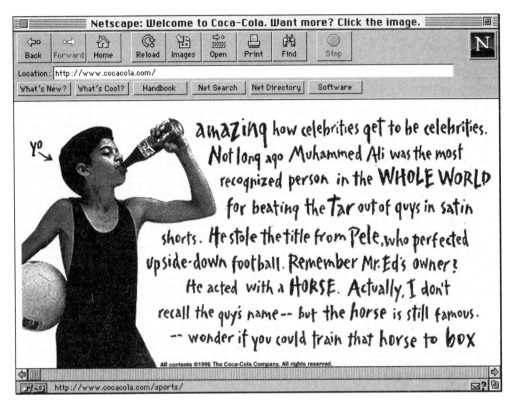

Figure 10.10   Coca Cola's Home Page

Summary

In this chapter we presented the culmination of all that has been explored in this work. Creating interactive Web-based systems that extend the enterprise directly to customers, trading partners, and other interested parties is the next great wave of Internet computing. Providing external services, such as catalogs, electronic commerce, customer support and marketing communications, all bring the essence, the products, and the services of the organization straight to those who want to know, to buy, and to sell. For business to be conducted in a manner consistent with the Information Age, Web-based services such as these are essential and will become as commonplace in homes and organizations as the telephone book.

REFERENCES

BOOKS

Aronson, Larry. *HTML Manual of Style*. Ziff-Davis Press, 1994.

Brinson, J. Dianne, and Mark F. Radcliffe. *Multimedia Law Handbook*. Ladera Press, 1995.

Bean, Greg. *Internet Servers: A Step-by-Step Guide on How to Build Them*. CyberGrp, 1994.

Carroll, Michael L. *Cyberstrategies*. Van Nostrand Reinhold, 1996.

Chandler, David M. *Running a Perfect Web Site*, Que Corporation, 1995.

Cheswick, William R., and Steven M. Bellovin. *Firewalls and Internet Security: Repelling the Wily Hacker*. Addison-Wesley, 1994.

Cox, Nancy, Charles T. Manley and Francis E. Chea. *LAN Times Guide to Multimedia Networking*. Osborne/McGraw-Hill, 1995.

Drummond, Richard, and Nancy Cox. *LAN Times E-Mail Resource Guide*. Osborne/McGraw-Hill, 1994.

Ellsworth, Jill. *Internet Business Book*. Wiley & Sons, 1994.

Garfinkel, Simson, and Gene Spafford. *Practical UNIX Security*. O'Reilly and Associates, 1991.

Lawley, Elizabeth L., and Craig Summerhill. *Internet Primer for Information Professionals: A Basic Guide to Internet Networking Technology*. Mecklermedia, 1993.

Liu, Cricket, et. al. *Managing Internet Information Services: WWW, Gopher, FTP & More*. O'Reilly & Associates, 1994.

Loukides, Mike, ed. *World Wide Web Handbook*. 1995, O'Reilly & Associates.

Lynch. Daniel C., and Marshall T. Rose. *Internet System Handbook*. Addison-Wesley, 1994.

357

McMullen, Melanie, ed. *Networks 2000: Internet, Information Highway, Multimedia Networks & Beyond.* Miller Freeman, 1994.

Pfaffenberger, Bryan. *World Wide Web Bible.* MIS Press, 1995.

Quarterman, John S. and Smoot C. Mitchell. *InterNet Connection: System Connectivity & Configuration.* Addison-Wesley, 1994.

Tilton, Eric, Carl Steadman, and Tyler Jones. *Web Weaving: Designing and Managing an Effective Web Site,* Addison-Wesley, 1996.

Wiggins, Richard. *Internet for Everyone: A Guide for Users & Providers.* McGraw Hill, 1994.

INTERNATIONAL STANDARDS, TECHNICAL PAPERS, AND RECOMMENDATIONS

Banan, Mohsen. Internet E-Mail Services. Arlington, Va.: Electronic Messaging Association, 1994.

Borenstein, Nathaniel, and Ned Freed. MIME (Multipurpose Internet Mail Extensions) Part One: Mechanisms for Specifying and Describing the Format of Internet Message Bodies, RFC 1521.

Common Messaging Call API. Version 2.0. Mountain View, Calif.: X.400 API Association, 1995.

Electronic Mail Privacy. Arlington, Va.: Electronic Messaging Association, 1992.

Introduction to Messaging APIs. Arlington, Va.: Electronic Messaging Association, 1994.

MAGAZINES AND NEWSLETTERS

Communications News

Communications Week

EMMS (Electronic Mail and Messaging Systems)

Information Week

Interactive Age

LAN Times

Messaging Magazine (Electronic Messaging Association)

Network Administrator

Network Computing

New Media

VR News

WebMaster

GLOSSARY

Acceptable Use Policy—A code of conduct addressing appropriate use of electronic services, such as messaging, news groups, bulletin board systems, chat, etc.

Access Control List—The means by which permission and denial of service for users and hosts is managed.

ACL—Access Control List.

Address—Computer notation representing the location of a device, host, user, or information on a network.

Address Mapping—The process by which an alphabetic Internet address is converted into a numeric IP address and vice versa.

Advanced Research Projects Agency Network—A leased-line, packet network funded by the federal government which eventually became the Internet.

Advertainment—Content that provides advertising as well as entertainment for the viewer.

Agent—Computer software program that performs specified tasks, seeks out information, etc., on behalf of a client or server application.

.aif—PC file extension for a sound file.

Aliases—Used to re-route browser requests from one URL to another.

Algorithm—A computing procedure designed to perform a task, such as encryption, compression, or hashing.

Alta Vista—A Web search engine developed by DEC.

American Standard Code for Information Interchange—A standard character-to-number encoding scheme in wide use in the computer industry.

Anchor Tags—Hyperlinks in HTML documents that enable a user to jump from one screen or page to another.

Anonymous FTP—A server that permits users to download files without having to supply a user ID and password to gain access to the remote computer.

API—Application Program Interface.

Applet—A small computer program or mini-program.

AppleTalk—A network protocol developed by Apple Computer, Inc., enabling Apple devices to communicate with each other.

Application—A computer software program performing functions for a user.

Application Program Interface—Computer code specifications detailing how one application can invoke and/or access another application.

Archie—A search mechanism for use on anonymous FTP servers.

Architecture—A framework for the design of a workable computer service or system.

ARPANET—Advanced Research Projects Agency Network.

ASCII—American Standard Code for Information Interchange.

Asynchronous Transfer Mode—A high-speed networking standard using fixed cells and providing dynamic bandwidth allocation.

ATM—Asynchronous Transfer Mode.

.au—PC file extension for a sound file.

AUP—Acceptable Use Policy.

Authentication—The process of establishing the true identity of a person or process; verifying the source of a message, transmission, or interaction.

Authoring—The process of developing HTML documents for use on the Web.

Authorization—The process of granting or denying access to a user or process.

Backbone—A high-speed line or collection of lines that form a major network highway. Usu-

ally refers to large data communications networks for messaging, the Internet, etc.

Bandwidth—The difference between the highest and lowest frequencies of a transmission circuit. More commonly, the total amount of data that can be carried on a transmission circuit.

BBS—Bulletin Board System.

Bit—The smallest unit of computer data represented by either a 0 or a 1. An acronym for "binary digit."

Bookmarks—Permits the Web browser user to capture a URL for later use.

Browser—The user interface or client for the World Wide Web enabling search and retrieval of information.

Bulletin Board System—A computer software application that provides messaging, file archival, and other services of interest to the users of the system.

Buttons—Clickable interfaces that link users to another location.

Byte—A sequence of eight bits.

CA—Certification Authority.

Caching—Performance-enhancing capability of storing large amounts of information on the server for frequent access.

Catalog Service Provider—A company that designs and may also host catalogs for other companies.

CERN—Conseil Europeen pour la Recherche Nucleaire.

CERT—Computer Emergency Response Team.

Certification Authority—A trusted organization that distributes and maintains public and private cryptographic keys for use in secure transmission environments.

CGI—Common Gateway Interface.

CGI-Bin Directory—A scripts directory located on the HTTP server.

Chameleon—Client software that enables connectivity to TCP/IP networks.

CIX—Organization of commercial Internet providers (http://www.cix.org).

Clear Text—See *Plain Text*.

Client—Software enabling users to interface with servers, making requests and receiving responses. Mosaic and Netscape are examples of World Wide Web clients commonly known as browsers.

Client/Server Architecture—A computer processing arrangement in which both the workstations and the server share the workload.

CommerceNet—A consortium of companies working to enable electronic commerce over the Internet.

Commerce Server—File server software developed to enable organizations to conduct electronic commerce activities over the Internet. Also known as Electronic Commerce Server.

Common Gateway Interface—A specification for how a server should communicate with server gateway programs.

Compiler—A program used to translate source code into executable program code.

Computer Emergency Response Team—A Carnegie Mellon University organization that distributes information about security threats to the Internet such as worms and viruses.

Conseil Europeen pour la Recherche Nucleaire—The European Laboratory for Particle Physics. CERN developed HTTP and HTML, which form the foundation of the World Wide Web.

Copyright—The exclusive right to publish, sell, reproduce, and distribute the contents of a literary or artistic work for a specified number of years.

CSP—Catalog Service Provider.

CU SeeMe—A videoconferencing application developed by Cornell University that runs on the Internet.

CyberCash—A company that provides software for secure payment systems for use on the Internet.

Cyberspace—A term describing the virtual world of computers.

Daemon—In UNIX, an independent, automated background program that performs specific functions.

Database Management System—Tools to administer and maintain a repository of electronic records known as a database.

DBMS—Database Management System.

DECnet—A proprietary networking protocol developed by Digital Equipment Corporation, enabling DEC devices to communicate with each other.

Decryption—Process of converting encrypted text to plain text that can be viewed and understood by humans.

Dedicated Line—See *Leased Line.*

Dial-up—A temporary network connection established over a telephone line using modems or dumb terminals.

Digital Signature—The act of electronically affixing a seal or token to a computer file or message in which the originator is then authenticated to the recipient.

DLL—Dynamic Link Libraries.

DNS—Domain Name System.

Domain—A managed community of users and host systems in the Internet hierarchy, such as .edu or .com.

Domain Name—A unique, alphabetic name following the @ symbol in an Internet address, identifying an Internet site. The name is generally composed of the organization's name and the top level host type, such as **organization.com**.

Domain Name System—A system used to look up and resolve host IP addresses. Maps alphabetic names to numeric IP addresses.

DOS—Disk Operating System.

Download—A process used to transfer or copy files from a host computer to your own computer.

Dynamic Indexing—The capability of automatically listing and sorting a group of URLs, records, etc.

Dynamic Link Libraries—DLL.

EDI—Electronic Data Interchange.

Edutainment—Content that is both educational and entertaining for the viewer or user.

EFT—Electronic Funds Transfer.

Electronic Data Interchange—The paperless process of exchanging business documents such as purchase orders and shipping notices electronically between trading partners.

Electronic Funds Transfer—The electronic transmission of money between financial institutions.

Electronic Commerce—Buying and selling goods and services and paying for them electronically over the Internet.

Electronic Mail—Application program that enables the exchange of computer-generated messages between users over a network.

Electronic Mail Address—A user identifier enabling the exchange of messages over a network such as the Internet. An Internet e-mail address is typically formatted **userid@organization.com**.

Encryption—Computer software used to scramble data located in files so as to make it unintelligible.

Ethernet—A network technology used in local area networks, providing coaxial cable connections for devices and a network speed of 10Mbps.

Eudora—A popular Internet e-mail package.

FAQ—Frequently Asked Questions.

FDDI—Fiber Distributed Data Interface.

Fiber Distributed Data Interface—A standard for local area networks using fiber optic media and offering a network speed of 100Mbps.

File Transfer—The process of copying a file from one computer to another over a network.

File Transfer Protocol—Format and methodology, based on TCP/IP, used to exchange files with remote computers.

Finger—An Internet resource that displays logged on users and information about them.

Firewall—Computer hardware and software that serve to permit or deny access to network resources. Used to separate a local area network from the outside world.

Flame—Harsh reproach transmitted in an e-mail message or posted to newsgroups or bulletin boards.

Forms—Fill-in text fields on home pages that provide interactive query and response for users seeking information or wishing to provide feedback.

Frequently Asked Questions—A listing of the most commonly received queries in a newsgroup, bulletin board system, etc., to which users may refer prior to posting their question.

Freeware—Software available for download and use on the Internet. Also referred to as Public Domain Software.

Front Porch—The access point to a secure network environment; also known as a firewall.

FTP—File Transfer Protocol.

Gateway—Computer hardware and software that translate between two disparate application programs or networking protocols.

GIF—Graphics Interchange Format.

Gopher—A text-based Internet browsing service developed at the University of Minnesota.

Graphical User Interface—Computer program code that resides between the user and the application program, enabling quick and easy access to information and program features using graphics, icons, buttons, and pull-down menus.

Graphics Interchange Format—A commonly used image file format.

Groupware—Computer software designed to facilitate collaboration among the users, such as scheduling, data conferencing, and document and task management.

GUI—Graphical User Interface.

Help Desk—The single point of contact for internal users for problem resolution.

Heterogeneous Network—A communications network using more than one protocol, such as IP, DECnet, and AppleTalk.

Hierarchy—A stratification of objects, all having relationships which descend from the topmost object, called the root, to lower levels of more and more specialized objects.

History List—A list of URLs and titles of documents accessed during a user's Mosaic session.

Home Page—The initial screen of information displayed to the user when initiating the client or browser software or when connecting to a remote computer. The Home Page resides at the top of the directory tree and functions as the entry way to the Web site.

Host—A computer that enables users to communicate with other user computers on a network.

Hosting Content—When an organization uses the facilities of an Internet Service Provider, consultant, etc., to run its Web site.

Host Address—The IP address of the host computer.

Host Name—The name of the user computer on the network.

Hot Buttons—Small images or icons hyperlinked to other HTML documents.

Hot Java—A Java-enabled browser developed by Sun Microsystems.

Hotlink—Hypertext links between documents on a Web site.

Hotlist—A list created by the user of URLs within a particular Web document.

Hotspot—A clickable area in an HTML document that automatically takes a user to another location.

HTML—Hypertext Markup Language.

HTTP—Hypertext Transport Protocol.

HTTPD—Hypertext Transport Protocol Daemon.

Hypertext Link—A location in a document that enables a user to jump to a location within the same document or another document. Links are identified by highlighted, underlined, or colored text or images.

Hypermedia—Documents containing several information types, such as text image, audio, and video.

Hypertext—Text documents that contain links to related content at other locations.

Hypertext Markup Language—A specific programming language, based on SGML, that enables the development of Home Pages and documents that can be accessed and displayed by WWW client software. HTML documents use the .html or .htm PC file extension.

Hypertext Transport Protocol—The rules, based on TCP/IP, that govern the exchange of information between WWW servers.

Hypertext Transport Protocol Daemon—A type of information server using the HTTP protocol.

ICE—Type of search engine.

Icons—Small images, generally uniform in size and appearance, that link users to other locations.

Imagemap—An image, such as a still photograph with embedded hypertext links, enabling users to click on the image and be transported to another location.

Infobots—Software agents that perform specified tasks for a user or application.

Infotainment—The combination of programs, processes, etc., that are both entertaining and informational in content.

In-line Image—A graphic image such as a still photograph or logo that is displayed within an HTML document.

Integrated Services Digital Network—A digital network for voice and data transmission, offering high speed and increased bandwidth.

International Standards Organization—An organization composed of interested parties in various countries who collaborate to create standards in such areas as communications and computers.

Internet—An international network of networks connecting computers in government, educational institutions, businesses, and other entities.

Internet Protocol—The basic set of rules that govern the exchange of data on the Internet.

Internet Relay Chat—An Internet resource that enables users to communicate with each other in real-time over the network.

Internet Service Provider—A company that links your host computer(s) with the Internet.

Internet Society—A non-profit organization of volunteers that collects and distributes information about the Internet, such as usage statistics, and supports on-going technical work to improve and enhance the Internet.

Internet Voice—A product enabling users to engage in telephone conversations across the Internet.

Internetwork Packet Exchange—A networking protocol used on Novell networks.

Internet Server Application Programming Interface—Microsoft's programming specification for Internet servers.

Intranet—The internal network within an enterprise based on Internet protocols.

IP—Internet Protocol.

IP Address—The 32-bit representation of the location of a device on the Internet. Takes the form of 111.111.111.111 and is also known as a dot address, host address, Internet address, or network address.

IPX—Internetwork Packet Exchange.

IRC—Internet Relay Chat.

ISAPI—Internet Server Application Programming Interface.

ISDN—Integrated Services Digital Network.

ISO—International Standards Organization.

ISOC—See Internet Society.

ISP—See *Internet Service Provider.*

ITU—International Telecommunications Union.

Java—An object-oriented programming language developed by Sun Microsystems.

Joint Photograph Experts Group—A methodology used to store images such as still photographs in a compressed digital format.

JPEG—Joint Photograph Experts Group.

Jughead—An Internet service that provides searching of Gopher sites.

LAN—Local Area Network.

Leased Line—A high bandwidth private line used by an organization to carry data communications transmissions (e.g. T1, T2, T3).

Link—See *Hypertext Link.*

Listserv—A program that automatically sends messages to a pre-defined distribution list.

Local Area Network—A network connecting multiple computers within a single location.

Lycos—A Web search engine.

MacTCP—Apple's network software that enables Macintoshes to connect to TCP/IP networks.

Mailbots—Software agents that perform specified electronic messaging functions on behalf of a user or application.

Management Information Base—In an OSI network, a repository designed to facilitate communications between network devices in open systems.

MBONE—Multicast backbone.

MIB—Management Information Base.

MIME—Multipurpose Internet Mail Extensions.

MPEG—Motion Picture Experts Group.

Modem—Hardware device that enables a computer to communicate with other computers using a telephone line by converting analog signals into digital and vice versa.

Mosaic—A computer program developed at the National Center for Supercomputer Applications that provides a simple graphical interface to the Internet.

Motion Picture Experts Group—A methodology used to store movie files in a compressed digital format.

Multi-Domain—The ability of an Internet server to host more than one domain.

Multimedia—An integrated collection or presentation of various information types such as text, audio, video, animation, graphics, 3-D images, etc.

Multimedia Messaging—Electronic messaging that contains text, audio, video, animation, graphics, 3-D images, etc.

Multimedia Networking—The capability of transmitting multimedia information types over traditional and emerging data communications paths.

Multipurpose Internet Mail Extensions—A protocol that allows a mail system to attach binary files such as graphics and spreadsheets.

Name Resolution—Mapping a name to its address.

NAPs—Network Access Points.

National Center for Supercomputing Applications—Originator of the Mosaic WWW browser client software located at the University of Illinois in Urbana-Champaign, Illinois.

Navigating—The act of moving through the pages of a Web site.

Navigator—Netscape's Web browser.

NCSA—National Center for Supercomputer Applications.

NDS—NetWare Directory Services.

Netiquette—Proper behavior on and appropriate use of the Internet.

NetSearch—An Internet search engine.

Netscape—A company that produces Internet and Web software.

Netscape Application Programming Interface—Set of programming specifications for use in Netscape applications.

NetWare Directory Services—Novell's distributed, replicated name service built into NetWare 4.X.

Network—A data communications system connecting computing devices over a physical medium.

Network Access Points—Nodes providing entry to the high-speed Internet backbone system.

Network Address—That portion of an IP address that designates the network.

Network File System—A set of rules that permits access to files contained on remote hosts as if they were on local disks.

Network News Transfer Protocol—A set of rules for the distribution of news articles over the Internet

Newbies—Novice Internet users.

News—Software that permits the reading and posting of messages on specific topics, read by NNTP.

Newsgroup—A collection of articles on a specific topic in Usenet.

NFS—Network File System.

NNTP—Network News Transfer Protocol.

NSAPI—Netscape Application Programming Interface.

Open Systems Interconnection—An international standard for data communications networks.

OS/2—IBM's operating system.

OSI—Open Systems Interconnection.

OSI Reference Model—The seven-layer architecture designed by ISO for open data communications networks.

Packet—A unit of data sent across a data communications network.

Packet Filtering—The capability of permitting only designated IP packets through a server or firewall to prevent unauthorized access to the network or the Internet.

Packet InterNet Groper—Software that permits a user to determine if a distant host is active on the network.

Page—A single HTML content file.

Patent—Exclusive right granted to an inventor to produce, sell, and distribute the invention for a specified number of years.

PEM—Privacy Enhanced Mail.

PERL—Programming language based on C.

PGP—Pretty Good Privacy.

PING—Packet InterNet Groper.

Plain Text—Unencoded or encrypted text that can be viewed and understood by humans.

Point of Presence—Location where access to a telecommunications network may be obtained.

Point-to-Point Protocol—A set of rules defining the manner in which packets are transmitted over a serial point-to-point link.

Post Office Protocol—A set of rules defining the manner in which messages from a server can be read by a single user host.

Posting—Sending an electronic message to a newsgroup or a bulletin board system.

POP—Point of Presence; Post Office Protocol.

PostScript—A page description language developed by Adobe Systems.

PPP—Point-to-Point Protocol.

Pretty Good Privacy—A freeware encryption utility.

Privacy Enhanced Mail—A software application that provides encryption for electronic messaging.

Protocol—A set of rules and formats governing the manner in which a transfer of data is conducted over a network.

Proxy—Software residing on a Web server or firewall that enhances security by creating a filter for authorized use.

Proxy Server—A Web server used for enhanced security services.

Public Key—The encryption algorithm that is publicized and made widely available.

Public Key Encryption—An encryption scheme where two pairs of algorithmic keys, one public and the other private, are used to encrypt and decrypt messages, files, etc.

Public Domain Software—See *Freeware*.

Private Key—The encryption algorithm that is maintained by the user in secrecy.

QuickTime—Apple's movie and audio file digital storage method.

Remote Access—The capability of interacting with a distant computer by means of dial-up, modem, etc., over a standard telephone line.

Request for Comments—The set of documents describing the Internet's protocols, standards, and other relevant items.

RFC—Request for Comments.

Root—In a hierarchy of objects, the top-most object; the object having no others above it.

Route—The path that network traffic takes from its source host to its destination host.

Router—A computing device that relays data communications traffic between other devices on a network.

RSA—A type of public key encryption.

Scripts—Executable programs used to perform specified tasks for Web servers and clients.

Search Engine—Software that permits the lookup of information on the Internet, such as Lycos or Yahoo.

Secure Hypertext Transport Protocol—Rules that enable secure Web transactions.

Secure Multipurpose Internet Mail Extensions—Programming specifications that enable the use of encryption for MIME messaging types.

Secure Socket Layer—A protocol providing privacy between the Web server and the client application.

Sendmail—In UNIX, the messaging transport utility.

Serial Line Internet Protocol—A set of rules defining the manner in which packets are transmitted over a serial network link such as a telephone line, permitting dialup connections to the Internet.

Server—A computer such as a file server or a name server on a network that responds to requests from clients.

SGML—Standard Generalized Markup Language.

Shell—In UNIX, the program that interprets the commands entered at the computer. A shell can be used to run simple programs called shell scripts.

S-HTTP—Secure Hypertext Transport Protocol.

Simple Mail Transfer Protocol—The set of rules and formats defining the manner in which electronic mail messages are transmitted between computers over the Internet.

Simple Network Management Protocol—The set of rules and formats defining the manner in which management information about computing devices on a network is collected.

SLIP—Serial Line Internet Protocol.

SMDS—Switched Multimegabit Data Service.

S/MIME—Secure Multipurpose Internet Mail Extensions.

SMTP—Simple Mail Transfer Protocol.

SNMP—Simple Network Management Protocol.

SONET—Synchronous Optical Network.

Spamming—Sending a large number of commercial and otherwise offensive messages to users on a mailing list. This is not considered an appropriate use of the Internet.

Spider—A software program used to search the Web for specified purposes, such as cataloging words in URLs.

SSL—Secure Socket Layer.

Standard Generalized Markup Language—An international standard for encoding textual information that specifies particular ways to annotate text documents separating the structure of the document from the information content. HTML is a specialized form of SGML.

Surfing—Navigating or moving rapidly through Web sites.

Switched Multimegabit Data Service—A high-speed network service offered by the telephone companies.

Synchronous Optical Network—A high-capacity network for fiber optic media providing high-speed data transmission.

T1—Network transmission speed of 1.544Mbps.

T3—Network transmission speed of 45Mbps.

Tagged Image File Format—A method of storing image files.

TCL—Programming language.

TCP/IP—Transmission Control Protocol/Internet Protocol.

TIFF—Tagged Image File Format.

Telnet—An Internet standard protocol used to access remote hosts.

Threats—Risks of security intrusions into the network.

Token Ring—A type of local area network in which the devices are arranged in a virtual ring using a particular type of message, called a token, in order to communicate with one another.

Topology—The arrangement of computing devices on the physical media of the network.

Trademark—A registered word, letter, or device granting the owner exclusive rights to sell or ditribute the good to which it is applied.

Transmission Control Protocol/Internet Protocol—A set of rules, based on IP, governing the reliable transfer of data between computers on the Internet.

Trojan Horse—A type of computer virus in which the malicious code hides inside an innocuous-looking file or executable.

Twisted Pair—A type of network physical media made of copper wires twisted around each other. Ordinary telephone cable.

Uniform Resource Locator—The address of a source of information located on the WWW. URLs take the form of "http://host/directory or file name" as in **http://www.scifi.com/listings**.

UNIX—A multitasking computer operating system developed by AT&T.

Upload—The act of copying files from your own computer to that of a remote computer.

URL—Uniform Resource Locator.

Usenet—A collection of newsgroups active on the Internet. See *News*.

Value Added Network—Typically, a data communications carrier offering basic and enhanced services for such applications as messaging and electronic commerce.

VAN—Value Added Network.

Veronica—Search software for filenames on gopher servers.

Viewer—A software program invoked when the file received is not supported on the client's workstation. For example, a user receiving a PostScript file must invoke a viewer in order to display the contents of the file.

Virtual Reality Markup Language—A computer programming modeling language for use in rendering 3-D simulated "worlds" on Web sites.

Virus—A malicious software program that replicates itself, causing damage to files and utilities in a computer system.

VRML—Virtual Reality Markup Language.

W3—World Wide Web.

WAIS—Wide Area Information Server.

WAN—Wide Area Network.

Web—A computer network based on Internet protocols and hypertext pages, forming a subset of the World Wide Web.

Web Crawler—A software program that searches the Web for specified purposes such as to find a list of all URLs within a particular site.

WebMaster—One who administers and manages the Web site.

Web Site—A collection of HTML pages forming a realm reachable by users from a single URL.

Web Server—Software that provides services to Web clients. Also, the file server that contains the Web HTML software and other applications forming the Web site(s).

Wide Area Information Server—Software that permits the searching of huge Internet indices by means of keywords or phrases.

WHOIS—An Internet resource that permits users to initiate queries to a database containing information on users, hosts, networks, and domains.

Wide Area Network—A network connecting multiple computers at multiple locations, often geographically dispersed.

Windows—A computer operating system developed by Microsoft. New versions include Windows 95 and Windows NT.

World Wide Web—An information system created at CERN enabling easy access to distributed hypertext information.

Worm—A type of malicious software that damages a computer or network.

WYSIWYG—"What you see is what you get."

WWW—World Wide Web.

X.25—A data communications protocol specification for use in OSI networks.

X.400—An international standard specification for the exchange of electronic mail messages.

X.500—An international standard specifying a model for a distributed directory system.

XBM—X bit map, a black and white image format.

Yahoo—An Internet search utility.

I N D E X